Global Trade in the Premodern World

Global Trade in the Premodern World offers an authoritative and expansive history of exchange and interaction across Eurasia from the prehistoric origins of trade to the integration of large parts of this world-system by the fifteenth century CE.

The book tackles questions that are critical to our understanding of premodern globalization. How did global trade in the premodern world take shape? Who did the trading and what motivated them? Which commodities were traded and how did different goods influence how trading networks functioned? How did geography change how and where people carried goods? How did states and communities seek to control the practice of commerce? And finally, what was the impact of trade on political structures and in the relationship between different states, empires, and communities?

Drawing on the fruits of research in history, anthropology, and archaeology, as well as primary sources produced by authors from Africa, Asia, and Europe, *Global Trade in the Premodern World* is a book of remarkable scope written engagingly and accessibly with scholars, students, and non-specialists in mind.

Richard L. Smith was Emeritus Professor of History at Ferrum College, Virginia. His teaching and research were driven by wide-ranging interests in trade across Afro-Eurasia, especially in the first millennium CE. Smith's publications include *Premodern Trade in World History* (2008) and numerous chapters and articles.

Edmond Smith is Professor of Economic Cultures at the University of Manchester, UK. Their research and teaching explore the cultural and institutional origins of globalization across the second millennium CE. Smith has published numerous articles, chapters, and books, including the prize-winning monograph *Merchants* (2021).

Global Trade in the Premodern World

Thematic Approaches to Routes, Realms, and Networks

Richard L. Smith and Edmond Smith

Routledge
Taylor & Francis Group
LONDON AND NEW YORK

Designed cover image Merchants in a camel caravan. Miniature painting by Yahya ibn Mahmud al-Wasiti, 1237 CE. Credit: Alamy 2B01RJ3.

First published 2025
by Routledge
4 Park Square, Milton Park, Abingdon, Oxon OX14 4RN

and by Routledge
605 Third Avenue, New York, NY 10158

Routledge is an imprint of the Taylor & Francis Group, an informa business

British Library Cataloguing-in-Publication Data
A catalogue record for this book is available from the British Library

ISBN: 978-0-367-51224-8 (hbk)
ISBN: 978-0-367-51223-1 (pbk)
ISBN: 978-1-003-05289-0 (ebk)

DOI: 10.4324/9781003052890

Typeset in Sabon
by KnowledgeWorks Global Ltd.

Contents

Note on Writing

When I was an undergraduate, I was very lucky to find a brilliant mentor who introduced me to some books that shifted my view of the world and led me to the first steps on my road studying histories of global trade and exchange. After getting hooked by classics by the likes of Braudel and Polanyi, Richard's *Premodern Trade in World History* was at the top of a pile of books that I enthusiastically consumed while trying to get some grasp of the basic relationship between humans, trade, and the long history of economic change that has shaped our world. His engagement with history across such broad geographies, long chronologies, and different cultures and languages inspired my own efforts, first as a researcher and especially when I eventually started teaching these topics myself. While I was never lucky enough to be taught by Richard, his brilliantly wide-ranging approach and enthusiasm for the topic sang through his book, a legacy that I hope I draw on and continue in my own teaching. It was with this in my mind that, when I was approached to help complete this book after he very sadly died, I was honored to do so.

The invitation to contribute to this book coincided with my own journey into teaching these topics over the past six years. During this time, I've designed and run two undergraduate modules at the University of Manchester that have covered many of the key themes of this book. The first is a wide-ranging survey course called "Silk Roads" and the second is a final-year elective called "Responses to Globalisation" – both of which take a long comparative perspective of globalization in the period crossing usual "premodern" and "early modern" designations. Additionally, my work on this book has drawn on my current research project INTRECCI, generously funded by the European Research Council, on institutional transformation and entangled commercial cultures in international trade. It is from my teaching and research, as well as my wider work on merchants and globalization, that my contribution to this book has grown.

Before he died, Richard had completed just over 40,000 words of his planned manuscript, or approximately half of this completed book, which drew on his years of experience teaching the subject as well as his keen engagement with scholarship and primary sources. I have maintained Richard's approach to citing primary sources, where possible, under the original author's name while also usually including information about where these have been translated into English – the hope being that the vast majority of primary sources cited in this book should be accessible for students to work with themselves.

Rather than finished chapters, the text Richard had written was collected for the most part into almost-finished blocks of text around particular themes that I have been able to include with only minimal editing. With these sections my time has been spent deciphering and adding in Richard's footnotes (which he kept only as handwritten notes, and I must admit, were a little difficult to decipher in places!) or adding a few additional sentences here and there to connect ideas across the book or push Richard's analysis a little further. These minimally altered segments ensure that there are significant parts of this book that present Richard's ideas very much as he intended. However, as a complete piece of work, it was necessary for me to develop a structure that diverged from Richard's original proposal. In part this was because his own completed sections didn't align precisely with the proposal, and I believe he was pushing into new directions as he was writing. In part it is also because I wanted to build my own work and experiences of teaching on these topics into the book. I have done my very best to integrate the ideas that Richard set out in his proposal and in his completed sections into the book, and I hope the structure I have chosen effectively presents these ideas as well as my own. I think it's been a fruitful collaborative effort.

Overall, sections of the writing Richard had completed appear in five of the six chapters that now make up the volume, and I have tried throughout to build on and develop ideas that bring out the aims and objectives that Richard had in mind for this volume. In places, of course, my own perspective comes through more, and my own ideas from teaching and researching around these and connected themes are also set out across the volume. Despite some differences in our approaches, I hope that my contribution has gelled well with his work, and that the book would, in its finished state, win his approval.

Edmond Smith

Introduction

A Book of Routes and Realms

Trade and Global History

Trade has shaped the world. It is among the oldest, most pervasive, and most important of human activities, serving as an engine for change in many other human endeavors. It takes place on scales that range from the everyday transfer of goods within a single community to the transportation of commodities from one continent to another. As Philip Curtin argued in his ground-breaking work, "trade and exchange across cultural lines have played a crucial role in human history", being "the most important single source of change and development in art, science and technology".[1] Not only did trade move goods, but with these were often carried ideas, technologies, and information, not to mention their role as a less welcome vector of disease. Yet, despite its importance, trade in the premodern world was a risky business. It required traders to leave their homes, travel on uncertain routes, and to work with people whose cultural practices might be very different to their own. The very presence of trade across such divides might come as something of a surprise: "people with a different way of life are strangers by definition; their ways seem unpredictable, and the unpredictable is probably dangerous as well".[2] In the decades since Curtin made these observations, interest and scholarship related to global trade in the premodern world has flourished. Across much of this work, the questions of how people did business with strangers; how traders reached across geographical and cultural divides that separated them from suppliers, partners, and customers; and how they organized their own activities on vast geographical scales have all puzzled and inspired historians.

In answering these questions, this book presents a long history of "globalization" that explores the linkages and processes of exchange in places and times that are too often excluded from histories of the topic. Here, globalization is understood as a process, rather than a finished state defined by a single global market. As James Belich, John Darwin, and Chris Wickham break it down, globalization often began with simple *contact* between regions, that was occasional and indirect; the second step was *interaction* that involved regular and ongoing contact, exemplified by luxury trade;

DOI: 10.4324/9781003052890-1

third was *circulation,* that saw bulk trade; and the final step was *integration,* where different sections of a system were mutually dependent parts of a single economic whole.[3] All four stages can be seen in different times and places in the premodern world. The Roman Empire, for instance, was in contact with China, interacted with India, and oversaw both circulation and integration in the Mediterranean. As this example suggests, distance was often a feature in the stage of globalization that was reached, and methods to shorten those distances (or more precisely reduce the time and risk taken to cross them) were an important part in increasing connectivity. Throughout this volume, an array of different methods that were used to reduce the risk and challenges of long-distance trade by premodern traders to bridge the gaps between distant markets are encountered and examined.

In this book, the extent of the "global" scale is limited to the Afro-Eurasian landmass, despite long-distance of course playing an important role elsewhere in the premodern world. The book returns repeatedly to interactions across the Eurasian steppe and in the Indian Ocean World: two "sub-global" regions that were nevertheless defined by interactions and connections across large and complex geographical areas.[4] This focus comes from a conscious effort to avoid writing an unwieldy "big history" of global trade that attempts (realistically or not) to cover all trade in all places at all times. Instead, it traces examples that draw out common themes and points of interest to dig more deeply into the shape and structure of global trade in the premodern world. At the largest scale, global economic interaction was achieved because different regions were linked into wider systems through interactions and exchanges that participants were barely aware of.[5] The early history of long-distance trade had been characterized by sporadic and unsystematic exchanges using down-the-line, trickle trade, relying on wider trade flows to carry goods onwards. Local exchange systems developed independently and incrementally. Eventually these began splicing together to form regional and interregional grids or webs of exchange. If indeed something like a "world system" came to exist during the millennium before 1500 CE, it was in the form of a series of interconnected overlapping regional markets. Such systems were composed of circuits, emporiums, transit points, and termini stretching from one side of Afro-Eurasia to the other and characterized by increased complexity, specialization, scale, and efficiency.

In trying to pin down the structure of the premodern world system at a global scale, it's easy to conclude that "China and India did the manufacturing, and the rest of the world paid in non-manufactures, such as spices, dyestuffs, horses, furs, and, especially, bullion".[6] That being said, similar dynamics were a common feature in many trading networks at sub-global, regional or smaller scales of analysis. At a local level agricultural commodities might be brought to a local urban market where they could exchanged for finished goods or access capital. Similar patterns can be seen in different contexts across the world, and as this book shows, goods were carried over routes that often intersected with multiple emporium and local markets, rather than passing from an origin to destination with nothing but empty space in between. Such a process was far from linear. Political, social, technological, and other variables impacted positively and negatively on trade and commerce, the fortunes of which oscillated from time to time and place to place. In the end, all but the most remote regions in Afro-Eurasia participated in these exchanges, although not with the same intensity nor on the same scale. The millennium before 1500 CE was a mixed bag of ups and downs, convergences and divergences, vigor and regression, with its fair share of decline, disorder, and catastrophe.

The book recognizes that the history of globalization is fundamentally a history of connectedness. This required mobility, and naturally the study of global trade requires a deep engagement with the people who passed over borders, moved between places, and lived lives that were often on the move. The human and natural environments through which people had to pass to connect with others informed how these connections took place. Often, this means looking at histories of people who are not tied to specific states, and nomadic and diasporic communities feature regularly and prominently throughout this book as essential agents of globalization. This mobility was certainly not only incentivized by trade, and people on the move included agents of violence like raiders and armies, as well as peaceful migrants, religious pilgrims and others. Sometimes, states and empires made efforts to impose borders and restrict movement, on trade or otherwise, in opposition to processes of globalization. At other times, states exploited connectedness, whether simply through taxing the wealth that these vectors transmitted, or otherwise using them as a means of extending their influence and power.[7] The history of connectedness presented here must inevitably be understood alongside the frictions and disconnections that were also certainly a part of the premodern experience.

These frictions are an important part of global history scholarship. As Sanjay Subrahmanyan and others have demonstrated, simply noting how communities in premodern contexts were connected or disconnected is ill-suited as a means for interpreting global encounter.[8] They warn against the habit of "celebrating the cosmopolitan" and push scholars to recognize that "the person who crosses cultural boundaries with a certain facility" was not "always valued in past societies".[9] Rather than "faceless globetrotters, colorless chameleons and invisible boundary crossers", premodern traders' lives were just as likely to take place in moments of "crisis and dislocation".[10] Too easily, global history can encourage focus on "encounters and exchanges at the expense of conflict", but to understand a long history of trade it is essential to understand the impact of borders and boundaries just as much as it is the means by which people overcame them.[11] In this way, global history can be most effective when it "investigates the connections between individual and context, between the regional, national and even the global" as a means of connecting "local communities and international networks".[12] Employing this method, and presenting examples for engaging across these different scales of analysis, is a key feature of this volume.

In doing so, the book builds on an array of existing studies on premodern trade that have sought to expose the connections and relationships that existed between different parts of the premodern world. Probably the most prominent focus of such studies has been on the so-called Silk Road. In 1877 Ferdinand von Richthofen (1833–1905) published the first of five volumes entitled *China, Ergebnisse eigner Reisen und darauf gegründeter Studien* [*China: Findings of My Own Travels and Studies Based Thereon*], the last volume of which appeared posthumously in 1912. He also produced other works. Von Richthofen was a German geographer and geologist who had traveled extensively in Asia and would ultimately settle down to the life of a well-respected university professor. In volume 1 he became particularly interested in a passage from Ptolemy (*c.*100–170 CE). This particular information had come rather roundabout since Ptolemy had borrowed much from another geographer, Marinus of Tyre, who, in turn, got his information from a Macedonian merchant named Maes (or Titianus).[13] Maes was involved in the silk trade and appears to have traveled at least part of the way to China, but the important part of the report came from his unnamed agents whom he had sent on. Having reached Ptolemy fourth hand, it is, not surprisingly, a rather obscure and difficult passage.[14] Merchants from the West like Maes came up from ancient Bactria (Afghanistan), crossed the Pamir Mountains, and in the Upper Alai Valley somewhere west of Kashgar connected with merchants coming from the East at a landmark called the Stone Tower. This was near a building referred to as the Hormeterion, which appears to have originally been a fortress but was at the time being used as a caravanserai.[15] One suggestion is that the Stone Tower was the modern city of Tashkurgan, which literally means "Stone Tower" except that other places in this general region also have that name and names changed over the centuries.[16]

Rather deep into his first volume, Von Richthofen coined a word, "Seidenstrasse": meaning "Silk Road". He did not include a definition, and he used it sparingly in the rest of the work, limiting it specifically to the route Maes and his agents traveled on the way to the Stone Tower.[17] After all, Von Richthofen had to be careful, he was working from a single source who got his information from a lone informant and without support from any archaeological evidence. Later in the book while discussing the silk trade, he casually refers to the "Seidenstrassen", that is, the plural form of his new word, indicating that there was more than one Seidenstrasse. However, he does not follow up on this, makes no attempt to extend it to other time periods, and does not seem to be using it in a generic way. On page 500, he delineated in an orange line on a map his idea of the location of the Silk Road, which appears a bit too straight to be an ancient trade route but rather more like modern engineers laying out tracks on a planning board. Indeed, it was Von Richthofen's eventual idea to run a railroad from Germany to China.[18]

Von Richthofen's evocative term did not catch on in his own time, and after a while he stopped using it himself. But it had made an impression on a few of his colleagues, especially August Hermann, who used *Seidenstrasse* in the title of his book and thereafter in various publications and on maps.[19] Hermann, however, never saw the forest for the trees and spent much of his efforts arguing over picayune matters involving times and places: but he did not question the basic concept of a Silk Road. That left the field open to Sven Hedin, a former Swedish student of von Richthofen, who came out with *Silk Road* in 1936. It was Hedin who tapped into the growing public appetite for adventures in exotic settings with the main character being a true-to-life archaeologist. Hedin's book devotes a good ten-page or so summary to the real Silk Road, but much of his book focuses instead on his own motor car expedition and its daring adventures.[20] The popularization of the term became widespread, and marketeers and movie makers added to its popularity, even as the term gained exposure as a political tool for describing China's growing global influence in the twenty-first century.[21]

The Silk Road (or roads) have provided an evocative framework for understanding long-distance trade in the premodern world, but they have always been just one part of much wider webs of exchange and communication that connected people across Afro-Eurasia. Even in the wide expanse of steppe that lay in northern Eurasia between China and Europe, trade and exchange took place in a much more complicated and multi-layered environment than classic accounts of the Silk Roads suggest. Goods did not need to travel to or from Europe to be part of exchanges taking place at a global scale, and flows of Chinese goods from these northern steppes into places like the Indian Ocean World, or that ignored the stepped entirely by taking the maritime routes, were much more significant that those that reached Europe directly. More to the point, Chinese goods were a small part of total trade in the premodern world, and multiple centers of productions and multiple networks of exchange were all part of the premodern world's commercial landscape.

Our understanding of premodern globalization needs to be broader than the infamous Silk Road, even as this route provides a fascinating insight into some of the ways people did business. Whether focusing on the Eurasian steppes or elsewhere, the practices and experience of trade and travel across the world have picked out common themes for analysis that introduce possibilities for how historians can approach the study of global trade in the premodern world. As noted here in the introduction and exemplified by examples across each chapter, long-distance trade was by no means only an occasional feature of the premodern world. Long-distance trade in luxury goods has a history stretching back to the prehistoric exchange of goods like obsidian, incense, and amber that led to ongoing interactions between different regions that were sustained over centuries and even millennia. Long-distance trade was undertaken through the bulk exchange of commodities too, and that systems of exchange in the premodern world could lead to the integration of different regional economic systems. In this way, the premodern world is well suited for study as a site of a globalizing process.

There are some common themes and questions that occur across this volume and shape the approach to premodern trade taken here. The book asks, how did global trade in the premodern world take shape, in different places and in different times? Who did the trading and what motivated these exchanges? Which commodities were traded and how did different goods influence the shape and structure of particular trading networks? How did geography change how and where people carried goods? How was trade conducted, and how did states and communities seek to control the practice of commerce? And finally, what was the impact of trade on political structures and in the relationship between different states, empires, and communities?

Scope and Structure

The millennium that stretched from the beginning of the sixth to the beginning of the sixteenth century was a dividing line in the history of Afro-Eurasia, representing a bridge from the ancient to the modern world. For trade and commerce this was the great age of connectivity, a process extending back to the Bronze Age but accelerating exponentially during this time. Shmuel Eisenstadt labeled it the "Age of Proto-Globalization", and indeed what had been distinct trade zones increasingly intersected and began to interweave. Markets became more integrated, linking supply and demand over distance, and commodity demand changed, as did the composition of those who made the process work: traders and merchants.

This book uses a thematic-comparative approach that breaks out of the traditional chronological-geographical approach. While there is a greater focus on the Eurasian steppe than other regions, in general the book is structured to answer key themes about how trade was organised in the premodern world and does so in each chapter across multiple geographies and chronologies. This book's structure is therefore guided by its analysis, which allows comparisons across a whole range of topics related to trade and commerce. What generalizations can be made about trade routes or merchants or commodities, and what was unique to each and why?

Premodern trade routes and systems were complicated in practice, trying to reconstruct them from surviving sources can verge on maddening. The most useful of contemporary observers like Ibn Khurradādhbih for the Abbasid Caliphate or Abū al-Bakrī for the trans-Saharan system can tell that a route ran from here to there and occasionally offer up an unexpected tidbit about something along the way. But most particulars are glossed over, and little attempt is made to make comparisons or draw larger conclusions. Authors often had only minimal interest in the practices of traders along the route: the who and the how of business interactions. Successfully sourcing a product is the beginning of tracing its course, from which emerges a trade route, a network, and finally a system. The very nature of the subject matter therefore means that this book takes an interdisciplinary approach, incorporating history and economics but also elements of geography, anthropology, and, where necessary, geopolitics.

Chapter 1, "The Origins of Trade", sets out the starting point for the rest of the volume and considers the origins of trade in the earliest days of human experience. It begins some 300,000 years ago with the exchange of obsidian over long-distances in East Africa and continues through to the neolithic period, before considering what the Cucuteni-Trypillia culture in prehistoric Ukraine and the metal-trading Markop people can tell us about early trade on the Eurasian steppes. Through these explorations, the chapter offers an overview of how prehistoric trade can be understood, and traces some of the lineages of prehistoric trade routes and practices into the first millennium BCE. The chapter ends with two case studies that show how experiences of trade bore some commonalities across the human experience while, inevitably, distinctions also arose shaped by the unique environmental, social and cultural conditions within which exchange took place. The first case study considers what might be seen as a classic, linear trade route, known as the Incense Road, which ran between southern Arabia and the eastern shores of the Mediterranean. The second case study presents the Amber Trails, which connected Scandinavia to traders across much of Europe, exchanges that took place across less defined and interlinked network of routes. In each case study, some of the key themes across the rest of the book are brought to the fore, including the role of different types of commodities, the influence of states, the impact of the environment, and the importance of intersections between local and trans-regional exchanges for long-distance trade.

Chapter 2, "Trade Across the Steppe", develops this story by focusing on the dynamics of trade in the Eurasian steppes over a very long period, from the last few millennia BCE through to the thirteenth century CE Mongol Empire, and questions how the particular social and economic structures of life on the steppe shaped processes of exchange. David Christian argued that "modern historiography has not fully appreciated the ecological complexity of the Silk Roads", an observation that could be applied to the approach taken to many premodern trade routes.[22] This idea is a founding principle of this and future chapters, where the importance of geography and environment are recognized as a key feature in how premodern trade developed and was structured. Building up from the lives of nomadic and pastoral peoples that lived in the vast expanse of land lying between the Hungarian plain in the west and Manchuria in the east, it considers how trade developed through exchanges within these steppes but also at its borders, as mobile societies and sedentary societies exchanged goods. Trade between agricultural and pastoral societies represents an archetypical form of exchange in the premodern world that had long lasting consequences for the way in which societies, empires, and economies functioned across Eurasia. By assessing forms of exchange that took place across the steppes, this chapter presents then an insight into premodern trade that traversed different geographies, cultures, and states.

Whereas the second chapter focuses on moments of exchange across the steppe frontier, Chapter 3, "Controlling the Steppe Frontier", continues the discussion of the nomadic-sedentary border by focusing instead on efforts by societies to limit exchange and movement in these same spaces. As well as potential trading partners on the steppe, this chapter begins by acknowledging the way fraught power dynamics affected how the nomadic-sedentary relationship was understood by contemporaries, leading to treatment of "outsiders" as potentially dangerous and in need of control. Beginning with the well-known Great Wall in China, and then efforts to barricade settled societies in western Eurasia against the lands of "Gog and Magog", the chapter focuses on how border societies used military force and massive infrastructure projects to try and manage, or perhaps more typically limit, exchanges on the frontier. In doing so, it highlights a counterpoint to the movement of goods and people that was so important for premodern trade. Markets and trade were shaped by states and societies in many ways, and it is essential to recognize that this was not always done to remove barriers and increase exchange.

Chapter 4, "Travel and Transport", pushes further beyond the steppes to show how trade, travel and transport across a wider Eurasian experience connected with the practices that defined long-distance steppe trade. It begins with an overview of how different people who engaged with long-distance trade sought to measure and map the wider world that they inhabited. From here, the chapter moves into an assessment of how geography and cross-cultural movement shaped the practice of travel overland in the premodern world, with specific attention given to some of the most challenging and famous trading routes that connected China, western Asia, India, and elsewhere. Here, there is also consideration of the practicalities of trade, both in the organization of roads and stopping points and the ways in which merchants organized their caravans and goods. These themes continue with a section considering the development of trade at sea, with a focus on the Arabian seas and connecting points between the Mediterranean, Indian Ocean, and wider Eurasian coastal trading world. Rather than particular routes, this section focuses instead on the challenges of travelling by sea and how states, ports and trading communities sought to take advantage of the remarkable mobility that maritime travel enabled while simultaneously overcoming the risks and challenges that it entailed.

In the final thematic chapter, Chapter 5, "Merchants and Networks", the focus shifts to the ways in which merchants organized themselves and their trade to take advantage of the exchanges detailed elsewhere in the book. Here, particular attention is paid to the institutions of premodern trade, including prominently the role of diasporic communities as vectors of trade in the premodern world. This underpins a consideration of the routes and systems that developed because of sustained trading interactions. Finally, the chapter concludes with an extensive case study of the Trans-Saharan trade, running between Morocco and the gold-producing regions of West Africa, which brings together themes from across the volume in a single geographical context.

Chapter 6, "Commodities of the Premodern World", offers something a little different, and it could be read separately to, before, or after the preceding chapters. Here, the global scope of premodern trade is presented through a deeper interrogation of five primary sources. First, the potential scale of trade in a globally significant emporium as detailed in Francis Balducci Pegolotti's fourteenth-century account of Constantinople is used as a starting point for understanding the integration of different trans-regional trading networks. The remainder of the chapter uses the texts of Ibn Battuta, Hamdallah Mustawfi, Ma Huan, and Tomé Pires to assess how premodern traders in mostly maritime Asia understood the commodities that shaped their commercial worlds. This covers natural commodities ranging from cereal crops to exotic species, mineral commodities like gold or gemstones, and manufactured goods like ceramics and textiles, which were produced and distributed from the very eastern to the very western markets of Eurasia. Together, material from these primary sources reveals the scope, scale and experience of global trade in the premodern world.

Notes

1 Philip Curtin, *Cross-Cultural Trade in World History* (Cambridge, 1984), p. 1.
2 Philip Curtin, *Cross-Cultural Trade in World History* (Cambridge, 1984), p. 1.
3 James Belich, John Darwin, and Chris Wickham (eds.), *The Prospect of Global History* (Oxford, 2016), p. 5.
4 James Belich, John Darwin, and Chris Wickham (eds.), *The Prospect of Global History* (Oxford, 2016), pp. 4–5.
5 Nicole Boivin and Michael Frachetti (eds.), *Globalization in Prehistory: Contact, exchange and the "people without history"* (Cambridge, 2018).
6 James Belich, John Darwin, and Chris Wickham (eds.), *The Prospect of Global History* (Oxford, 2016), p. 8.
7 James Belich, John Darwin, and Chris Wickham (eds.), *The Prospect of Global History* (Oxford, 2016), p. 15.
8 Sanjay Subrahmanyam, *Three Ways to Be Alien: Travails and encounters in the early modern world* (Waltham, MA, 2011), pp. 21–2.
9 Sanjay Subrahmanyam, *Three Ways to Be Alien: Travails and encounters in the early modern world* (Waltham, MA, 2011), p. 22.
10 John-Paul Ghobrial, "The Secret Life of Elias of Bablylon and the Uses of Global Microhistory", *Past & Present* 222 (2014), p. 58, pp. 51–93.
11 Filippo de Vivo, "Microhistories of Long-Distance Information: Space, Movement and Agency in the Early Modern News", *Past & Present* 12, issue supplement 14 (2019), p. 180, pp. 179–214.
12 Filippo de Vivo, "Prospect or Refuge? Microhistory, History on the Large Scale", *Cultural and Social History* 7:3 (2010), p. 392, pp. 387–97.
13 Claudius Ptolemy, *The Geography*, trans. Edward Stevenson (New York, 1932), p. 33.
14 Kurakichi Shiratori, "On the Ts'ung-ling Traffic Route Described by C. Ptolemaeus", *The Memoirs of the Research Department of the Toyo Bunko* (1957), pp. 1–34.
15 Aurel Stein, *Innermost Asia: Detailed report of explorations in Central Asia, Kan-su and eastern Iran* (Oxford, 1928).
16 Kurakichi Shiratori, "On the Ts'ung-ling Traffic Route Described by C. Ptolemaeus", *The Memoirs of the Research Department of the Toyo Bunko* (1957), pp. 4–5.
17 Daniel Waugh, "Richthofen's 'Silk Roads': Towards the Archaeology of a Concept", *The Silk Road* 5:1 (2007), pp. 5, 10.

18 Tamara Chin, "The Invention of the Silk Road, 1877", *Critical Inquiry* 40:1 (2013), pp. 194–219.
19 Albert Herrmann, *Die Alten Seidenstrassen Zwischen China und Syria* (Berlin, 1910).
20 Sven Hedin, *Silk Road* (London, 1938). Discussed in Daniel Waugh, "Richthofen's 'Silk Roads': Towards the Archaeology of a Concept", *The Silk Road* 5:1 (2007), p. 5.
21 Warwick Ball, "Following the Mythical Road", *Geographical* 70:3 (1998), p. 18; Peter Frankopan, *The New Silk Roads: The Present and Future of the World* (London, 2018).
22 David Christian, "Silk Roads or Steppe Roads? The Silk Roads in World History", *Journal of World History* 11:1 (2000), pp. 1–26.

1 The Origins of Trade

Trade and Human Society

Trade has existed for an extraordinarily long time. Probably the earliest form of exchange was between people who knew each other and were part of the same communities. It was hand-to-hand, face-to-face, and likely incidental and discontinuous. This was more a matter of swapping items between people and households, and was rooted more in behaviors like sharing, loaning, gift-giving, and reciprocity than in gaining an economic advantage. Those taking part were largely self-sustaining and were independent from each other for basic needs, but they were desirous of having something someone else had, or perhaps they perceived that they had something someone else wanted. Such trade followed no regular pattern; it did not require markets or trade routes, and was instead likely an almost constant part of daily life and the quantities involved were very small. Within communities, items traded were primarily goods intended for practical everyday use, such as tools; household items like pots, pans, cups, and other wooden and stone utensils; pottery; cloth; leather; food; and food-related items like grinding stones, horn mattocks, and knives. The goods passed back and forth were assumed to be of equivalent value, but chances are no one kept close track.

That is not to say that this trade was inconsequential. Prehistoric trade in this form shaped communities and established practices of trading and exchanging goods for others that could be carried outside the community.[1] It was likely not long before people learned not only to exchange goods among themselves but also recognize the benefits of trade beyond their specific locality. Resources, whether natural or human, were not evenly distributed across the globe, and the simple incentive of trading surplus from one area for surplus from another provided an essential motivation for trade. Recent research by paleoanthropologists has shown that long-distance trading networks existed as long as 300,000 years ago (perhaps even before the emergence of *Homo sapiens*). Rather than everyday items that were traded intra-communally, this trade depended on the transportation of rarer material that was prized by people across a wider area: in this case obsidian.[2] For rarer and more valuable commodities, early

DOI: 10.4324/9781003052890-2

people were willing and able to exchange goods across great distances by land, river, and sea.

Over the following millennia, trade shaped the development of human societies across the world, as a means of communities to support themselves by distributing their goods among themselves, and increasingly in relation to the cross-communal exchange of material. Trade represented a viable alternative to conflict as a means of distributing resources and was fundamental for the emergence of complex human societies. Alongside physical goods, trade facilitated the movement of people and ideas. By around 10,000 years ago, in the early neolithic period, many settled communities were connected by some form of inter-community or external trade.[3] Transportation was primitive, and traveling among strangers or letting outsiders into one's own community, let alone dealing with them in exchanging goods, could be risky business. But if matters of security could be overcome, the most natural swapping partners for farmers were probably hunter-gatherers, a grain-and-cloth for meat-and-skins exchange that underpinned more complex systems that supported trade in rarer and far-flung commodities.[4] As the foraging economy faded, agriculturalists turned to pastoralists with dairy products now included, and nomadic and semi-nomadic societies were deeply connected with sedentary communities and urban markets. Farming communities also swapped with each other, which was essentially a social act symbolizing a relationship that would probably include ritual and ceremonial ties bonding communities together.[5] While some societies distinct specialisms within the exchange economy, others blended agriculturalist, and mobile pastoralist activities.[6] Even as they were shaped by different local environments, cultures, and politics, societies across the world engaged in trade with their neighbors.

In time, communities became more deeply linked into networks of contacts providing support and mutual assistance in times of need or danger. Such networks were more likely to be in the form of chains rather than clumps or blocks and, if large enough, between different ecological zones. This helped address the issue of matching products: adjacent villages would have little incentive to trade their grain for their neighbors' grain, but trade was likely to flourish between complementary ecologies. Typically controlled and directed by their leaders, some communities came to be capable on occasion of engaging in large scale exchange operations. Nevertheless, market mechanisms were not yet directing such exchanges, which still did not involve entrepreneurial behavior as we would recognize it today. The objective was still to maximize social relations: this is not to say such motives were purely altruistic, indeed they were likely to be very calculative.[7]

Mundane trade, such as the exchange for grains for dried fish, preceded long-distance trade and would have taken place on a much larger scale. For long-distance trade to make an attractive proposition to participants it required a demand for something thought of as especially valuable in a particular local context. Despite the long distances that some commodities were exchanged across, most early trade of such mobile goods would not have seen goods carried far by any individual. Instead, the initial method of exchange involving adjacent communities in its most incidental form has been referred to as "trickle trade" and in its slightly more active form, the "down-the-line" approach. Goods were transferred from community to community, some of which would be consumed at a particular point and some passed on again, percolating through the genesis of what might be called a proto system.[8] In this manner some goods might travel considerable distances over time, potentially taking a long time to move from one owner to the next. Sometimes large amounts of surplus staples could be used to buy a much smaller amount of more valuable products. Expanding trade from basic needs and ritual items came to include functional items that were lent value beyond their efficacy as tools. An early example would be polished axes made with unusual stones such as chocolate colored flint, which in some places was associated with spiritual qualities. Whether or not a particular stone was more or less effective in felling trees was not the decisive issue.[9] Obsidian is volcanic glass found only in certain places. In the world before metals, it produced the sharpest cutting edge, and was both functional and prestigious.

More direct exchanges also took place at large meetings of affiliated communities to share in celebratory and ceremonial activities and gift giving.[10] Ritual items believed to be imbued with supernatural powers and body decorations such as necklaces were special items of exchange. Such gatherings appear to have had their roots as far back as the late paleolithic period – some 15,000 years ago. If ceremonial gatherings were the earliest method of directly moving goods between two places not adjacent to each other, a more certain practice came with the development of "directional trade" in which goods were sent directly to a specific location bypassing areas in between. This was conducted over bodies of water, particularly rivers, but also along coastlines like the Aegean Sea and the Black Sea. It was especially useful in transporting bulk goods like salt and unfinished stone. Large scale overland directional trade would eventually come with the creation of group expeditions for protection. Even so, the exchange of goods would take place between communities with whom there was some preexisting relationship.

By the seventh millennium BCE, there is evidence of the widespread exchange of various commodities across prehistoric societies, sometimes over substantial distances. Obsidian from deposits in eastern Anatolia and Armenia were reaching Jarmo in Mesopotamia in significant amounts, Jericho near the Mediterranean coast in lesser amounts, and even Cyprus in very small amounts. Subsequently Armenian obsidian appeared in the Persian Gulf region. Trade in one commodity, like obsidian, soon led to other products changing hands, most of which are archaeologically invisible. In some places trails blazed in the early obsidian trade became the trade routes ultimately incorporated into more permanent long distance commercial networks.[11] Hand-to-hand circulation was too slow and unpredictable for long distance trade in items like specialized axes and obsidian, so indirect distribution systems involving intermediaries, meaning strangers, became part of the process. Places began to concentrate on what they did best. Some developed special niche products either because they had access to resources like unusual stones, or they developed exceptional handiwork and craft skills, as in carving. This added value to a product, and some places became increasingly geared to producing goods for distribution in distant markets. Specialization became more pronounced, systems expanded, and goods were disseminated over wider ranges. Transportation, however, was a problem, and most goods had to be carried by people themselves unless there was a river or coastline nearby. Long distance trade was still sporadic and of very low volume. The longer a route reached, the more expensive the goods that were carried over it became. Nevertheless, settlements on their way to becoming towns were connected, if not quite within a systematic arrangement, at least more than haphazardly and with some measure of continuity.

While the overwhelming majority of items being exchanged were basically utilitarian and had some functional use, a class of goods that was largely not utilitarian or may have had very minimal functional use also came into circulation. These were objects that had social meaning attached to them. They were prestige goods, that is, items whose function was to bring prestige to their owners like jewelry made of precious materials or crafted weapons. Their perceived value could come from the material they were made of, the specialized work that went into making them, their rarity or exoticism due to the distances over which they had traveled, or some intangible feature. Neolithic craftsmen in Taiwan were producing jade for export as early as the fourth millennium BCE that were distributed across southeast Asia as part of ongoing maritime trade that lasted much of the next 2500 years. Decorative objects like nephrite adzes, bracelets, bell-shaped beads, and tubular beads from Taiwan have been found in sites including nearby Ludao and Sabtang islands, in the Philippines at Luzon, and in Thailand and Vietnam. In each case, alterations to the jade, probably by local artisans, suggest that the value of jade justified its transportation and exchange, even as different communities lent it particular cultural meaning.[12] Having access to foreign and especially exotic goods motivated by the desire of elite groups to enter regional social relationships greatly expanded exchange networks.

As specialization and sophistication increased the supply of prestige goods and they became more prominent in communities that evolved from being basically egalitarian and acephalous to becoming ranked and socially stratified. Wealth and power became concentrated in fewer hands and was often displayed through the physical objects that showed an owner's material supremacy.[13] However, while prestige items were generally an element of directional trade they did not have to form a discrete class. Exchanges might include grain, household goods, obsidian blades, unusual stone axes, specially crafted ceramics, and shells from coastal regions hundreds of miles away. Textiles and skins could be of the most commonplace variety or come from very exotic materials. Salt was a staple and a bulk item but could be found only in particular places often a considerable distance from where it was needed. As with obsidian, some old salt trails became the basis of later trade routes, while the regular exchange of other mundane goods along prestige objects like jade helped establish long-lasting trading networks.

From the earliest exchange as long as 300,000 years ago to the emergence of sustained long-distance commerce between communities in the last ten millennia, trade has been an important part of human development. Although simple in its premise – exchanging one good for another considered of equal value – the exchange of goods within and across communities required the development of practices and behaviors that made it easier to do business with strangers. As trade became more common, both the production and transportation of goods took on greater complexity, and this was shaped by and helped to shape early societies. Repeated and repeated across time, whether a single generation, a century or even a millennium, these practices became standardized and accepted across larger spaces. The impact of trade went far deeper than the geographical pathways that travelers wore into the land as they carried goods across the earth: it also shaped how humans interacted with each other.

Long-Distance Trade in Prehistoric Eurasia

By the neolithic period, there are numerous examples of long-distance trade taking place in locations including Egypt, Mesopotamia, and other early civilizations.[14] However, rather than focusing on trade in societies that concentrated wealth and power through agricultural intensification and urbanization, the focus here will instead fall on the Eurasian steppes and patterns of exchange that were shaped by the mobility of pastoral peoples. In doing so, it sets out avoid the risk of "flattening Eurasia" and reducing people living within the steppes to "passive participants of interactions between the agrarian empires".[15] Additionally, as well as setting the scene for the emergence of the most well-known premodern long-distance trade route – the so-called Silk Road – this grounding will also serve to highlight the diffusion and impact of long-distance trade on societies across the world, and establish that mobility is an essential factor for understanding the structure and practices of exchange across the world.

Archaeological evidence seems to indicate that long-distance trade moved west to east across the steppes starting from southeastern Europe. The Danube River provided a great highway linking the Black Sea region and the steppes with Central Europe, over which much movement of goods took place. What may be the most long-lived and most impressive of the Copper Age cultures in this part of the world was the Cucuteni-Trypillia culture. At its largest size it reached from the Carpathian Mountains to the Dnieper River and lasted from approximately 5200 to 3500 BCE. In the early centuries of its development, its economy centered on the production of cereal grains and livestock husbandry, especially cattle. Its tools were still made from knapped and polished stone, including flint and some obsidian, as well as wood, bone, and for certain jobs antler. Unlike many of its contemporaries, the Cucuteni-Trypillia appears to have been a generally peaceful society in which weapons were used mostly for hunting. Settlements, which were often along large rivers, were high density and included some very large towns, with some estimates of the largest having populations in the 20,000 plus range.[16] Trypillia (Central Ukraine), one of the eponymous sites, had more than fifteen hundred houses that were very similar in size spread across a plain.[17] Periodically these settlements appear to have been deliberately burned down and then rebuilt, a peculiar practice that may be connected with a long lost religious rite.[18]

In these large, complex settlements, a number of different commodities have survived in the archaeological record that reveal how the people of the Cucuteni-Trypillia culture were connected with networks of exchange that crossed southern Europe and western Asia. Its long-distance trade evolved from the provision of basic goods like salt, which came from salt works in Romania, the Carpathian Mountains, and the Black Sea coast, and could be moved in bulk mostly by river. Eventually, smaller and more valuable products like the pigments used to decorate ceramic vessels, which came from specific locations mostly in Romania were added, as were mineral resources, foremost of which was copper.[19] At the very twilight of this culture, bronze items produced in a variety of places began to come in as imports. Close contact was maintained with neighbors to the east, the peoples of the steppes, including those of the Yamnaya culture and settlement fortresses in the Don River region and the Crimea.[20] In their heyday, the people of the Cucuteni-Trypillia culture would have had one of the most advanced societies, technologically, in the world.[21]

Copper production is evident in the last few centuries and helps provide a deeper understanding of the Trypillia economy. In Trypillia, some copper came from relatively nearby mines at Volyn (Ukraine) and deposits along the Dnieper River, but it was also imported from the Balkans in both raw and finished form, indicating the establishment of trade carrying goods hundreds of miles. Long-distance trade in metals was a common feature in the establishment of commercial exchanges between communities and it continued to be important in subsequent millennia. Metals, from copper in the prehistoric period to lithium or nickel in the twenty-first century, are found in geologically specific geographies and their distribution requires transportation and exchange. Considering the wide-ranging applications of metals, their role as key trade commodities across human commercial history is not surprising. When technology entered the age of metallurgy, the first phase being the Chalcolithic (Eneolithic) or Copper Age in the fifth millennium BCE, the most prominent use of copper was initially not for tools but to make personal ornaments, an important class of prestige items. As for weapons, flint daggers replaced polished battle axes, but they in turn would be replaced by bronze daggers in the third millennium BCE. Bronze and later iron made much more effective weapons than copper, so as states became larger and more aggressive, their armies grew and so did the demand for metals. Much of the new weaponry would likely be channeled through the original systems that had been developed to move polished stone battle axes. Some steppe people who had access to deposits and were noted for their metallurgical skill became associated with a particular metal, whether the Scythians of the first millennium BCE for gold or the Türks of the first millennium CE for iron. The end of the Cucuteni-Trypillia culture corresponds roughly to the early centuries of the Bronze Age. A peaceful society moving into a very warlike period with potentially rough neighbors to the east offers an easy explanation as to what happened to these people and their culture. This can be combined with the other usual suspect in downfalls, climatic change in the form of a drier, colder environment to which pastoral societies like the Yamnaya were better equipped to adapt to than were agriculturalists.[22]

Alongside the expansion of metallurgical practices across Eurasia, a slow-moving yet radical transformation was taking place in how goods could be transported: the development of horse power. While people had been domesticating animals since the beginning of the neolithic period, among the earliest being goats, sheep, cattle, and swine. Initially these were food animals, living storehouses for meat and later milk. Horses, which appear to have been domesticated in the fourth millennium BCE in what is today northern Kazakhstan by a people known as the Botai, were a comparatively late animal to arrive in human history, but their importance for trade can scarcely be overstated.[23]

Horses were foremost a means of transport. Most evidence seems to indicate that pulling came before riding, and using carts and wagons for peaceful purposes came before war chariots. Exactly when and where the wheel-and-axle principle originated has been a matter for speculation since it seems to have popped up abruptly in several places.[24] Donkeys were pulling wheeled carts in Mesopotamia in the fourth millennium BCE, and two- and four-wheeled closed wagons pulled by cattle were used in eastern and central Europe and on the Pontic steppes above the Black Sea. The crucial breakthrough came in advancements in cart mechanics and the invention of spoked wheels, an innovation associated with the Sintashta and Andronovo cultures of Bronze Age Russia. Early domesticated horses were smaller than modern horses, another indication that they more likely pulled vehicles than supported riders. The great leap in popularity for the horse in places beyond the Eurasian steppes came in the second millennium BCE with the diffusion of the light chariot. Horse-drawn chariots spread across the Caucasus to appear in eastern Anatolia, northern Syria, Central Europe, and southward to the Mycenaeans of Greece. To the southeast, Indo-Iranians and Aryan tribesmen rode on chariots into Iran and northern India and directly eastward along the Gansu Corridor, finally reaching China during the late Shang dynasty.[25]

The importance of horses extended beyond their role as a means of transport. In places like the Eurasian steppes where lush grass grew thick but outright agriculture was generally not a good idea, the herding of animals was often the best strategy for survival. Horses could not match cattle in producing meat and milk, and they required better pasture than goats, sheep, or camels; nevertheless, nomadic pastoralists often kept huge herds of horses. Everywhere the horse was a status symbol, and in places it became an element of cult worship. Its popularity had an obvious source. Warriors don't ride cattle, goats, or sheep into battle and only sometimes camels, donkeys, and mules. During the premodern centuries the horse was the ultimate war machine on land.[26]

When not at war with each other, mobile pastoral societies by the nature of their lifestyle interacted frequently over immense distances exchanging ideas, beliefs, technologies, and, above all, goods. On steppes and deserts, and in mountains among herders who practiced transhumance, shared lifestyles and culture reinforced contact. And pastoralists provided commercial links not just with other pastoralists but with settled folk eventually linking, however indirectly, the western and eastern sides of Eurasia. That is not to say that nomadic pastoralists wandered aimlessly. They followed migratory cycles, sometimes based on older hunting trails or followed water sources like river basins. They did not evolve into a class of professional traders or even carriers; their business remained the herding of animals. But as a supplement to their livelihood, they often transported goods from points of supply to points of demand on their annual rounds. Pastoral routes laid the groundwork for what over the centuries coalesced into more formal structures that became trading networks.[27]

Exchange routes leading to trade networks were not created in one fell swoop like an interstate highway or transcontinental railroad but rather incrementally with sections developing on their own momentum before gradually fusing. Local exchange systems spliced together creating regional and later interregional systems with increased organization, complexity, scale, and efficiency. Segments intermeshed to form what would later become parts of larger mega-systems.[28] An exchange network reaching across large areas of Western Europe was distributing jadeite polished axes in the late Neolithic. By the late fourth millennium BCE, an indirect distribution system was bringing special crafted ceramics from across the highlands of Iran to the lowlands of Mesopotamia. As the third millennium BCE crossed into the second millennium, a full-blown long distance trading system, including regular caravan service and the establishment of merchant colonies, was transporting woolen textiles, tin, and silver between Ashur in northern Mesopotamia and Kanesh in Cappadocia in Central Anatolia. The operators were private entrepreneurs motivated by profit making.

The scale of such prehistoric trading networks can be seen in the archaeological record of societies across Eurasia, even those that might traditionally have been seen as too distant or too insignificant to have made much of a contribution to the emergence of Eurasian trading systems. Indeed it is here that some of the strongest evidence for very long-distance trade taking place can be found, as well as material that shows the importance of trade in shaping the development of human societies across the world. Around the same time that the Cucuteni-Trypillia culture was flourishing, there are indications long-distance trade on the western Eurasian steppes was tied to a trading system centered in southeast Europe known the Carpatho-Balkan Metallurgical Province. This involved the exchange of both raw material and finished products mostly in copper and some gold, and may have reached into the steppes as far east as the lower Volga River.[29] However, more certain evidence comes from the mid-fourth millennium BCE once bronze technology diffused into the area around the Black Sea and in particular to the people of the Markop Culture (3700–3200 BCE), who lived tucked away southeast of the Sea of Azov where the steppes give way to the foothills of the northwest Caucasus Mountains in the Kuban River basin (Russia). Manifestations of this culture are found as far north and east as the lower Don River and the western Caspian region.

The people of the Markop built kurgans, raised barrows that served as elaborate mortuary complexes at the heart of which were wooden structures covered by massive stone mounds up to ten meters high and 200 meters in circumference. Different counts put the number of these kurgans at between 150 and 250, with each requiring thousands of days of collective labor to build.[30] The tombs inside the kurgans were loaded with spectacularly rich grave goods, including rare luxury, prestige, and ceremonial items. Thousands of precious metal items have been recovered, including jewelry, figurines, vessels, and silver rods of tubing with bull figures perhaps used as staffs or wands. One body had clothing decorated with ornaments, including gold appliques that had been attached. Accompanying all of this gold and silver were turquoise and carnelian beads, and stone and ceramic vessels. Nor was bronze neglected. Along with ceremonial prestige weapons such as daggers and axes were some items that appear to have been utilitarian, such as adzes and hoes. There were also bronze bowls and cauldrons perhaps used during bouts of prodigious consumption at ceremonial feasting.

The Markop kurgans and their luxury grave goods raise obvious questions beginning with why the kurgans were built, why they were so lavishly furnished, and how they were paid for. The short answer is metallurgy. The longer answer is the exchange of metal ores and finished metal goods. This was the Bronze Age, metal-working technology was spreading, and in some places metals were being produced on a large scale. The Caucasus Mountains proved to be a great source of ore deposits, particularly copper. Ore, perhaps in the form of ingots, was brought through one or more corridors in the Caucasus to Markop, from where it was distributed east and west across Eurasia. The wealth, and thus the power, of those who were in control at Markop came from their position as middlemen in the metal business. As an indication of how far Markop trade may have reached, at least indirectly, what have been identified as Markop-style ceramic vessels have turned up in Syria and northern Mesopotamia.[31] The kurgans, the fabulous grave goods, and the long distance trade all signaled that important interrelated processes were transforming Markop society: social differentiation and stratification, hereditary inequality and formalized leadership, and the emergence of an elite. As they gained status and power, elites like those who had the Markop kurgans built became plugged into an exchange network of high value prestige goods, allowing them to acquire the exotica and symbolic items that marked them off as special people within their society.

If the rise of the Markop elite foreshadowed the development of social structures elsewhere, it was due, in part, to the special geographical location of Markop as an entry point into the wider Eurasian economy. Across the steppes, most people still practiced transhumance agro-pastoralism with cattle as their principal animal, and the accumulation of wealth, the advance of social differentiation, and the concomitant development of long-distance exchange were gradual processes fueled by demand for metals. This was sustained using wheeled vehicles that enabled the transportation of heavy ores far beyond riverine or coastal trading routes. The mobility of people on the steppes was likely beneficial on a very broad scale, and their ability to act as middlemen in emerging networks of exchange across Eurasia made them sought after trading partners. The people who lived north of the steppes in the taiga forest and beyond had their own goods to trade, foremost of which were skins and furs from animals not available on the steppes like bears and sable, and other wild animal products like horns, antlers, tusks, and castoreum as well as some wild plant products used in various concoctions for medicine.[32] As well as connecting the steppe with sites such as Markop, goods like these that could be obtained by steppe traders were also in demand by those who lived to the south and east of Eurasia in settled agricultural areas, including China, where the domestication of rice and millet had taken place as early as 6000 BCE. This transit trade was sustained by a demand for metal products in the north.[33]

Interregional contacts across the steppes greatly increased during the second half of the second millennium BCE and by the beginning of the first millennium BCE contacts were becoming networks.[34] The impact of these growing links has been identified as a major factor in changing burial patterns in Mongolia and southern Siberia, between 1400 and 1000 BCE, with the construction of khirigsuurs. These monumental burial mounds with stone enclosures used for human internment, smaller surrounding heaps of stones, and stone pathways, all together comprised a ritual landscape.[35] Khirigsuurs were often associated with deer stones, steles standing up to fifteen feet high. These stones had detailed carvings showing deer in what is referred to as "synchronized flight" with snouts pointed upward. They could also contain renderings of other forest animals as well as circles, weapons, and, rarely, a human head. The deer, in the most likely interpretation, was supposed to be accompanying the deceased to the afterlife.[36] Khirigsuurs and deer stones did not include grave goods, but clearly these were memorials to important and powerful people. Other burial sites of a slightly later period from the Khangal Valley (Mongolia) lacked the imposing khirigsuurs and deer stones but did contain imported items made of bronze as well as jade and turquoise from far to the south. The Karasuk people who lived in the Minusinsk Basin of the Yenisei River and the river valley bottoms of the Altai Mountains (Siberia) made their own prestige goods including bronze ornaments and stylized weapons that they exported westward to the central regions of the steppes and southeast through Mongolia to the borderlands of China. The copper in this bronze came from local mines, but the tin had to be imported, signs that something like a trading system was at work.[37] Social inequality and the concentration of power had come to the far corners of the eastern steppe, a process accompanied by the accumulation of high value exotic goods acquired through long distance exchange whether or not these goods ended up being buried with their owners as had been done in the Markop kurgans.

As commercial exchange grew, commodities would become increasingly valued for their exchange potential than for the status they brought as prestige items. By the second millennium BCE, tangled webs of long-distance trade linked Mesopotamia, Persia, Egypt, and the Eastern Mediterranean south through the Persian Gulf and east to the Indus River Valley. To the north and east, precocious well-fortified urban settlements along with productive irrigation-based agricultural settlements in Central Asia became woven into this expanding commercial fabric. More economically, culturally, and politically advanced places became increasingly dependent at certain levels of their economies on expanding their wealth from regional and long-distance trade. This interconnectedness reached to the borderlands of what is today northwest China, but very sporadically and indirectly. The embryonic structure of a trans-Eurasian exchange system was taking shape.

Case Study: The Incense Road

The Incense Road offers an excellent early example of an enduring trade route that grew from the exchange of one particularly prominent commodity – incense. It is an interesting example of a route with origins in the early millennia BCE that took the shape of a dominant backbone for mainstream traffic with features that were defined by the region's unique geographic, geological, and climatic conditions.

The Incense Road stretched across the Arabian Peninsula from the southeast to the northwest although more at an angle than a straight line. This was because the Incense Road went through Yemen in the southwest. For international trade Yemen was the most promising location in the Arabian Peninsula, situated at the intersection of the Red Sea and the Gulf of Aden in the corner where two continents came together. To the east and south lay the Indian Ocean basin, the only ocean-spanning commercial network of the time stretching from the shores of East Africa to India and eventually China via Southeast Asia. To the north was the Mediterranean basin, more compact but a center of ancient trade and commerce. Geography made Yemen the linchpin for maritime and overland trade. During the first millennium BCE this combination of factors allowed for the emergence of true kingdoms, among the most important of which was Saba. Ancient writers characterized them as being prosperous and productive with beautiful cities, causing this region to be dubbed "Arabia Felix" (depending on translation, "the Blest", "the Happy", or "the Fortunate").[38] Goods arrived from India to the port of Eudaimon Arabia (Aden) lying to the east of the Bab el-Mandeb, the straits that separated southwestern Arabia from the African continent at the mouth of the Red Sea. There they were exchanged for goods coming from Egypt and the Mediterranean as well as the local products of Arabia.

The precise origins of the Incense Road are unclear, and the earliest accounts suggest only sporadic exchanges, rather the establishment of an effective commercial system. As early as the fifteenth century BCE, the Egyptian Pharoah Hatshepsut's celebrated expedition to Punt may have brought back frankincense or myrrh trees, and various forms of incense reached ancient Egypt overland along the Red Sea shore.[39] Some south Arabian incense also reached Mesopotamia and Syria but sporadically and not through an organized system. Another early reference to the trade has been suggested in the Queen of Sheba's reported journey to meet King Solomon in Jerusalem around the tenth century BCE, for which she was accompanied by "a great caravan of camels loaded with spices, large quantities of gold, and precious jewels.[40] This trade in frankincense and myrrh would have been possible following the domestication of the dromedary, a process that was completed by the twelfth century BCE.[41] By the time the Queen visited Jerusalem, ongoing trade relations between Israel and southwest Arabia over an existing route was operational, by land and sea, but the scale of these exchanges remain unclear.[42] Some historians have pointed out a number of problems in using the Solomon story as straight history: to begin with, frankincense is not specifically mentioned in the Biblical passage, but rather the much broader term "spices" is used. In the ancient world frankincense and myrrh could be included as such, but so could a lot of other forms of incense not to mention what is thought of today as actual spices like cinnamon and pepper. More importantly, it is not likely that camel domestication had reached the point where long-distance camel caravans were the norm. If frankincense, myrrh, or a similar form of incense was used in Old Kingdom Egypt and elsewhere at such an early time, it likely came from Red Sea trade rather than across the desert in western Arabia, which does require camels. Finally, the Sabaean kingdom probably did not exist in the tenth century BCE, and when it did come into being, it was not ruled by queens. Furthermore, the use of Arabian frankincense seems to pick up considerably at the northern end of the Incense Road in places like Syria, Palestine, and Greece only towards the end of the seventh century BCE, when the Incense Road became fully developed as a regularly used trading route.

Greek and Roman authors writing in the final centuries of the last millennium BCE understood that unique conditions in Southern Arabia and the Gulf of Aden region provided their much-in-demand products in the form of frankincense and myrrh. Strabo was aware that "the part of Arabia that produces the spices is small" but that it was "from this small territory that the country got the name of 'Blest', because such merchandise is rare in our part of the world and costly. To-day, to be sure, the Arabs are well to do and even rich, because their trade is extensive and abundant."[43] These "spices" were the source of gum resins that were used as incense burned for both religious and domestic purposes and were highly sought after in the wider Mediterranean world. They were used in sacrifices and other ceremonies, since it was believed the gods had a particular liking for their fragrances, and at funerals to mask the odor of rotting or burning flesh. They were also made into perfumes, scented oils, and ointments and used for fumigating buildings when necessary. Eventually they became important ingredients in medicines. The center of their production was to the east of Yemen, where myrrh (*Commiphora myrrha*) and frankincense (*Boswellia sacra*) trees grew across Hadramaut and Dhufar, the coastal regions of south central and southeastern Arabia. Together with Somalia and the island of Socotra, these sites were the only sources for these expensive commodities that had been in demand since the days of the pharaohs.

Yet, even as these commodities were prized and the journey to their source increasingly representing a well-trodden trading route, the distance and exotic rarity of the goods meant that knowledge of their origin remained ambiguous. In Dhufar at the southern end of the Incense Road, Herodotus reported that frankincense trees were guarded by tiny, winged snakes that could be driven off only by burning storax resin. He also thought that cinnamon and its related product cassia were Arabian products. According to the story he related, cinnamon was collected from some unknown source by great birds and stored in nests perched on unreachable cliffs. To obtain the cinnamon, Arabian merchants cut up the carcasses of large animals, which they placed below the cliffs for the birds to gather. Eventually the greedy birds accumulated so much meat it broke their nests, which fell to the ground allowing the Arabians to collect the cinnamon.[44] Subsequent writers recognized that cinnamon came from trees, but they, too, believed it originated in Arabia. Cinnamon, frankincense, myrrh, and other fragrant trees were said to be guarded by "a multitude of snakes, the colour of which is dark red, their length a span, and their bites altogether incurable; they bite by leaping upon the victim".[45] This warning was passed down from Herodotus to the second century BCE geographer Agatharchides of Cnidus, whose work was the source for reports in both Diodorus Siculus and Strabo. Such scary, fantastic stories were potentially conjured up and spread by those Arabian merchants who actually controlled the sources and transport of frankincense and myrrh to discourage interlopers. Cinnamon and cassia were not products of Arabia or nearby Somalia, which was given the appellation "Cinnamon Country"; cinnamon actually came from Sri Lanka and cassia from southern China and Southeast Asia. They were from Arabia and Somalia only in the sense that they passed through these countries on the transit trade via the port of Ocilia south of Muza at the tip of the Bab el-Mandeb.

For the goods that were produced in Arabia, frankincense and myrrh, they were exported through two common routes. One option was to transport them through the port of Kane lying far eastward of Eudaimon Arabia. The alternative was a long overland haul westward through Yemen, then due north: it was this latter option that formed the much-storied trade route system known as the Incense Road. The core of this route was a low volume-high value trade in luxury commodities destined for the super-rich and powerful. Tracing this route using Pliny and Strabo starts at the source of frankincense, an area which Pliny refers to as Sariba, meaning "secret mystery". This was a region of impenetrable rocks and inaccessible cliffs to which only a people he calls the Astramitae had access. From there, Pliny reported that frankincense was transferred to the Minaeans along one narrow road: "It was these people who originated the trade and who chiefly practice it ... none of the Arabians besides these have ever seen an incense tree."[46]

Arab merchants carried their precious cargo to Yemen, where the Incense Road made a sharp turn to the north. This was a path that required specialist knowledge and skills to traverse safely, and was described as a long stretch of sandy barren soil with a few palm and thorn trees. Water had to come from wells, and the people lived in tents and tended camels. The route ran inland parallel to the Red Sea and the mountains of al-Hijaz through oasis stops like Yathrib (Medina) and Dedan (al-Ala). The only product that may have been available along the way at select places was gold. Strabo does make one curious observation as to the methodology of trade along the route that may be easily misinterpreted: "Those who live close to one another receive in continuous succession the loads of aromatics and deliver them to their neighbors as far away as Syria and Mesopotamia."[47] He seems to be describing relay trade, the ancient way of passing goods down-the-line. More likely he is referring to circuit trade in which caravans operated in linked, segmented regional circuits using hubs rather than making complete round trips from one side of the system to the other. It was not only individual merchants who grew rich from exploiting this trade.

The Incense Road did have other routes that intersected it at strategic points. The first bifurcation came at Nagram, where the road was not quite out of Yemen. This went northeast to the Persian Gulf and from there by boat to Mesopotamia. The second came at Yathrib but then split again, one part heading straight to southern Mesopotamia, others going north to the Levant and Anatolia or northwest to the Red Sea, then by boat to the Egyptian coast. The third, at Dûmâ, again headed northeast but this time into the wadi system, which could take travelers farther northeast or northwest.[48] For caravans that stayed all the way on the central route, the normal trip took about seventy days. The principal northern hub of the Incense Road was Petra, which started as a series of caves and became a city carved out of rock. The local people, the Nabataeans, had been herdsmen and occasional bandits who figured out that offering merchants services like food, water, protection, and cool places to rest was more profitable and safer than trying to rob them.[49] Cities like Palmyra and Petra, located in well-resourced pockets on the edges of the Syrian Desert, became important centers of trade through their supply of merchant caravans. They would also, along with larger states, come to take a more prominent role in policing and taxing the traffic that sustained them. Through these exchanges, Arabia's rare and precious commodities would reach markets that were more welcoming to traders from a wider world of trade, who would take them on the next steps of their journey to destinations across Europe, North Africa, and Western Asia.

Partly due to its challenging desert geography and partly to the tremendous wealth it generated in profits and taxes, polities that lay across the route most of the time attempted to ensure the route's safety and stability when they weren't trying to steal chunks of it from each other. One positive consequence of this was that it was a much straighter system with caravans funneled along a more pronounced, well protected backbone with well-defined water resources and refreshment stations. Stable government eased the establishment of essential institutions and infrastructure. On a more negative side, the caravans were easy pickings for the taxman, and charges imposed by states or small, local powers along the way drastically increased transaction costs for the journey. Pliny described how, after the frankincense was collected, it had to be brought to the local capital city of Sabota, where priests extracted a tithe; it was a capital crime to avoid this. The caravans then passed on to the country of the Gebbanitae, where the king levied a tax. Following this Pliny counted sixty-five stages where taxes, dues, fees, and expenses as well as mandatory gifts and bribes were expected to be paid. This was, of course, in addition to the normal costs of transport:

> All along the route they keep on paying, at one place for water, at another for fodder, or the charges for lodging at the halts, and at the various tolls-gates; so that the expenses mount up to 688 denarii [a coin of 3.89 grams 98% pure silver] per camel before the Mediterranean coast is reached; and then again payment is made to the customs officers of our empire.[50]

Considering these charges, the profits on incense needed to be considerable to justify merchants taking this challenging route and it's not surprising that as the Red Sea's maritime trade increased during this same period, that alternative routes carry goods to the coast quickly, rather than the arduous journey overland, became more popular.

Following the inception of Roman control over the region after 106 CE, who came to control the northwestern corner of Arabia directly and wielded considerable influence over the rest, demand for the products of the Incense Road peaked during the halcyon days of the empire. However, the Romans were never able to establish control over the sites of production to the south of the peninsular. By the time the Romans came, Arabia Felix enjoyed a long-standing reputation for fabulous wealth. Pliny complained that Arabia along with India and China were responsible for the huge balance of payments deficit the Roman Empire had run up amounting to one hundred million sesterces a year (a sesterce was worth one-quarter of a denarius).[51] Under Augustus an expedition was sent to find the land of frankincense and myrrh: "He conceived the purpose of winning the Arabians over to himself or of subjugating them," Strabo notes. "They [the Arabians] were very wealthy ... but never expended with outsiders any part of what they received; for he [Augustus] expected either to deal with wealthy friends or to master wealthy enemies."[52] In the end he did neither. The expedition's guide, a Nabataean official, led the Romans on a wild goose chase up and down the peninsula. After six fruitless months the Romans returned to Egypt; the land of frankincense and myrrh remained safe from outsiders.

If the Romans did not come to occupy western and southern Arabia, they did work to expand trade in the area mostly through the Red Sea from their base in Egypt. Overland trade across the Incense Road went into slow decline in favor of ports on the western coast of the Red Sea that opened to caravan routes going to the Nile. In 363 CE Petra was partially destroyed by an earthquake, and eventually traders stopped going there. It was abandoned in the seventh century CE. The slow but irreversible decline of the Roman Empire from the third century CE on would have a profound impact on trade and commerce. The economy of the western half of the empire deteriorated and eventually collapsed. The economy of the eastern half faltered, then transitioned under what became the Byzantine Empire. The elite classes of what had been the Roman Empire still desired luxury products, and the Christian church and Byzantine court demanded certain items including incense, spices, and silk. But the decline in wealth meant a weakening in buying power and a slackening of demand. A new market was opening in China, where Buddhism was gaining ground. Earlier only elite families burned incense, but Buddhist rituals mandated it, so the demand greatly increased.[53] Of course, the Incense Road ran from east to west whereas China was far to the east of Dhufar and Hadramaut. China-bound frankincense and myrrh would not be going over this particular route.

As for the trade across western Arabia, there were various desert tracks, the most prominent of which is sometimes seen as a revamped version of the Incense Road. However, the traffic in incense was largely gone, and the remaining trade was mostly regional. Nevertheless, along this route marketplaces and commercial hubs did a brisk business, and Arab intermediaries who bought and sold, lent capital, and serviced the caravans prospered although not to the degree of the earlier era. In the sixth century CE the southern end was anchored in the Kingdom of Himyar, which was presumed to play the same role as its more illustrious predecessors. However, this was a more rough-and-tumble world than earlier, and Himyar was not Saba. When the Himyarite king, Yusuf, who was Jewish, captured the Christian town of

Najran, a crossroads for caravan traffic, and massacred the local clergy, the Christian kingdom of Ethiopia retaliated by invading and taking control over the southern end of the western Arabian caravan trade. This lasted for four decades, at which time the Persians replaced them. In the meantime, the old Incense Road had succumbed to the inevitable rises and falls of history as had its next-door rival, the Red Sea maritime route. The challenges of transporting goods across the desert had incentivized the use of specialist traders to carry goods along a well-defined route for hundreds of years, but as markets shifted, the costs of maintaining such a linear traffic were just too high.

Case Study: The Amber Trails

Conversely, the Amber Trails present an early example of a trading network that was structured very differently to the linear Incense Road in Arabia.[54] Despite the similar importance of a single commodity – amber in this case - the paths taken by traders were not limited to a single, distinct route, but rather formed a web of intersecting corridors that carried similar goods in roughly the same directions. Early Europe had its share of regional systems circulating polished ceremonial axes, flint daggers, obsidian blades, and similar items, but as systems fused together in response to demands for particular products, the most notable to merge for long-distance exchange had their source not in a single geographical location, but in a number of coastal sites in the continent's distant north where amber was in rich supply. Amber is a yellowish to brownish translucent fossilized resin found in various parts of the world. Chemical analysis confirms that in the case of the ancient European Amber Trails this particular amber originated in the Baltic Sea area.

Amber could be found across a wide geography in Scandinavia and there was no possibility of a single region monopolizing production (as was the case with incense). Perhaps as a consequence, there is limited interest or material on the part of ancient authors to understand its origins, although there is also less interest in general in these northern geographies. Rather than mysterious tales of flying snakes, Herodotus took little interest. He referred to amber only in a negative context, in his survey of the "outermost reaches of the world". After covering "the most remote countries" in Asia and North Africa ("Libya"), he says he has "no reliable information to pass on about the western margins of Europe, because I at any rate do not accept that there is a river which the natives there call the Eridanus said to issue into the northern sea and to be the source of amber".[55] Pliny, writing some 3000 years or more after the amber trade had been in operation, offers some more specific suggestions about the origins of amber. He noted that, "it is well established that amber is a product of islands in the Northern Ocean",[56] meaning the seas to the north of Germany. Amber could be mined, quarried, or dredged from the sea, but in this instance, "the amber is washed upon the shores of the mainland",[57] where it was simply collected by people walking on the beach. While Pliny claimed that the amber came from a specific location the

Romans called Glass Island,[58] in fact, it was much more widespread, with Denmark, especially Zealand and Jutland, the main location. The collection area probably reached at least to Poland and in the opposite direction, according to Pliny, to the southeastern coast of Britain, "being swept along so easily that it seems to hover in the water without settling on the sea-bed".[59]

As a precious commodity that could be collected with relative ease across a wide geography, it's not surprising that it came to be traded at a very early date. The spread of Baltic amber was wide ranging and it could be found across Europe by the fourth millennium BCE, as seen in the recent discovery of an amber bead recovered in a Late Neolithic funerary cave in northeastern Iberia[60], but it was transported in its largest volumes across routes running southward from the Baltic to the major trading centers of the ancient Mediterranean. Amber was hard but lightweight and took a fine polish. It was an elite product not used for utilitarian purposes; its function was ornamental, mostly in the form of jewelry as pendants, carved beads, and above all necklaces, some of which were very elaborate and multi-stranded. Where it was not common (i.e., outside the Baltic region), amber was in high demand. During the Bronze Age, possession of amber was considered a source of prestige and status at a time when social ranking and political hierarchies were transforming northern and central Europe. Before it was ever bought and sold as a commodity, amber was an important element in prestige-chain exchanges that linked alliance networks of higher and lower chiefdoms. However, there is also evidence of much broader engagement with the amber trade. Amber finds from Thy in northern Jutland associated with the Early Neolithic Funnelbeaker Culture (4000–3300 BCE) and from a Late Bronze Age (1100–500 BCE) settlement, have helped show how the amber trade could take place outside elite control and contributed to shifting local, regional, and international connections across this long period.[61] The rapid scaling up of local amber collection at Thy took place in response to international demand – an engagement with trans-regional patterns of exchange that were understood and responded to by common households.[62] Of course, exchange required reciprocity and that was provided by the northward flow of metal products, especially bronze. Denmark, in particular, was noted for its high-quality flint but lacked metal resources. Amber and probably furs, which are archaeologically invisible, became the business of those who controlled the bronze trade.[63]

The various branches of the Amber Trails traveled up and down river valleys between chiefly centers establishing long distance interregional exchange networks. The Oder and Vistula rivers, both of which were navigable through most of their courses and both of which branched into sizeable tributaries, became trade corridors linked to the Danube. Forts and then towns grew up along the routes. Amber crossed the Alps in the west and the Carpathians in the east and in the second millennium BCE moved down the Balkans to Mycenean Greece, where some of it was deposited in the shaft graves of elite burials in places like Mycenae and Pylos. It was widely traded in central and southern Britain during the Wessex Culture (2000–1650 BCE), a period associated with the building of Stonehenge and the use of barrows for burying the princely dead. Along with some superbly crafted gold objects and daggers from as far away as Mycenaean Greece, Wessex amber, most of which appears to have been imported, was made into an extraordinarily beautiful variety of jewelry. Across much of Europe, elites shared common practices and technologies that were transmitted, at least in part, through trade routes that linked the Baltic to Britain, the Aegean, and beyond – routes that were as important for conveying ideas as they were for carrying commodities like Egyptian glass, metals like tin and gold, and of course Baltic amber.[64]

In western Europe, the density of the trading networks that carried amber from Scandinavia have been described as a "triangular Middle Bronze Age trade system" that also included copper from the Italian alps and tin from Britain.[65] First, by around 1500 BCE, amber was transported from coastal communities of Jutland and northwest Germany down the Weser river that led directly to one of the centers of the Tumulus Culture with rich Middle Bronze Age burials, where numerous complex necklaces including Baltic amber have been uncovered. At the same time, the origin of copper in Danish bronze artifacts was increasingly likely to have been found in Italy, with a lesser trade bringing copper from Slovakian deposits. As well as trading copper north, the North Italian Terramare Culture also represented a hub linking these European networks into wider Mediterranean commercial circuits. As well as this north-south route, a further link was established on an east-west axis with tin producing Cornwall, in southern England. An analysis of the presence of foreign swords in burials across these routes suggest high levels of interaction and even the possibility of "well organized caravans protected by warriors moving on a regular basis between the hubs in local chiefdoms". As this suggests, the Amber Trails represented the nascent development not just of an intermittent trade or the slow transfer of goods between neighbors, but rather a highly organized form of early commodity trade, that was able to transport large quantities of goods across great distances and across cultures.[66]

Yet, despite this scope, and the significance of these trading routes in prehistoric Europe, there is only limited textual evidence to explain how these functioned. There is an interesting story in Herodotus, who lived about half a millennium before Pliny, that has often been associated with amber and the practice of gift-giving. It concerns a people called the Hyperboreans, who lived "beyond the north wind". The report comes from the island of Delos, legendary birthplace of Apollo:

> The Delians say that sacred objects are tied up inside a bundle of wheat straw and are transported from the Hyperboreans first to Scythia, then westward as far as possible – that is, to the Adriatic – through a chain of successive neighboring tribes.[67]

Finally they reached the Greek world, where they were passed from city state to city state until they arrived at Delos: "The purpose of their visit was to bring Eileithyia tribute they had undertaken to pay in exchange for a quick and easy labour at childbirth."[68] This down-the-line route Herodotus describes running to the north and east of Greece from the Black Sea region, across Scythia and into the interior of Asia, is often associated with an early version of the Steppe Road, that long-distance system that was in operation before the Silk Roads and ran parallel to it several hundred miles to the north.[69] It has often been speculated, perhaps because of where the Hyperboreans were said to have lived, that the sacred items inside the straw were amber.[70] In describing how the amber gets from source to market, that is, over the Amber Trails, Pliny was disappointingly brief: "It is conveyed by the Germans mostly into the province of Pannonia [Hungary and neighboring territory]. From there it was first brought into prominence by the Veneti ... who are close neighbors of the Pannonians and live around the Adriatic."[71] By Pliny's time the main hub for the amber trade in Pannonia was Carnuntum on the Danube River east of Vindobona (Vienna). How it traveled across northern Europe, a trip, Pliny admits, of 600 miles, invites speculation.

Despite the limited interest in the amber trade by ancient writers, there is evidence showing that, as the practice of prestige-based gift-giving faded, amber became a true commodity handled by a profit-seeking professional merchant class in a market-based economy. In the first millennium BCE as Europe transitioned from the Late Bronze Age to the Iron Age, the demand for amber moved farther into the Mediterranean region. Workshops were in operation on the Adriatic, and in Italy the Etruscans became noted for their skill in carving amber. Baltic amber went far beyond its immediate distribution chain, having been found in a burial site in Mongolia from the early first millennium BCE.[72] In the West, with the rise of the Roman Empire, that part of the Amber Trails system running through Germany remained outside imperial territory, but the passage from Pannonia to the Adriatic came under the In the sixth century CE Romans, who paved parts of it, making it, in a sense, an actual road. Tribal migrations periodically cut the system, some of which had to be reestablished during Nero's reign.[73] In the sixth century CE Pannonia came under the control of the Lombards and then the Avars, a Türkic-speaking nomadic people who established an empire stretching into the Balkans. When the Danube frontier was lost to the Romans, the Amber Trail disintegrated. The Avar Empire in turn was defeated between 791 and 796 in wars against the rising empire of Charlemagne and thereafter collapsed. Sections of the Amber Trails were revived under the Carolingians, and today parts of the old system can be traced by archaeologists through coin finds particularly around the Danube.[74]

Across these contexts, the long-distance trade in amber from Scandinavia to sites across Europe took place across a complex web of exchanges that followed no singular route and was certainly not managed by a single state or group. As such, while the survival of amber in the archaeological record makes it especially useful for tracing these early interconnections, it is also indicative of a much broader array of exchanges. The movement of goods like amber coincided over very long distances with the exchange of walrus tusks and furs, as well as the movement of people, including enslaved captives, traders, and soldiers.[75] While not necessarily part of the classic Amber Trails, these exchanges supplemented and expanded the scope of that trade into the North Sea, and, especially into mercantile networks that ran from the Baltic to the Black Sea and into the Eurasian steppes.[76] As this suggests, long-distance trade in the premodern world was not limited to the exchange of luxury goods across well-defined routes, but rather these were part of much larger networks of exchange that crisscrossed and intersected with each other from one end of Eurasia to the other.

Notes

1 For definitions and discussion of prehistoric trade and exchange, see: Marcel Mauss, *The Gift: Forms and functions of exchange in archaic societies* (London, 2002 [1925]), p. 3; C. Refrew, "Trade and Culture Process in European Prehistory", *Current Anthropology* 15 (1969), p. 152, pp. 151–69; K. Polanyi, "Traders and Trade" in J. A. Sabloff (ed.), *Ancient Civilizations and Trade* (Alburquerque, 1975), pp. 133–4, pp. 133–54; C. Runnels and T. H. Van Andel, "Trade and the Origins of Agriculture in the Eastern Mediterranean", *Journal of Mediterranean Archaeology* 1:1 (1988), p. 92, pp. 83–109; M. D. Sahlins, "On the Sociology of Primitive Exchange" in S. Gudeman (ed.), *Economic Anthropology* (Cheltenham, 1998), p. 82, pp. 82–140.

2 Alison Brooks et al., "Long-Distance Stone Transport and Pigment Use in the Earliest Middle Stone Age", *Science* 360 (2018), pp. 90–4.

3 Johan Ling, Richard Chacon, and Kristian Kristiansen (eds.), *Trade Before Civilisation: Long distance exchange and the rise of social complexity* (Cambridge, 2022), pp. 1–20.

4 Thomas N. Headland and Lawrence A. Reid, "Hunter-Gatherers and their Neighbors from Prehistory to the Present", *Current Anthropology* 30:1 (1989), pp. 43–66.

5 Robert Wenke, *Patterns in Prehistory: Humankind's first three million years* (Oxford, 2006); Peter Bellwood, *Prehistory of the Indo-Malaysian Archipelago* (revised edition) (Sydney, 2007).

6 Benjamin S. Arbuckle and Emily L. Hammer, "The Rise of Pastoralism in the Ancient Near East", *Journal of Archaeological Research* 27 (2019), pp. 391–449.

7 For debates about the commercial incentives in prehistoric trade, see: Rahul Oka and Chapurukha M. Kusimba, "The Archaeology of Trading Systems, Part 1: Towards a new trade synthesis", *Journal of Archaeological Research* 16:4 (2008), pp. 342–6, pp. 339–95.

8 Robin Skeates, "Neolithic Exchange in Central and Southern Italy" in Christopher Scarre and Frances Healey (eds.), *Trade and Exchange in Prehistoric Europe: Proceedings of a conference held at the University of Bristol* (Oxford, 1992), pp. 109–14.

9 Albert Ammerman and Christopher Polglase, "The Exchange of Obsidian at Neolithic Sites in Italy" in Christopher Scarre and Frances Healey (eds.), *Trade and Exchange in Prehistoric Europe: Proceedings of a conference held at the University of Bristol* (Oxford, 1992), pp. 101–8.

10 Jeremy Sabloff and C. C. Lamberg-Karlovsky (eds.), *Ancient Civilization and Trade* (Albuquerque, 1975), p. 102; Elizabeth Brumfiel and Timothy Earle, *Specialization, Exchange and Complex Societies* (Cambridge, 1997), pp. 1–37.
11 P. Petrequin, F. Jeudy, and C. Jeunesse, "Neolithic Quarries, the Exchange of Axes and Social Control in the Southern Vosger" in Christopher Scarre and Frances Healey (eds.), *Trade and Exchange in Prehistoric Europe: Proceedings of a conference held at the University of Bristol* (Oxford, 1992), pp. 45–60.
12 Hsiao-Chun Hung et al., "Ancient Jades Map 3000 Years of Prehistoric Exchange in Southeast Asia", *Proceedings of the National Academy of Sciences of the United States of America* 104:50 (2007), pp. 19,745–50.
13 Sarah Semple, "Materializing Inequalities in Past, Present and Future", *World Archaeology* 54:4 (2022), pp. 493–501.
14 Rafi Benvenisti, *Economic Life at the Dawn of History in Mesopotamia and Ancient Egypt: The birth of market economy in the third and second millennia BCE* (Berlin, 2024), pp. 6–26.
15 Ursula Brosseder and Bryan K. Miller, "Global Networks and Local Agents in the Iron Age Eurasian Steppe" in Nicole Boivin and Michael Frachetti (eds.), *Globalization in Prehistory: Contact, exchange and the "People Without History"* (Cambridge, 2018), p. 162, pp. 162–83.
16 Aleksandr Diachenko and Francesco Menotti, "The Gravity Model: Monitoring the formation and development of the Tripolye culture giant-settlements in Ukraine", *Journal of Archaeological Science* 39:8 (2012), pp. 2810–17; John Chapman, "The Standard Model, the Maximalists and the Minimalists: New interpretations of Trypillia mega-sites", *Journal of World Prehistory* 30:3 (2017), pp. 221–37.
17 Bisserka Gaydarska (ed.), *Early Urbanism in Europe: The Trypillia megasites of the Ukrainian forest-steppe* (Berlin, 2020).
18 Dragoş Gheorghiu, "A Fire Cult in South European Chalcolithic Traditions? On the relationship between ritual contexts and the instrumentality of fire" in Dragoş Gheorghiu, D. Barrowclough, and C. Malone (eds.), *Cult in Context: Reconsidering ritual in archaeology* (Oxford, 2007), pp. 269–84.
19 Cornelia Magda-Mantu, Gheorghe Niculescu, and Ana-Maria Vlad, "Painting pigments for ceramic decoration in the Cucuteni-Tripolye cultural complex" in F. Draşovean (ed.), *Festschrift für Gheorghe Lazarovici zum 60. Geburstag* (Timişoara, 2001), pp. 191–210; J. Chapman and B. Gaydarska, "The Provision of Salt to Tripolye Mega-Sites" in A. Korvin-Piotrovsky, V. Kruts, and S. Rizhov (eds.), *Tripolye Settlement-Giants* (Kiev, 2003), pp. 203–11.
20 E. E. Kuzmina and Victor Mair, *The Prehistory of the Silk Road* (Philadelphia, PA, 2015), p. 48.
21 James Mallory, *In Search of the Indo-Europeans: Language, archaeology and myth* (London, 1989).
22 Marija Gimbutas, *The Goddesses and Gods of Old Europe: 6500–3500 BC: Myths and cult images* (London, 1982), p. 1; Henrietta Todorova, "The Neolithic, Eneolithic and Transitional Period in Bulgarian Prehistory" in Douglass Bailey, Ivan Panayotov, and Stefan Alexandrov (eds.), *Prehistoric Bulgaria* (Madison, WI, 1995), pp. 79–98.
23 Marsha Levine, Colin Renfrew, and Katie Boyle (eds.), *Prehistoric Steppe Adaptation and the Horse* (Cambridge, 2003): chapters by Sandra Olsen, "The Exploitation of Horses at Botai, Kazakhstan", pp. 83–104; and Norbert Benecke and Angela von den Dreisch, "Horse Exploitation in the Kazakh Steppes During the Neolithic and Bronze Ages", pp. 69–82.
24 David Anthony, *The Horse, the Wheel, and Language: How Bronze-Age riders from the Eurasian steppes shaped the modern world* (2007); Phil Kohl, "The Ancient Economy, Transferable Technologies and the Bronze Age World System: A view from the northeastern frontier of the ancient Near East" in Michael John

Rowlands, Larsen Mogens, and Kristian Kristiansen (eds.), *Centre and Periphery in the Ancient World*, pp. 143–64.
25 M. A. Littauer and J. H. Crouwel, *Wheeled Vehicles and Ridden Animals in the Ancient Near East* (1979); Jan Albert Bakker et al., "The Earliest Evidence of Wheeled Vehicles in Europe and the Near East", *Antiquity* 73, 282 (1999), pp. 778–90; Katheryn Linduff, "A Walk on the Wild Side: Late Shang appropriation of horses in China" in Marsha Levine, Colin Renfrew, and Katie Boyle (eds.), *Prehistoric Steppe Adaptation and the Horse* (Cambridge, 2003), pp. 139–62.
26 Robert Drews, *Early Riders: The beginnings of mounted warfare in Asia and Europe* (Abingdon, 2004).
27 Luc Kwanten, *Imperial Nomads: A history of central Asia, 500–1500* (Leicester, 1979), p. 208.
28 Nicole Boivin and Michael Frachetti (eds.), *Globalization in Prehistory: Contact, exchange and the "People Without History"* (Cambridge, 2018).
29 Philip Kohl, *The Making of Bronze Age Eurasia* (Cambridge, 2007), pp. 31–4.
30 Philip Kohl, *The Making of Bronze Age Eurasia* (Cambridge, 2007), p. 74.
31 Philip Kohl, *The Making of Bronze Age Eurasia* (Cambridge, 2007), p. 74.
32 Xinru Liu and Lynda Norene Shaffer, *Connections Across Eurasia: Transportation, communication, and cultural exchange on the Silk Roads* (New York, 2007), pp. 10–11.
33 Katherine Linduff and Jianun Mei, "Metallurgy in Ancient Eastern Asia: Retrospect and prospects", *Journal of World Prehistory* 22: 3 (2009), p. 274, pp. 265–81.
34 William Honeychurch, *Inner Asia and the Spatial Politics of Empire: Archaeology, mobility, and culture contact* (New York, 2015), p. 149.
35 William Honeychurch, *Inner Asia and the Spatial Politics of Empire: Archaeology, mobility, and culture contact* (New York, 2015), p. 113.
36 William Honeychurch, *Inner Asia and the Spatial Politics of Empire: Archaeology, mobility, and culture contact* (New York, 2015), pp. 116, 120.
37 William Honeychurch, *Inner Asia and the Spatial Politics of Empire: Archaeology, mobility, and culture contact* (New York, 2015), pp. 166–8.
38 Strabo, *Geographica*, vol. 16, book 4, part 2; Pliny, *Naturalis Historia*, book 5, chapter 11; Claudius Ptolemy, *The Geography*, trans. Edward Stevenson (New York, 1932), p. 137.
39 Filip Taterka, "Hatshepsut's Expedition to the Land of Punt – Novelty or Tradition?", *Current Research in Egyptology 2015: Proceedings of the Sixteenth Annual Symposium* (2016), pp. 114–23.
40 1 Kings 10:11.
41 Jan Retsö, "The Domestication of the Camel and the Establishment of the Frankincense Road from South Arabia", *Orientalia Suecana,* 40 (1991), pp. 187–219; Ludovic Orlando, "Back to the Roots and Routes of Dromedary Domestication", *Proceedings of the National Academy of Sciences of the United States of America* 113:24 (2016), pp. 6588–90.
42 Robert R. Stieglitz, "Long-Distance Seafaring in the Ancient Near East", *The Biblical Archaeologist* 47:3 (1984), pp. 134–42.
43 Strabo, *Geographica*, vol. 1, book 2, part 32.
44 Herodotus, *The Histories*, trans. Robin Waterfield (Oxford, 2008), pp. 214–15.
45 Diodorus Siculus, *Bibliotheca Historica*, vol. 3, book 47, part 3.
46 Pliny, *Naturalis Historia*, book 12, chapter 30.
47 Strabo, *Geographica*, vol. 16, book 4, parts 18–19.
48 Michael MacDonald, *Literacy and Identity in Pre-Islamic Arabia* (Surrey, 2009), pp. 334–5.
49 Tali Erickson-Gini and Yigal Israel, "Excavating the Nabataean Incense Road", *Journal of Eastern Mediterranean Archaeology & Heritage Studies* 1:1 (2013), pp. 24–53.

50 Pliny, *Naturalis Historia*, book 12, chapter 32.
51 Pliny, *Naturalis Historia*, book 12, chapter 41.
52 Strabo, *Geographica*, vol. 16, book 4, parts 22–3.
53 Olivia Milburn, "Aromas, Scents, and Spices: Olfactory culture in China before the arrival of Buddhism", *Journal of the American Oriental Society* 136:3 (2016), pp. 441–64.
54 For an overview of changing conceptions of the prehistoric amber trade, see: Arnold Spekke, *The Ancient Amber Routes and the Geographical Discovery of the Eastern Baltic* (Stockholm, 1957); Joan Todd, "A Reappraisal of the Prehistoric and Classical Amber Trade in the Light of New Evidence", *Journal of Baltic Studies* 5:4 (1974), pp. 295–314; Cat Jarman, *River Kings: A new history of Vikings from Scandinavia to the Silk Roads* (London, 2021).
55 Herodotus, *The Histories*, trans. Robin Waterfield (Oxford, 2008), p. 216.
56 Pliny, *Naturalis Historia*, book 37, chapter 11.
57 Pliny, *Naturalis Historia*, book 37, chapter 11.
58 Pliny, *Naturalis Historia*, book 4, chapter 13.
59 Pliny, *Naturalis Historia*, book 37, chapter 11.
60 M. Murillo-Barroso, A. Martín Cólliga, and M. Martinón-Torres, "The Earliest Baltic Amber in Western Europe", *Scientific Reports* 13 (2023), article 14250.
61 Timothy Earle, Jens-Henrik Bech, and Chiara Villa, "New Early Neolithic and Late Bronze Age Amber Finds from Thy", *Antiquity* 97:391 (2022), pp. 70–85.
62 Timothy Earle, Jens-Henrik Bech, and Chiara Villa, "New Early Neolithic and Late Bronze Age Amber Finds from Thy", *Antiquity* 97:391 (2022), p. 83.
63 Stephen Shennan, "Exchange and Ranking: The role of amber in the earlier Bronze Age of Europe" in Colin Renfrew and Stephen Shennan (eds.), *Ranking, Resources and Exchange: Aspects of the archaeology of early European society* (Cambridge, 1982), p. 40, pp. 33–45.
64 Kenneth Wardle, "Wessex and Mycenae: A rapprochement?", *Athens University Review of Archaeology* 4 (2020), pp. 461–70.
65 Kristian Kristiansen and Johan Ling, "A Triangular Middle Bronze Age Trade System of Amber, Copper and Tin, 1500–1300 BC" in C. C. Bakels, Q. P. J. Bourgeois, D. R. Fontijn, and R. Jansen (eds.), *Local Communities in the Big World of Prehistoric Northwest Europe* (Leiden, 2018), pp. 41–5.
66 Kristian Kristiansen and Johan Ling, "A Triangular Middle Bronze Age Trade System of Amber, Copper and Tin, 1500–1300 BC" in C. C. Bakels, Q. P. J. Bourgeois, D. R. Fontijn, and R. Jansen (eds.), *Local Communities in the Big World of Prehistoric Northwest Europe* (Leiden, 2018), p. 42.
67 Herodotus, *The Histories*, trans. Robin Waterfield (Oxford, 2008), p. 246.
68 Herodotus, *The Histories*, trans. Robin Waterfield (Oxford, 2008), p. 246.
69 Geoffrey Hudson, *Europe and China: A survey of their relations from the earliest times to 1800* (London, 1961), pp. 28–39, 48.
70 Herodotus, *The Histories*, trans. Robin Waterfield (Oxford, 2008), pp. 648–9.
71 Pliny, *Naturalis Historia*, book 37, chapter 11.
72 William Honeychurch, *Inner Asia and the Spatial Politics of Empire: Archaeology, mobility, and culture contact* (New York, 2015), pp. 281–2.
73 W. W. Tarn and G. T. Griffith, *Hellenistic Civilisation* (London, 1952), p. 259.
74 Michael McCormick, *Origins of the European Economy: Communications and commerce, AD 300–900* (Cambridge, 2001), pp. 370–81.
75 Søren Michael Sindbæk, "Local and Long-Distance Exchange" in Stefan Brink, *The Viking World* (London, 2008), pp. 150–8.
76 Cat Jarman, *River Kings: A new history of Vikings from Scandinavia to the Silk Roads*.

2 Trade Across the Steppe

Pastoralists, Nomads, and Steppe Society

Trade in the premodern world did not require clearly delineated trade routes or carefully set out marketplaces. These could certainly concentrate and ease trade in certain places and times, but over large swaths of territory often there are what would be more accurately described as trade flows. In these spaces, the movement of goods took place across numerous routes, in different places at different times, and included both bilateral exchanges and multiple, interlinking exchanges of goods to carry commodities to their ultimate consumers. In the premodern world, one place where recognizing the presence of this widespread movement of goods was the ecotone (an area where two communities meet and integrate) between the lands of the steppe nomads and that of the settled peoples, the agriculturalists and urban dwellers. Because they lived in different environments, they had access to different resources and could produce different products, which under normal circumstances leads to trade. One of the most celebrated examples of nomadic pastoralists lived on the steppes of Inner Asia.

The steppes extended latitudinally in a belt across Eurasia about five thousand miles long all the way to the Hungarian plain in the west and Manchuria in the east. In the north it was bordered by the taiga forests of Siberia and in the south by dry lands, beyond which were great mountain ranges. Because of its light annual precipitation and high rates of evaporation, the steppe was moisture-deficient, the southern section more than the northern. Steppe was prime grassland, at least for drought-resistant varieties with well-developed root systems. This enormous swath of grazing land had pronounced seasonal swings with green, bountiful springs, summers that can be lush in some places and dried brown in others, and frozen winters racked by icy winds. The steppe was par excellence the home of pastoral nomadic societies, in ancient times various Indo-European speaking groups of the Iranian branch and later Türkic-Mongol peoples.

As a form of subsistence economy, pastoral livestock herding appeared in the fourth millennium BCE as some people moved away from a mixed system of food production based largely on crops but including some animal

DOI: 10.4324/9781003052890-3

husbandry to a more specialized exploitation of domestic livestock and a more mobile way of life. This appeared first on the western steppes north of the Black Sea and diffused eastward due, it is generally assumed, to climate change and population pressure. Domesticated cattle, which had been on the steppes at least since the late seventh millennium BCE, appear to have been the principal animal in the west, as were horses in the central, and sheep and goats later in the eastern regions.[1] Different environments led to different pastoral strategies, that is, the appearance of regional diversity but also diversity within regions. In the eastern region, for example, among groups that had not practiced agriculture, pastoral strategies developed from earlier hunting strategies. This seems to be the case also with some groups who lived north of the Caucasus Mountains and the Caspian Sea, which is considered to be part of the western region. Nevertheless, by the mid-second millennium BCE a certain degree of cohesion did exist across the vast Eurasian steppes; in terms of economic and social structure rather than the existence of a common political system.[2]

People discovered that an animal could be more than just a storehouse for the one-time consumption of meat, what is referred to as "live food-on-the-hoof", since for most pastoralists who were not on the higher end of the tribal pecking order, meat from their domestic animals was not an everyday occurrence. After the widespread adoption of the practice of milking, animals became a renewable source of food. Young males were culled before winter and consumed, probably in ritual feasting. Products from the herd could be used for most immediate needs.[3] Animals provided fibers in the form of wool, skins, and hair for use in making garments and apparel as well as tents and other shelters. In an environment lacking in wood, dried dung was a suitable substitute to heat and cook with, and large animals provided power for pulling wagons and carts. Bones were suitable material for making some types of tools and weapons. Although pastoral peoples required much more land than farmers to produce the same amount of food, there was a surfeit of grassland that was suitable for grazing but not for agriculture. Grass would feed people indirectly by being cycled through domesticated herbivores. In eastern Eurasia, where highlands more commonly breached the steppes, pastoralists practiced vertical transhumance, taking goats and sheep upland and downland according to season.

Across the steppes, pastoralists had a wide range of resources to draw from, and their diets were usually more varied than may be assumed.[4] Along with animal husbandry, steppe economies included a range of secondary subsistence activities that could be easily adapted to a life of herding, such as foraging for wild food and fishing if a river or lake was nearby. The hunting of large and small mammals such as deer and hare, and some birds, was especially important in the eastern zone of the steppes and northward toward the forest. However, over the centuries the importance of these activities tended to fade as emphasis on herding became more pronounced.

In the past, a common misconception has been that nomadic pastoralism represented a transition economy between hunter-gatherers and settled agriculturalists. On the contrary, mixed farming came first, and only later did nomadic pastoralism develop from it. Nomadic pastoralism was a specialization, a strategy created by people who lived on the Eurasian steppes based on the tending of domestic animals and a mobile lifestyle. It required the use of the wheel in order to migrate with the herds by wagon. The people of the Yamnaya culture (also referred to as the Pit Grave culture), who lived on the Caspian steppes during the late fourth and third millennium BCE, are thought to have been especially important in the introduction and spread of animal husbandry on the steppes. With their horses and wooden wheel carts, they migrated eastward spreading their pastoral economy and accompanying lifestyle, which took many forms as they adapted to local conditions.[5]

Varying degrees of animal husbandry came to exist across a wide spectrum, the key determinants being the amount of mobility necessary to sustain livestock and the level of dependence of the herdsman on his animals. This could produce very complex systems, but in its simplest forms it ranged from the oasis grain and fruit farmers who kept a few animals for work and provided a small portion of food all the way to the full-blown nomadic pastoralists who drove their flocks and herds from pasture to pasture, season to season, and depended on their animals for most if not all necessities. Herodotus provided an example in his description of the Sauromatians, whom he located on the other side of the Tanais (Don) River. The Greeks had a special interest in these people, believing them to be the descendants of Amazon warriors who had once fought against the Greeks, and indeed grave sites identified with this culture contain the remains of women buried with weapons and armor. The Sauromatians lived in a country "entirely bare of both wild and cultivated trees", that is, the steppes. Modern archaeology has expanded their grazing land farther to the east on the lower Volga and Ural rivers, from where they drove their herds in a yearly cycle of hundreds of miles. This started in the north during the milder months and ended far to the south in a drier but warmer climate for the deep winter.[6] Ban Gu's description of the Wusan, who lived on the steppes north of Kashgar, is much the same: "The people do not work at cultivating the fields or planting trees but in common with their stock animals they go in search of water and pasture."[7]

Where the herders went was dictated by the availability of grass, that is, the carrying capacity of pastures, which, in turn, depended on moisture usually in the form of rain. Herds generally included more than one species of animal in order to best utilize available resources. In the case of the Sauromatians, for example, this included horses, sheep, and Bactrian camels. Mixing animals, however, could become complicated since different animals had different needs, as, for example, between larger animals and smaller animals, grazers and browsers, those that preferred long grass and those that would settle for short grass, and those that needed watering twice a day or once a day, or in the case of camels, every several days.[8]

Over time groups could transition from one spot on the spectrum to another in both directions. Some pastoral groups became increasingly nomadic. The more they grew their herds, the more land they needed to feed them, and the more difficult it became to stay in one place.[9] This was not arbitrary wandering but rather systematized and regulated within specific boundaries. On this spectrum the purely nomadic groups were comparatively rare in relation to the agro-pastoral groups that fell somewhere in between, combining agriculture with herding. Fan Ye in the *Hou Hanshu* describes, for example, the people of Eastern Jumi on the northern slopes of the Tian Shan: "The people live in tents. They go in search of water and pasture. They farm a bit ... They are nomads."[10] Such agro-pastoralists might live part of the year in settled quarters or share villages with neighbors who were more purely agriculturists. Much of the soil on the steppes was rich in humus due to climatic factors, principally the amount of rainfall and the short growing season. Agriculture was possible only in fringe or favored areas such as the delta of the Oxus River (Amu Darya), where some pastoralists took up irrigation agriculture.

The fertile of flatlands of Ferghana (Kyrgyzstan and southeast Uzbekistan) on the upper course of the Jaxartes River (Syr Darya) was almost surrounded by mountains but connected into trade flows across the steps that centered on Kashgar. It was lauded for its big, beautiful horses that the Chinese thought had originated in heaven but were actually bred and raised on the region's lush fields of alfalfa. The people there were once nomads but came to grow enough wheat, grapes, and eventually even rice to support an urban population. Nomads and farmers fused over time to form not only a single economic system but a single society and culture. In the *Hou Hanshu* they were known for making prodigious quantities of wine that could be kept for decades without spoiling.[11] At the same time, they maintained their extremely rich pasturelands and were formidable cavalrymen.[12] Nor was such switching confined to Central Asia. In Sind between the seventh and eleventh centuries CE large groups of migratory people including Jats and even some Afghans settled into a life of agriculture and went from plundering to protecting commerce.[13] In other places groups were known to have gone from farming to herding and back to farming over several centuries. Much depended on climatic fluctuations as in changes from cool and humid to hot and dry, but human factors, particularly invasions and migrations, often played a role in the decision to shift from one mode of subsistence to another.

Animal husbandry required lots of territory, but by the late second millennium BCE the richest and most fertile lands across the steppes had been occupied, and even marginal areas like the usable parts of the deserts and mountains were being exploited. This situation became aggravated by a climatic downturn in the form of an abrupt cooling of temperatures. The result was a new strategy, the "drive-to-pasture" system, which altered herd composition somewhat in favor of animals more fit for migration. This meant more sheep, the wooly fleece type first having appeared in the

Caucasus Mountains region from which they spread to Mesopotamia in the late fifth millennium BCE and were in widespread use in Central Asia by the third millennium BCE.[14] The wool and skin from sheep would become valuable trade commodities and in settled places provided the basis for large-scale textile production. The new system also favored horses since, like sheep, they proved more successful than other herd animals at getting to grass that was covered by snow.[15] If a group needed to expand, it had to dislodge someone else or move into lands occupied by cultivators. Unlike arable land, animals are moveable property and can be stolen if unprotected, die from inclement weather, or be eaten by wolves, leaving their owners with the option of starving or plundering someone else. Animals also came to represent accumulations of wealth, allowing for the emergence of tribal elites. Raids led to war in which those groups with better weapons were more likely to prevail, hence the connection between livestock husbandry and metallurgy.

Nomadic pastoralists, agro-pastoralists, and other groups on the steppes and in neighboring areas lived in segmented societies of tightly knit family units that traveled together and periodically met with kindred groups to renew and reinforce their relationships. When one group enjoyed a surplus of animals or other goods, they often lent to each other, creating ties that formed the basis for alliances in dangerous times. Families were joined together in larger extended kinship groups comprised of clans that sometimes cooperated and sometimes competed with each other. Clans could be united into tribes held together by the usually fictitious notion that way back in time they descended from a common ancestry. Clans shared common rights to specific pasturelands and other natural resources such as mines, but tribes were basically alliances of clans and could dissolve when their components took to feuding with each other.[16] This was a highly localized, diversified, and decentralized society with a minimum of political infrastructure designed to serve a mobile population whose wealth was in livestock and whose seats of power were inside of wagons. At this level states were by and large superfluous.[17]

The economy of nomadic pastoralists was delicate since everything depended on the herds and flocks. Under the right conditions these could expand rapidly prompting one group to encroach on the pastures of another, probably weaker, group. However, any kind of climatic problem, such as a drought, prolonged frost, heavy snowstorm, or zoogenic disease could wipe out entire herds or flocks. And the steppe was a place of limited resources in the form of grasslands, which easily led to periodic overpopulation of people. Such conditions produced instability and a sense of insecurity. One option was for tribes to unite into confederations especially if they felt threatened from more powerful or aggressive groups. Larger entities could better compete for pasturelands, exercise trading advantages over expanded areas and fight common enemies. Control of trade routes often became the most important consideration in inter-tribal relations.

The rise of powerful states in neighboring settled lands could prompt nomadic pastoralists who otherwise might be rivals to come together in common cause. This helps to explain the cyclical pattern in Chinese-nomad relations: when China was enjoying periods of strength, that often led to the rise of strong nomadic confederations. Marriages binding elite families from different tribes helped to hold such confederations together. Normally confederations were mobilized in times of war, but, even then, they were not inevitable results of this system. The Qiang, for example, who lived on the southwestern frontier of China in the Kunlun Mountains, on the Tibetan Plateau, and in parts of Gansu, Sichuan, and Yunnan, were a populous people divided into 150 separate tribes, but seemingly constant conflict with each other was the likely reason why they never coalesced into a confederation.[18]

Hostile groups, whether clans, tribes, or confederations, spent much of their time and energy struggling with each other over grazing and hunting rights and the prerogative to protect or extort from passing merchants. Across a constantly oscillating landscape, groups of horsemen dislodged each other, pursued each other, and absorbed each other. Often this took the form of chain reactions like billiards knocking into each other, flying off in different directions, one dislodged group dislodging another, who, in turn, repeated the process if it could find a weaker neighbor. With notable exceptions, annihilation was not a common consequence when confederations expanded into empires. More people equaled more power: people were too valuable, unless the intent was to make some kind of statement as was the case during the building of the Chinggisid Mongol Empire. Fragments of defeated groups sometimes combined. Migrations could be set off by empire building. In the *Hou Hanshu*, Fan Ye described how when a group migrated, it carried peoples along its way, shedding portions in its wake while absorbing new elements.[19] Their historical names, another convenience of history, were usually given to them by outside observers or reflected a ruling clan name rather than what in more modern times would be considered as an ethnicity or nationality. Such practices accounts for the maddening catalog of names that appear, then disappear, sometimes quickly; only a few of the more long-lasting, noteworthy, or notorious escape this phantom-like existence in steppe history.

Confederations and the empires that occasionally developed out of them were not homogenous states; they were temporary alliances of groups that shared common interests. Such polities may qualify to be called "empires", but as to whether they fit the definition of statehood is less certain.[20] One way of looking at an empire is simply to see it as a larger, more consolidated confederation having somewhat more of a formalized power structure dependent on a more established set of elites. Or, adding a touch of complexity to this model, a steppe empire can be seen as representing a unified entity when dealing with war and foreign affairs involving rival nomads or settled states but completely decentralized in internal matters with its various components going their own ways.[21] They have been called "state-like", "minimalist states", or even "statelets" and defined as a particular type of state with its own set of features different from the sedentary, agrarian-based, bureaucratically and administratively structured states of the traditional mold.[22] It may be all a matter of typology, but part of the confusion does come from assuming that nomadic "states" should simply be copies of settled states. Also, many early standard-type sedentary states were not actually as unified, integrated, and stable as they are typically assumed to have been.[23]

Nomadic political entities evolved out of a different tradition based on an alternative configuration of statehood and carried much of their old baggage into their new forms. It is somewhat remarkable that people with a scanty population who lived vast distances apart and who may have been on the move part or all of the year were able to coalesce even into a minimal political structure. In place of bureaucracies, they were held together at a lower level by consanguineous relations and on a higher level by personalities. And since all able-bodied men were expected to fight when necessary, they were allowed varying levels of input into the decision-making process. Major decisions were expected to be the result of consensus. After all, common warriors as individuals had the same military capacity as anyone else, high status or low, who fought in this kind of military force. The institutions these structures created could be hugely effective, and made it possible for the state to impose itself in the lives of subjects across vast distances.[24]

Nevertheless, in some of the larger and longer-lasting empires this kin-based pattern became more formalized, stratified, and hierarchical, dividing an aristocratic elite from the mass of commoners.[25] Even when this did not happen, the nomads of the steppes did not live in a totally acephalous society with no lines of power. Clans had leaders who believed themselves to be linked to other clan leaders by kindred ties; above them tribes and confederations were led by chiefs and ultimately high chiefs. Outside observers like Chinese, Persians, Greeks, and Romans often thought the highest of these were kings since that was how they understood power relations in their own political traditions. Both Herodotus and Ban Gu referred to Scythian leaders as "kings". Likewise, the Xiongnu ("Evil Slaves"; this is what the Chinese called them along with the appellation "Northern Scoundrels"; since the Chinese left written records, in such instances this is all that has come down) had their Chanyu, the Yuezhi ("Meat Eaters") their Yabguhu, and the Wusun their Kunmo. These titles are sometimes rendered as high chief (or highest chief), but a more generalized title like supreme leader or paramount ruler is more likely. The Türks and Uyghurs had qaghans (khaghans), "an Altaic word for emperor, roughly equivalent to, though more exclusive than 'khan'"[26] although ultimately the term "khan" became widespread. The Chinese also had derisive names they applied to specific Wusun leaders, including "the Fat King" and "the Mad King".[27]

Nomadic empires were different from kingdoms in important ways, perhaps most easily simplified in their divergent definition of the limits of their power: kings were interested in ruling over specific territories while chiefs were interested in securing followers and controlling interregional trade. A nomadic empire has been likened to a "super complex chiefdom".[28] The concept of kingship is very much like that of statehood: it is a culture-bound interpretation. The position of chief was a matter of inheritance, and there were always rules of succession, however vague. Sometimes they were followed. Succession could be vertical, meaning primogenital, that is, passing from father to son, although not necessarily the oldest son, or horizontal, meaning fraternal in which succession was determined by age seniority within a given generation, going laterally from brother to brother, then skipping to the oldest member of the next generation. Mothers usually had to come from some acceptable, meaning powerful, affinal clan. Rarely did everyone play fair, and even rarer was everyone satisfied with the outcome. Sometimes at the death of the founder and always at the passing of a dynasty's last great man did the ruling clan spiral into competing claims and internecine bloody feuds. Outside forces used such opportunities to encourage divisions by offering support to the side that could do the greatest damage.

In lineage-based societies, not all clans were considered to be equal: one clan was usually recognized as being dominant. Herodotus referred to the "Royal Scythians", who claimed to be superior to all the other Scythian tribes they considered to be their "slaves".[29] However, the chief of this clan was closer to being first-among-equals than to being supreme master when dealing with the heads of subordinate clans. The nomadic lifestyle did not lend itself well to the concentration of power. In the thirteenth-century Mongol empire, these tensions were clear between the imperial government and the Chinggisid princes who viewed its territories as their own personal possessions. Here, the inheritance structures of the Türko-Mongolian nomads created conditions for uncertainty. Traditionally, the youngest son inherited the home pastures while elder brothers were expected to acquire their own. However, when Chinggis Khan apportioned his empire among his sons, Jochi was given territory in the west as his patrimony "as far in that direction as the hoof of the Tartar horse has penetrated". Tolui received much of Mongolia, while Chaghadai received Mawarannahr and much of Kyrgyzstan and modern Xingjiang, and Ogodei's territories overlapped with modern Xinjiang, Mongolia and Kazakhstan. Known as *uluses*, these patrimonies were subordinate to the Khan but each prince held considerable autonomy. Over time, the central imperial state sought to establish a more formalized civil government, but this was often layered over the top of existing local government forms that continued throughout the empire and survived following its dissolution.[30] As in all matters dealing with power relationships in this society, the position of dominant clan was always subject to change as one group replaced another at the top.

Such challenges were perhaps inevitable when steppe empires were conquest-based, rather than developing from confederations. The imposition of power on subjects inevitably created the conditions for resistance. Empires were not built following a blueprint. The only plan was an unbridled expansion in whatever direction was open with the steppes offering an easy topography to thunder across and the horse a means of traversing vast distances in a relatively short time. Empires depended on external expansion to support the elite groups and loyal followers who kept it together. This required a constant stream of goods obtained from plunder or tribute from settled peoples and the wealth that accrued from control over trade. Contemporary observers usually credited the founding of empires to exceptional men, charismatic figures with domineering personalities who could gain the support of other chiefs through their leadership abilities and military prowess that overrode ethnic, linguistic, religious, and even hereditary considerations. Exceptional individuals could gain power rapidly, reflecting the flexible nature of politics on the steppe. Such a ruler had to be absolutely ruthless, prepared to do away with any real, perceived, or imagined threats often by decimating his closest relatives.

While in some instances there is an element of historical accuracy in this interpretation – Chinggis Khan being the most obvious example – in most instances the theme of the charismatic leader is a convenient way to understand the rise of empires. The words most often used in describing steppe empires are "ephemeral", "unstable", "fragile", and "short-lived". This is, however, rather simplistic: a deeper look will usually reveal social, economic, and political forces at play, and as usual in this society, one size never fits all.[31] An empire or even a big confederation held together as long as the charisma and whatever else was holding it together lasted. Beyond that there was only the power that could be mustered by force of arms. Empires put together by their very nature harbored their own seeds of implosion especially if a significant portion of the subject population consisted of other pastoral tribesmen. Any indication of weakness at the center was a signal to revolt, and even if the empire survived such a challenge, it likely would be left weakened and on the downswing. The very success of creating an empire could stimulate other tribes and confederations to oppose it out of fear or envy. Friends and foes in this geopolitical muddle could change rapidly. An old empire could be devoured by the rise of a confederation on its own trajectory to becoming a new empire. Or centrifugal force could finally catch up to it in the form of civil wars in which the empire would fragment into its disparate elements.

Forms of Exchange

Whereas many steppe societies relied on the movement of their herds, sedentary societies that lived on the periphery of the steppe instead depended on the outputs of particular territories that required careful management. In areas where agriculture was possible, nomadic pastoralists had a less than clear-cut set of relationships with settled folk, whether peasant cultivators, townspeople, or passing merchants. From one perspective, the nomad-settled relationship can be seen as essentially symbiotic, grounded in mutual dependence and economic collaboration, each side complementing the other within a unified economic system. Pastoralists often made arrangements with farmers as in allowing their animals to graze on the field stubble after harvest in return for fertilizing the field with their droppings. As the eleventh-century scholar Mahmud Kashgari put it: "there is no Turk [nomad] without a Tadjik [sedentary], there is no hat without a head".[32] From an opposite perspective, the nomadic side of the equation has been characterized as being parasitic and predatory, and the sedentary as controlling and destructive to mobile ways of living.[33]

The balance centered on the opposite poles of trade and raid, but the reality was much less clear-cut, and it is probably better to see such relationships as reaching across a broad continuum of contacts that were ever shifting. These range from trade and other forms of exchange that were reciprocal along with providing services often of a commercial nature, to providing protection that usually meant dependency, to trade that was uneven and carried on under direct or implied duress, to providing subsidies or paying tribute often under the face-saving guise of giving gifts, to straight out blackmail and extortion, to casual and erratic raiding, to chronic raiding usually at harvest time, to looting and plundering, to conquest, and finally, on occasion, to complete destruction. Likewise, nomadic herders faced restrictions to the movement of their herds, often by force, as sedentary communities sought to expand or control greater territories or essential passes and routes between them. Neither side could assume that conditions would remain immutable: often they were fragile and fluid. Nor should too rigid a line be drawn in the interplay of parties. Sections of a nomadic tribe sometimes would become semi-sedentary and play the role of liaison between groups.

For the pastoral nomad, getting certain goods from the settled peoples, whether by some form of exchange, extortion, or confiscation, ranged from desirable to vital. The traders did not have to be from the tribal group involved; mercantile people like the Sogdians could travel between steppe communities and settled folk. What the pastoralist wanted from settled peoples included a broad range of goods best examined on a scale at one end of which were staples and other needed goods and at the other end luxury or desired goods. Living on the steppes or in the desert or mountains on marginal lands at the edges of the economic world, generally the nomad was not entirely self-sustainable. Just how essential such goods were for the subsistence of the typical nomadic pastoralist is something of a judgment call. For this particular economy, good times and bad times were worlds apart. It is safe to say that most needs were addressed by their primary economic activity, which was herding ruminant livestock. But could this address all their needs? Here an argument is often made that although the life of nomadic herding was one of considerable self-sufficiency, the limited resources of the steppes made at least some trade necessary.[34] Pastoral economy for the most part was based on maximizing returns from marginal areas, thus realizing only modest surpluses when compared to agricultural economy.[35]

The most common commodities sought by steppe traders were grains: wheat, millet, barley, and, at a somewhat pricier level, rice, to supplement the nomad's meat and dairy diet. According to Wei Shu (551–4 CE), in instances when the Chinese government exchanged grain for horses with powerful nomadic confederations and empires, this could involve hundreds of thousands of bushels of grain and thousands of horses.[36] Other foodstuffs, including a range of vegetables, dried fruits, and, when available, fresh fruits such as melons and grapes, were added to the nomad's diet. In an odd twist, the Chinese themselves sometimes imported fruits and vegetables from the nomads although these were grown in the oasis states to the west and only transported by the nomads. Alcoholic beverages ranging from homemade peasant rotgut to mead and fine grape wines were welcomed. Tea was added as early as the Tang period and flourished during the Southern Song (1127–1279 CE) in the trade it had with the Jin state, created by invaders from Manchuria, which controlled much of northern China. The demand for tea became so strong the Jin tried to expand its own production in the part of China it controlled, but the quality proved inferior to that grow in Sichuan, which was under Southern Song control. The balance of trade became so lopsided the Jin had to export silver to the Southern Song to compensate. The Southern Song also enjoyed a lively tea-for-horses exchange with Tibet. The demand grew again under the Ming (1368–1644): in a single year the Chinese exported northward an estimated one million tons of black tea in return for twenty thousand horses.[37]

The mobile life was not generally conducive to craft specialization and the manufacture of handicraft goods. And it did not lend itself easily to the carrying around of heavy, bulky items like furniture. Wealth was vested in more portable goods; in trade, cloth was next to food in importance. Cotton, linen, hemp, and even the lowest grade of silk made more comfortable clothing than the wool and leather steppe people had. This might include coats, trousers, stockings, and even hats and boots; for the tribal elite, there were the most elaborate of embroidered robes. As nomadic pastoralists moved from being wagon dwellers to pitching tents and constructing yurts, they turned even more to textiles. A tent would be made from the most basic of their products: animal skins and woolen felt. But the inside of a tent could be quite grand. Walls could be decorated with beautiful tapestries, floors covered with lush carpets, and beds draped with quilts to provide warm sleeping quarters. When Ibn Battuta met the ruler of the Chagatai Khanate Sultan Tarmashirin (1326–34), he "found him seated on a chair, resembling a mosque-pulpit and covered with silk embroidered in gold. The interior of the tent was lined with silken cloth of gold, and a crown set with jewels and precious stones was suspended over the sultan's head."[38] Simply holding court in a venue that could be moved certainly did not remove opportunities for ostentatious displays of wealth and power.

Nomads were able to make some textiles on their portable looms, and other craftsmen produced ceramics and lithic and metal products such as tools, utensils, and weapons. The raw metal often originated in mountains or other places controlled by the nomads, and some steppe peoples became accomplished metalworkers in their own right. However, the flow in finished metal products usually went from the settled lands to the steppes when trade was open. Often it was not for fear that any iron that went to the nomads would be used by them to produce weapons. A Chinese law of 1488 allowed the Mongols to barter animals, furs, and similar products for silks and some unspecified iron products.[39] The iron products were probably tools; nevertheless, this was somewhat unusual.

Craft specialization was commonly based in urban areas, from which a higher quality of product could be had, and goods manufactured in towns and cities were often aimed specifically for sale to the peoples of the steppes. Finely manufactured goods in demand by pastoral elites such as ceremonial weapons, black and red wood lacquered products, mirrors, even musical instruments like horns and drums almost always originated outside of nomadic society and came into it by trade, which was sometimes disguised as presents, or by plunder. This was also the case for ornate jewelry, cosmetics, and medicines even when the ingredients may have originated on the steppes or in the forest. According to one observation, women of the ruling family "were the chief consumers of goods commercial and cultural".[40] As the explorer Zhang Qian reported to the Chinese emperor on returning from Central Asia (*c.*115 BCE), "barbarians are greedy for Han goods".[41]

Typically, the closer a particular nomadic group lived to a sedentary area, the more it came to depend on the products there. To use an extreme example in reverse, the most self-sufficient of all nomadic pastoralists may have been certain tribes of Tuareg camel herders who lived very deep in the remotest section of the Sahara Desert. Elsewhere, the products of settled life provided the beams that supported the nomadic political structure. Through trade or other means, nomadic rulers could obtain enormous quantities of goods from settled folk in staples and luxuries, the most notable example of the latter being silk from the Chinese. Part of these goods was then redistributed to a leader's retinue and to allies and lesser chiefs in return for their loyalty.[42] It allowed the heads of member tribes in a confederation or empire to obtain luxury products or have trading privileges they might otherwise not have had access to. This trickle-down effect with higher-ups cultivating the support of their clients down the political and social ladder not only reinforced the power, importance, and prestige of the high chief but helped solidify the position of tribal elites in general. By the time the trickle got to the bottom, the average herdsman may not have been the beneficiary of silks or gold and silver jewelry, but he should have been getting enough grain, cloth, and other products including alcohol to maintain his loyalty to the system.

Agrarian societies, notably the Chinese, considered themselves to be essentially self-sufficient; as for trade with nomadic pastoralists, they could take it or leave it. Nevertheless, nomadic pastoralists did have commodities that settled peoples wanted even if they did not absolutely need. Edibles such as milk, butter, other dairy products, and meat probably topped the list at the lower end of the trade scale when nomads and farmers dealt directly with each other. Livestock could be exchanged on an individual level or in large quantities on the state level. In places like the Great Hungarian Plain, domesticated cattle were being exported in regional exchange in the early fifth millennium BCE; such a product had the advantage of transporting itself.[43] Above these came products such as skins, hides, hair, wool, felt, and horns; raw leather often came back to the nomads as finished products like saddles and boots.

The pastoralist's most important commodity was the horse; it was most in demand as a mount animal for the prestige associated with it, for its use in warfare, and, on a more mundane level, as a draft animal. Horses were transported in vast herds across Eurasia for trade, including, by the fourteenth century, from Azov to the north of the Black Sea all the way to India.[44] Another trade item in considerable demand that was especially popular among the urban populations in Islamic countries were enslaved people captured in the numerous intertribal raids and wars steppe peoples waged against each other. On a more exotic level, the Uyghurs, who lived to the west of China, brought a combination of trade, tribute, and presents to the Tang and succeeding courts of the Five Dynasties period. Their special products included "jade-yaks, green wild horses, one-humped camels, white minks, antelope horns, sal ammoniac, seal testicles, diamonds, red salt, and the skins of wild horses".[45] Steppe societies generally recognized the value of trade and encouraged and facilitated it. When trade was on the decline, as in many parts of Eurasia during the fifth century CE, nomadic and sedentary groups were more likely to struggle with each other over whatever commercial opportunities were left than during times when trade was flourishing and there was plenty to go around.

Beyond providing specific products, nomads also played a vital role in the structure of long-distance trade since caravan routes had to pass through their territories, and only they could guarantee safety. This was often done through agreements with particular rulers or societies that involved payment for protection. Under such agreements nomadic warriors were obligated to protect travelers not the least from their own proclivities. This practice can be traced into the practices of the rulers of states including the Mongol empire, where merchants were protected while travelling across the Eurasian Silk Roads.[46] Along with the roles of protector and escort, nomadic people often served as guides, carriers, and tenders of pack animals as well as renting out pack animals and supplying whatever else passing merchants might need. Furnishing services and exacting passage duties provided a much-needed supplementary income. They were important in communicating information and sometimes engaged in the carrying trade themselves, using their expertise in long-distance travel to exploit opportunities that arose in distant markets. Relay systems also existed between allied or friendly tribes. Without the range of services nomadic pastoralists provided, long-distance trade on a transcontinental scale could not have existed, at least on the level that it did. They were the intermediaries of trade.

In straight trade, which is to say when no threats, overt or implied, were involved, the agriculturalist had the advantage. Settled folk, particularly those engaged in agriculture, were not as dependent on the products of the nomadic pastoralists as vice versa. Animal products were produced in the settled world in limited quantities, while the lifestyle of the typical nomad nixed the option of growing one's own grain. While these were complementary economies that reflected some degree of dependency on both sides, the need to exchange was more urgent for the pastoralists: they needed grain and cloth more than farmers needed whatever the pastoralists had to offer. And herding animals meant that the nomadic pastoralist could not linger indefinitely to haggle for the price he wanted; the needs of his animals meant that he had to be off to new grasslands. Nor were times of windfall for the pastoralist necessarily the best of times. Herds and especially flocks could grow or be reduced quickly. An abundance of wool or skins had to be traded off at bargain prices; too many low-quality horses in one gestation period soon led to too many more low quality horses if no one decided to buy. On the other hand, too little wool and skins or too few horses may not have equaled the same value as the grain and cloth the pastoralist needed. In trade between the Northern Song Dynasty (960–1127 CE) and the Khitans, whose homeland was to the northeast but who had moved into part of northern China, the Khitans got the usual cloth, including silk, and rice, and the Chinese got the usual horses and other livestock. But the value of the Khitan products did not equal that of the Chinese, and the Khitans had to make up the difference in silver.[47]

The structure of trade taking place across this border was strongly influenced by the power of rulers, governments, and political, military, and social elites – on both sides of the nomad-sedentary frontier. However, how much control political authorities had over trade and commerce and whether they pursued policies and practices to stimulate and support the commercial sector differed greatly. As much as trade itself, control of exchange on the steppe frontier centered on controlling the movement of people, the protection of particular populations, and the ability of either nomadic or sedentary states to impose their control over borderland territories. One reality underlies this discussion. Generally, governments did not bother to become involved in commercial matters to promote the welfare of the community they represented or society at large, but rather to directly benefit those in charge of the government and the elites they represented. Priorities centered on state power rather than private profit. The major goal in attempting to control or interfere in trade and commerce was to extract wealth to use for personal and political purposes. Rulers were sometimes directly engaged in trade, and the ancient practice of gift exchange had not entirely disappeared. More importantly, states waged wars that are sometimes attributed to economic factors such as control over trade routes, trade nexuses, or valuable resources.

The generally held assumption is that peace promotes trade whereas violence undermines it. This comes with some provisos. States could and often did provide protection and order, which for merchants meant predictability, a most valued asset. Another assumption, although somewhat less generally held and with many more provisos, is that political centralization or at least a strong government was desirable or even necessary for commercial prosperity and a market-based system to work. In fact, a system of trade and commerce can work effectively under adverse political conditions if the promise of profits holds out. Of course, it was preferable for those who made the commercial system work to be in some kind of partnership, however tacit, with those who controlled the political system. That being said, much of the long-distance trade that we can trace in the premodern world took place across numerous boundaries and cultures, and the idea that there was a common set of institutional practices imposed by any state of community across these geographies seems fanciful. Instead, a more useful interpretation is to recognize that economic institutions of this sort can be generated within and across communities and enforced through social and cultural compacts rather than by any form of outside governance.

Rather than facilitating trade or providing governance for cross-cultural exchange, states were much more likely to have direct contact with mercantile communities through the levying of exactions in one form or another. Direct and indirect taxes, customs, duties, *cesses* (in India), other imposts and forms of tribute together with the cost of licenses, passports, tolls, "presents", and the payment of fees and fines were all experienced by traders operating in premodern Eurasia. Not only governments assumed the authority to collect, but many other organizations did as well, including trade organizations such as guilds and certain temples. In Song China innkeepers could charge their own tax. Some of this income went to provide for protection and the upkeep of infrastructure that facilitated transportation. Much of it also went to support the lavish lifestyle of courts or the ambitions of political and military elites, and not a small amount disappeared into the hands of rapacious officials.

Taxes varied by commodity and according to who was being charged. This could appear very arbitrary. For one reason or another, some commodities and traders were exempt, but generally strangers were subject to higher taxes as were luxury products such as spices and aromatic drugs. Duties could range from two percent to fifty percent on imports and exports, and were paid as a percentage of the goods, or in a lump fee by the shipload, wagonload, or camel and donkey load. For many merchants such payments represented a major share of transaction costs; as for governments such income was most welcome to the chronically strapped, but the large imperial states relied primarily on land taxes for support. When exactions became so onerous as to impact too heavily on profits, merchants changed routes or customers. Maritime travel lowered costs since under normal circumstances payment would have to be made only coming and going but not in between.

Trade was often held hostage by powerful settled states that could open, increase, restrict, or close frontier markets with nomads. Powerful nomads, on the other hand, could force settled peoples to trade on unfair terms, which often meant overpricing their goods. Such was the case in the Uyghur horse trade, an exchange that was subsidized by the Chinese, who willingly paid inflated prices for inferior steeds to keep an alliance with the Uyghurs. At times the Chinese agreed to trade with their nomadic neighbors or send goods through their territories to be taxed more as a stratagem for keeping potential enemies placated than for purely commercial purposes. Nevertheless, certain goods the nomads wanted were often restricted or prohibited by state authorities, the most obvious being weapons. Smuggling was common along the frontier.

Trade often determined war and peace on borders and where there were no borders. Tribal groups fought each other over control of routes and commercial hubs. Wars against settled states occurred when a state closed its borders and denied tribesmen access to trade. When nomadic empires or powerful confederations collapsed, the price of goods at both ends of a trade route as well as in between were likely to rise. War on the steppes was disruptive and contrary to everyone's interest, except, of course, the eventual winner. However, if that winner imposed a pax (as, for example, the Mongols did during the thirteenth and fourteenth centuries CE), it could prove to be a great boon for commerce.

Lying between trade and raid was the paying of tribute. Collecting tribute was not a reciprocal act in the sense of a two-sided exchange of goods, but it was, or it was supposed to be, non-violent unlike raiding. The payers officially recognized their status as subordinates in return for protection (usually from the same tribesmen) by the granting of subsidies on a scheduled or irregular basis. This could go both ways. Nomads could be forced to recognize the supremacy of a powerful sedentary state after being defeated in war or to be allowed access to markets. But more typically, nomads would impose their will over settled peoples, particularly if they were dissatisfied with trading arrangements. Whatever the given rationale, the threat of violence underlay such relationships. This may be interpreted as a form of extortion or blackmail with payment dependent on the ratio of power between the parties and both sides accepting the situation without a whimper. For the nomads it was safer just to collect payment rather than risk the bloodshed of their own people, which raiding, even when successful, might bring. For settled peoples, paying tribute it was likewise preferable to suffering invasion, looting, and pillaging, and almost always it proved to be cheaper. As one Chinese emperor admitted when faced with an invasion, the best strategy was "to roll up our armor and put away our weapons and tempt them with jade and silk. The vain pride of those stubborn barbarians will begin from this point to cause their decline. This is to say, if we wish to take from them, we have to give to them."[48]

In paying tribute to one group of nomadic pastoralists, settled people usually gained a protector against other groups. Sometimes this meant establishing a relationship with a neighboring tribe to use as a buffer; at other times it meant establishing a relationship with a group beyond one's neighbors if the neighbors were the problem. However, tribute-paying on a large scale could get out of hand. In the late fifth and early sixth centuries

CE a powerful nomadic empire built by a people known as the Hephthalites ("White Huns") forced the Persian government under the Sasanian dynasty (224–651 CE) to pay enormous sums of tribute for many decades after killing the Persian king Peroz I in battle in 484 CE. In one instance this amounted to as many silver coins as could be carried on the backs of thirty mules.[49] This flow of Persian silver, in the long run, is credited with helping to monetize the economies of large sections of Central Asia.

Over the centuries, great powerhouse states like the Chinese and Persian empires witnessed ever-changing relationships with their nomadic pastoral neighbors. Uneasy peace on the rim separating the settled, agricultural-based civilizations on one side and the nomadic pastoralists on the other was more likely to prevail when the balance of power was roughly equal. Mighty empires on both sides of the line often came and went together. This was less the case in the relationship between the settled peoples of Central Asia who lived in smaller more self-contained entities like the oasis city-states in the Tarim and Turfan basins or territorial kingdoms in Transoxiana, Bactria, Ferghana, and some parts of the mountainous regions between China and India. Some of these places had flourishing bazaars and at the same time contained significant nomadic groups within their own populations. Small states sometimes fought with each other, at which time having the support of a nearby nomadic group could prove crucial.[50] Security for such places ranged from ragtag militias to mercenary and professional forces, but they were small reflecting their resource base. Geography made them commercial people, and as such they were already deal-makers, a skill they extended in dealing with the nomads that surrounded them.

Nomadic groups were especially fond of controlling river valleys like the Ordos between Mongolia and China, and the Orkhon between Mongolia and Siberia. In some places the nomads themselves settled captured people to grow crops, produce manufactured goods, and even serve as garrisons. In one instance, Fan Ye in the *Hou Hanshou* recorded that the Xiongnu deported more than 6,000 people from the Barkol valley (eastern Xinjiang) north of the Jade Gate to the western side of the Tian Shan Mountains because the local ruler in some way offended the Chanyu.[51] The settled peoples of oasis, river valleys, and smaller territorial states were much more dependent on daily trade with pastoralists, which was much more essential to their overall economy than it was to the settled peoples of the larger states beyond the steppe. They were also much more vulnerable to exploitation. This did not have to be a military action. Just the threat of nomads suddenly appearing out of the steppes or desert driving their herds and flocks into the fields and gardens of cultivators to trample their crops would be a frightening enough scenario to ensure compliance with whatever arrangement the nomadic pastoralists imposed. For most nomads, however, the settled peoples outside the powerful states were generally considered to be a precious resource to be protected, not to be spoiled by overexploitation. Here relationships were more symbiotic.

For nomads, if threats and intimidation did not work, raiding was often the alternative under a number of various circumstances: if there was no agreed upon relationship with a particular settled group; if the nomads had been closed out of markets and were unable to trade; if the nomads had suffered the loss of their animals by various means; or if the nomads were just running amuck on indiscriminate pillaging expeditions. Raiding with the intention of making off with plunder, was, after all, a glorified form of stealing that could result in death, whereas raiding on behalf of a polity was awarded a form of legitimacy.[52] Raids tended to be of the hit-and-run variety, and much depended on what kind of defense the perpetrators expected from their victims. Whether nomadic pastoralists in general preferred war or peace is a matter of controversy since neither archaeology nor any other evidence generated by the nomads themselves can definitely answer this. The Chinese believed that tribal elites were better served by trade, which was a more likely way of obtaining luxury goods as presents from the Chinese court, while the more common herdsmen did better with raids, which were more likely to produce food and other staples.[53] Since both trade and raid had the same goal – to obtain certain needed or desired goods – it was, as one observer put it, a matter of cost effectiveness; given a particular circumstance, which strategy would work best.[54] As usual in history, much depended on circumstance.

The world of trade and commerce also had to deal with the abuse of power. In some places, corruption was endemic especially among border and port officials with inspectors as the most notorious. Extorting bribes came as loose free-for-all extortion or disciplined, structured extortion. In the marketplace swindlers practiced fraud by selling adulterated, shoddy, and defective goods, and brokers practiced scams but in turn had to pay off officials to be allowed to operate. In fairness, most governments had some system of market inspection in more urbanized areas, and occasionally reformers would come along to clean up a system, however temporary. But from the official perspective, crimes directly impacting on the state's authority, such as embezzlement and smuggling, particularly the contraband trade in such items as weaponry, were of higher priority.

Mention too should be made of the outliers of steppe society, the brigands, plunderers, outlaws, and the like, who engaged in dissolute behavior indiscriminately. They certainly existed, and their impact on trade and commerce could be very negative in causing merchants to alter routes, hire guards, and engage in other strategies that made trade less efficient and thus more expensive. Traveling great distances and sometimes across multiple borders with a tempting load of merchandise could be hazardous. One threat came from fellow humans in the form of robbery, extortion, and murder at the hands of professional bandits, part-time brigands, and freebooting soldiers. Such villainy was most common in regions farthest from government control. Where it was rampant, detours were used, and trade withered. Such places were often given names, such as the "haunt of thieves" or the "place of great fear". Islamic rulers generally provided for safety on the roads, and in places such as India, mercenaries were hired as guards. Protection costs often exceeded transport costs. Other problems included spillage and petty thievery by employees and fellow travelers; camel drivers on certain trans-Saharan routes were particularly infamous.

The Steppe Road to the north of the Silk Roads was a better way to get from western Eurasia to China than the Silk Roads; for caravans and especially wagons traveling over grasslands was much preferred to traveling across deserts and mountains. Nevertheless, for much of the first and into the second millennium CE, the steppes were not often safe, and commercial traffic generally preferred natural dangers to human dangers. The *Han Shu* warns that the Wusan "people are hard-hearted and greedy; they are unreliable and much given to robbery".[55] The *Hou Hanshu* issues a similar warning several centuries later regarding the people of Yizhi much farther to the east around Lake Barkol: "These people are brave and handy in combat. Robbery and pillage are their normal occupations. They all have disheveled hair."[56] It should be remembered, however, that in the premodern world of trade the steppes were not unique in being a risky place for travelers.

A quick glance at the *Hudūd al-Ālam*, which does not mince words when it comes to bad behavior in its survey of the world (as its author knew it) in the tenth century CE, provides sufficient warnings. In the district of Sarvan in Khorasan (eastern Iran), the people were "professional thieves". Moving eastward, the Kumijiyan (Kumeji), perhaps a remnant of the ancient Saka, are "courageous and warlike and professional thieves". Of the Njina Türks: "The people are professional thieves and looters of caravans ... They go far looting to a distance of 40 and 50 *farsangs* from the periphery of their district." Nun-Kat in the Türkic Khallukh country was a town "now desolate and is a thieves haunt". Nor was such inequity confined to Central Asia. In Arabia, Najran, at one time a crossroads for the incense trade, was "a prosperous borough in which lives the tribe of Hamdan. From it comes brigands who rifle the region of Yemen". Every part of the world suffered its share of bad actors. Farther west in the Sudan this was the Laba, who "are thieves, poor, naked, and the most despicable of all this country".[57]

During periods of warfare, anarchy, and chaos, the pastoral nomads of the steppes engaged in their fair share of looting, brigandage, and mayhem; it was considered as both a tactic to weaken the enemy and the opportunity for a payoff. This was much less the case when great confederations and empires were in control and parts of the steppes enjoyed relative peace. But in war and peace most nomadic pastoralists were not considered to be "professional thieves" by the norms of the time. Such people lived in particular places and belonged to identifiable groups, and the *Hudūd*, at least, attached to them a special label. Such categorization, however, needs to be flexible. Best to put outright thievery, plundering, raiding, and straight warfare across a range of negative behaviors, which under certain circumstances could be easily slid across.

The nomadic pastoralists of the steppes were special in a related if much broader way. Their lifestyle produced a superior, if not always invincible grade of warrior. There is some controversy as to when the warrior ethos became central to this society. In the more standard version, this is evident at least by the time of Andronovo culture in the second millennium BCE, which was actually a number of similar local Bronze Age sub-cultures that shared common traits. Andronovo culture seems to have originated north of the Caspian Sea between the Volga River and the southern Urals, but over the millennium it spread eastward. Their advances in bronze weaponry made them collectively an irresistible force. Among their terrible instruments of death were socketed two-bladed javelins and arrows (although curiously, they sometimes still made arrowheads from bone), single-edged knives, and above all the light two-horse war chariot.[58] Once one group mastered the use of the horse in warfare, its neighbors, and even those who may have been quite far away, had better learn the new techniques quickly or risk being overwhelmed. An opposite view, using the same archaeological evidence, also sees the same tribesmen on the move but not in warlike invasions. Rather, these are seen to be peaceful and protracted migrations of stock breeders who enjoyed frequent interaction with settled folk, trading products that included copper and tin.[59]

Whichever was the case, by the time of Herodotus, who provides the first written report in the period dominated by Scythian-Saka tribes, this had become a highly militarized society.[60] The horse was the central element. Nomads were superb horsemen, mobile and elusive on their hardy steeds. Children raised in the saddle were trained from an early age. Hunting was an important supplement in the economy of nomads, and the transfer of hunting to martial skills was easy. At a minimum, pastoralists had to protect their herds, but defensive skills could easily be converted to offense. They made exceptional cavalrymen whose weapon of choice was the powerful long range double curved bow, which they could fire with accuracy while at a full gallop without stirrups. Steppe warriors flowed back and forth, protecting their grazing grounds, plundering the herds and flocks of their enemies, and occasionally crashing into the settled communities on their borders.

Cavalries were operating on the steppes by around 600 BCE.[61] Tactically, nomads generally preferred raids and harassment to pitched battle unless someone was trying to build an empire. In raiding, horsemen relied on surprise, suddenly striking deep into an adversary's territory, gathering as much plunder as they could handle, then disappearing back to wherever they came from before an effective defense could be rallied or a retaliation mounted. They were masters of ambush, encirclement, and feigned retreats in which they would suddenly do an about face and charge back into their unsuspecting and probably disorganized pursuers. Of the military advantages the nomadic warriors enjoyed, one was intangible: their ferocity magnified their potency in the eyes of less combative peoples. This may have blended with a primal terror summed up as: "people with a different way of life are strangers by definition; their ways seem unpredictable, and the unpredictable is probably dangerous as well".[62] For sedentary populations across Eurasia, the nomadic societies of the steppes represented the ultimate strangers. They seemed impervious to the roughness of a life others would find untenable. This made them fearless and their adversaries fearful.

Notes

1 Michael Frachetti, "Multiregional Emergence of Mobile Pastoralism and Non-uniform Institutional Complexity across Eurasia", *Current Anthropology* 53:1 (2012), pp. 2–38.
2 Paula Doumani Dupuy, "Bronze Age Central Asia" in Oxford Handbooks Editorial Board (eds.), *The Oxford Handbook of Topics in Archaeology* (Oxford, 2014), p. 3.
3 Claudia Chang, *Rethinking Prehistoric Central Asia: Shepherds, farmers and nomads* (London, 2019), p. 66.
4 Claudia Chang, *Rethinking Prehistoric Central Asia: Shepherds, farmers and nomads* (London, 2019), p. 10.
5 Michael Frachetti, "The Multiregional Emergence of Mobile Pastoralism and the Growth of Non-Uniform Institutional Complexity Across Eurasia", *Current Anthropology* 53:1 (2012), p. 8; For concepts of environmental adaptation, see Tim Ingold, *The Perception of the Environment: Essays of livelihood, dwelling and skill* (London, 2000).
6 Herodotus, *The Histories*, trans. Robin Waterfield (Oxford, 2008), pp. 271–3.
7 Ban Gu, *Han Shu*, trans. Anthony François Paulus Hulsewé and M. A. N. Loewe (eds.), *China in Central Asia: The Early Stage: 125 BC–AD 23; an Annotated Translation of Chapters 61 and 96 of the History of the Former Han Dynasty* (Leiden, 1979), p. 144.
8 K. N. Chaudhuri, *Asia before Europe: Economy and civilization of the Indian Ocean from the rise of Islam to 1750* (Cambridge, 1990), p. 285.
9 David Christian and Craig Benjamin (eds.), *Silk Road Studies II: World of the Silk Roads: Ancient and modern* (Turnhout, 1998), p. 57; Roger Cribb, *Nomads in Archaeology* (Cambridge, 1990), p. 16.
10 Fan Ye, *Hou Hanshou*, trans. John Hill, *Through the Jade Gate to Rome: A study of the Silk Roads during the later Han Dynasty 1st to 2nd centuries, vol.* 2 (2009), p. 47.
11 Fan Ye, *Hou Hanshou*, trans. John Hill, *Through the Jade Gate to Rome: A study of the Silk Roads during the later Han Dynasty 1st to 2nd centuries, vol.* 2 (2009), p. 132.
12 Saidov Abdukakhor, "The Ferghana Valley: The pre-colonial legacy" in S. Frederick Starr (ed.), *Ferghana Valley: The heart of central Asia* (Armonk, NY, 2011), pp. 3–28.
13 André Wink, *Al-Hind: The making of the Indo-Islamic World* (Leiden, 1990), p. 169.
14 Philip Kohl, *The Making of Bronze Age Eurasia* (Cambridge, 2007), p. 223.
15 Philip Kohl, *The Making of Bronze Age Eurasia* (Cambridge, 2007), p. 159.
16 C. C. Lamberg-Karlovsky, "The Bronze Age *khanates* of Central Asia", *Antiquity* 68:259 (1994), pp. 401–2.
17 David Christian and Craig Benjamin (eds.), *Silk Road Studies II: World of the Silk Roads: Ancient and modern* (Turnhout, 1998), p. 59.
18 John Hill, *Through the Jade Gate to Rome*, vol. 1, p. 151.
19 Fan Ye, *Hou Hanshou*, trans. John Hill, *Through the Jade Gate to Rome: A study of the Silk Roads during the later Han Dynasty 1st to 2nd centuries, vol.* 2 (2009), pp. 145, 150–3.

20 Claudia Chang, *Rethinking Prehistoric Central Asia: Shepherds, farmers and nomads* (London, 2019), p. 131.
21 William Honeychurch, *Inner Asia and the Spatial Politics of Empire: Archaeology, mobility, and culture contact* (New York, 2015), p. 53.
22 David Christian, "State Formation in the Inner Eurasian Steppes" in David Christian and Craig Benjamin (eds.), *Silk Road Studies II: World of the Silk Roads: Ancient and modern* (Turnhout, 1998), pp. 51–76.
23 William Honeychurch, *Inner Asia and the Spatial Politics of Empire: Archaeology, mobility, and culture contact* (New York, 2015), p. 58.
24 Timothy May, *The Mongol Empire* (Edinburgh, 2022), pp. 76–93.
25 Claudia Chang, *Rethinking Prehistoric Central Asia: Shepherds, farmers and nomads* (London, 2019), pp. 99–100.
26 James Millward, *Eurasian Crossroads: A history of Xingiang* (London, 2007), p. 31.
27 Ban Gu, *Han Shu*, trans. Anthony François Paulus Hulsewé and M. A. N. Loewe (eds.), *China in Central Asia: The Early Stage: 125 BC–AD 23; an Annotated Translation of Chapters 61 and 96 of the History of the Former Han Dynasty* (Leiden, 1979), pp. 149, 154–6.
28 Michael Frachetti, "The Multiregional Emergence of Mobile Pastoralism and the Growth of Non-Uniform Institutional Complexity Across Eurasia", *Current Anthropology* 53:1 (2012), p. 25; Susan Keech McIntosh (ed.), *Beyond Chiefdoms: Pathways to complexity in Africa* (Cambridge, 1999), pp. 1–30.
29 Herodotus, *The Histories*, trans. Robin Waterfield (Oxford, 2008), p. 242.
30 Timothy May, *The Mongol Empire* (Edinburgh, 2022), pp. 91–3.
31 Sechin Jagchid and Van Jay Symons, *Peace, War, and Trade along the Great Wall: Nomadic–Chinese interaction through two millennia* (Bloomington, IN, 1989), p. 13; Peter Golden, "The Qipcac of Medieval Eurasia: An example of stateless adaption in the steppe" in Gary Seaman and Daneil Marks (eds.), *Rulers from the Steppe: State formation on the Eurasian periphery* (Los Angeles, CA, 1991), p. 138; David Christian, "State Formation in the Inner Eurasian Steppes" in David Christian and Craig Benjamin (eds.), *Silk Road Studies II: World of the Silk Roads: Ancient and modern* (Turnhout, 1998), pp. 51–76.
32 Mahmud al-Kashgari, *Dīwān Lughāt al-Turk* [Compendium of the Languages of the Turks], quoted in A. M. Khazanov, "Characteristic Features of Nomadic Communities in the Eurasian Steppes" in W. Weissleder (ed.), *The Nomadic Alternative: Modes and models of interaction in the African-Asian Deserts and Steppes* (The Hague, 1978), pp. 119–26.
33 For two perspectives on this issue, see K. N. Chaudhuri, *Asia before Europe: Economy and civilization of the Indian Ocean from the rise of Islam to 1750* (Cambridge, 1990), pp. 143, 276; Thomas Barfield, *The Perilous Frontier: Nomadic empires and China* (Oxford: 1989).
34 Luc Kwanten, *Imperial Nomads: A history of central Asia, 500–1500* (Leicester, 1979), p. 208; Morris Rossabi, *China and Inner Asia: From 1368 to the present day* (London, 1975), p. 40; A. M. Khazanov, "Characteristic Features of Nomadic Communities in the Eurasian Steppes" in W. Weissleder (ed.), *The Nomadic Alternative: Modes and models of interaction in the African-Asian Deserts and Steppes* (The Hague, 1978), pp. 119–26.
35 K. N. Chaudhuri, *Asia before Europe: Economy and civilization of the Indian Ocean from the rise of Islam to 1750* (Cambridge, 1990), pp. 142–3.
36 Wei Shu, *The Book of Wei*, quoted in Sechin Jagchid and Van Jay Symons, *Peace, War, and Trade along the Great Wall: Nomadic–Chinese interaction through two millennia* (Bloomington, IN, 1989), p. 171.
37 Morris Rossabi, *China and Inner Asia: From 1368 to the present day* (London, 1975), pp. 98, 102.

38 Ibn Battuta, *The Rihla*, trans. H. A. R. Gibb and C. F. Beckingham (eds.), *The Travels of Ibn Battuta, AD 1325–54*, 4 vols. (London, 1994).
39 Karl Reinhold Haellquist (ed.), *Asian Trade Routes: Continental and maritime* (London, 1991), p. 53.
40 S. A. M. Adshead, *Central Asia in World History* (London, 1993), p. 50.
41 Ban Gu, *Han Shu*, trans. Anthony François Paulus Hulsewé and M. A. N. Loewe (eds.), *China in Central Asia: The Early Stage: 125 BC–AD 23; an Annotated Translation of Chapters 61 and 96 of the History of the Former Han Dynasty* (Leiden, 1979), pp. 211, 217.
42 William Honeychurch, *Inner Asia and the Spatial Politics of Empire: Archaeology, mobility, and culture contact* (New York, 2015), p. 275.
43 Andrew Sherratt, "Mobile Resources: Settlement and exchange in early agricultural Europe" in Colin Renfrew and Stephen Shennan (eds.), *Ranking, Resource and Exchange: Aspects of the archaeology of early European society* (Cambridge, 1982), pp. 13–26.
44 Ibn Battuta, *The Rihla*, trans. H. A. R. Gibb and C. F. Beckingham (eds.), *The Travels of Ibn Battuta, AD 1325–54*, 4 vols. (London, 1994), pp. 478–9.
45 Sechin Jagchid and Van Jay Symons, *Peace, War, and Trade along the Great Wall: Nomadic–Chinese interaction through two millennia* (Bloomington, IN, 1989), p. 167.
46 Colleen Ho, "Overland Trade in the Mongol World" in Michael Hope and Timothy May (eds.), *The Mongol World* (New York, 2022), pp. 484–504.
47 Colleen Ho, "Overland Trade in the Mongol World" in Michael Hope and Timothy May (eds.), *The Mongol World* (New York, 2022), p. 168.
48 Colleen Ho, "Overland Trade in the Mongol World" in Michael Hope and Timothy May (eds.), *The Mongol World* (New York, 2022), p. 42.
49 Étienne de la Vaissière, trans. James Ward, *Sogdian Traders: A history* (Leiden, 2005), p. 111.
50 Fan Ye, *Hou Hanshou*, trans. John Hill, *Through the Jade Gate to Rome: A study of the Silk Roads during the later Han Dynasty 1st to 2nd centuries, vol.* 2 (2009), p. 3.
51 Yan Fe, *Hou Hanshou*, trans. John Hill, *Through the Jade Gate to Rome: A study of the Silk Roads during the later Han Dynasty 1st to 2nd centuries, vol.* 2 (2009), p. 47.
52 Brian Boeck, *Imperial Boundaries: Cossack communities and empire-building in the age of Peter the Great* (Cambridge, 2010), pp. 40–53.
53 Thomas Barfield, *The Perilous Frontier: Nomadic empires and China* (Oxford: 1989), p. 239; Sechin Jagchid and Van Jay Symons, *Peace, War, and Trade along the Great Wall: Nomadic–Chinese interaction through two millennia* (Bloomington, IN, 1989), p. 14; A. M. Khazanov, trans. Julia Crookenden, *Nomads and the Outside World* (Cambridge, 1984), pp. 222–7.
54 Gary Seaman and Daniel Marks, *Rulers from the Steppe: State formation on the Eurasian periphery* (Los Angeles, CA, 1991), p. 134.
55 Ban Gu, *Han Shu*, trans. Anthony François Paulus Hulsewé and M. A. N. Loewe (eds.), *China in Central Asia: The Early Stage: 125 BC–AD 23; an Annotated Translation of Chapters 61 and 96 of the History of the Former Han Dynasty* (Leiden, 1979), p. 144.
56 Fan Ye, *Hou Hanshou*, trans. John Hill, *Through the Jade Gate to Rome: A study of the Silk Roads during the later Han Dynasty 1st to 2nd centuries, vol.* 2 (2009), p. 47.
57 Anon., *Hudūd al-Ālam* [Boundaries of the World], trans. Vladimir Minorsky, *A Persian Geography, 372 AD–982 AD* (London, 1970), pp. 97, 106, 120, 146, 165, 362–3.
58 E. E. Kuzmina and Victor Mair, *The Prehistory of the Silk Road* (Philadelphia, PA, 2015), pp. 99, 101.

59 Philip Kohl, *The Making of Bronze Age Eurasia* (Cambridge, 2007), pp. 136, 140, 214, 236–7, 245, 250–1.
60 Herodotus, *The Histories*, trans. Robin Waterfield (Oxford, 2008), pp. 645–57.
61 Xinru Liu and Lynda Norene Shaffer, *Connections Across Eurasia: Transportation, communication, and cultural exchange on the Silk Roads* (New York, 2007), p. 14.
62 Philip Curtin, *Cross-Cultural Trade in World History* (Cambridge, 1984), p. 1.

3 Controlling the Steppe Frontier

Strategies for Border Security

Global historians tend to agree that during periods of increasing integration and exchange (such as moments where trade was expanding across the steppe frontier), states, empires, cities, and individuals who were concerned about the implications of these changes sought to more effectively define their territory and impose their sovereignty.[1] Growing connectivity often encouraged efforts to more effectively control who could connect with whom.[2] Rather than national perspectives, state-led and imperial interpretations of territorialization, understanding the steppe frontier requires a shift in perspective.[3] Here, a focus on border-making processes, rather than strict territorialization, helps to show that borders could be meeting points where cultures, states, and economies connected, competed, and were contested, rather than strict geographical demarcations between distinct polities.[4] In the premodern world, clearly defined territorial delineations were not the main concern for many people, even if some states, as we shall see below, sought to impose strict territorial limits on their subjects.[5] Instead, premodern communities cared about the movement of people, and the movement of goods.[6] While a state could, for example, regulate borders for commercial contact as a means of combatting disruption caused by international exchange, it was rarely possible for them to entirely restrict access across borderlands. Such spaces had too many well-defined crossing points, and informal flows of trade were almost impossible to stop.[7]

That being said, states certainly did try to control their borders along the steppe frontier. As noted in the previous chapter, trade was not the only form of exchange between nomadic and settled communities, and violent border crossings, ranging from small scale raiding to major invasions, were threats that appeared time and time again. When purely material factors are taken into consideration – matters like demographics, economic production, or overall military strength – the balance of might between nomadic pastoralists and settled peoples should favor the latter, at least on paper. Using population as an example, reasonable estimates for China range from 50 million during the Han and Tang periods to between 80 and 100 million during

DOI: 10.4324/9781003052890-4

the Song. All of Inner Asia, on the other hand, is thought to range between 1 million and 5 million over the same period.[8] Yet, despite this seeming imbalance, the mobility and militarization of steppe societies often meant that the settled populations were far from safe from them neighbors.

That the balance of might often did not favor settled peoples led to three basic strategies among them: diplomacy, aggressive military action, and defensive fortification. The first included typical practices of diplomatic exchange, and more often than not also combined bribery and subterfuge backed up with silver, silks, and other valuables, and sometimes with royal marriages. Negotiated royal marriages along with favorable alliance compacts and trade arrangements were couched in auspicious terms, including "to seal the friendship" or even "to establish brotherly relations", according to Fan Ye. Often this was accompanied by the emperor bestowing grandiose titles, such as "Performer of Heroic Deeds Who Cherishes Virtue" or "Conqueror of the Scoundrels". But such strategy could also be used in a more aggressive way to turn confederation against confederation, tribe against tribe.[9] Such tactics could also be used to manipulate politics within a tribe or inside a royal clan, turning potential candidates for a chiefdomship into murderous rivals. Sometimes this required a strategically applied element of force. In 36 BCE when five rivals vied for the position of Chanyu among the Xiongnu, the Chinese decided which one best suited them. This led to a brief invasion that was resisted by the strongest of the rival contenders. The Chinese candidate was elevated, and the recalcitrant rival and his whole "line" were "exterminated".[10]

The diplomacy strategy could become quite complicated. This was especially the case when efforts to control borders essentially stopped or significantly limited the flow of goods across the steppe. In the relationship between China and the Türk empire, the Türks were very interested in trade both with the states to the west, principally the Byzantines and the Sasanian Persians, and to the east, meaning China. The major product in demand in the west was Chinese silk, but there were problems on both ends. In the west "Anxi [Persia] wishing to control the trade in multi-colored Chinese silks, blocked the route to prevent the [Romans and subsequently the Byzantines] getting through [to China]".[11] In the east the Chinese showed little interest in Türkic products to pay for the silk the Türks needed to send west. For a while this was addressed by forcing the Chinese to pay tribute, but this changed when China came under the powerful Sui Dynasty (581–618 CE). The first emperor of that dynasty, Yang Jian, initially suspended silk payments to the Türks; when they were resumed, it was explicitly in the form of "gifts" in return for large payments in horses. Trade had replaced extortion. The balance of power between the two empires was shifting. The Türk Empire was splitting into an eastern confederation and a western confederation over issues involving succession and inter-tribal rivalries.[12] The Sui exploited this by fomenting dissention between the two groups and supporting the eastern branch against the stronger western branch.

Yang Jian also took the opportunity to turn his allies, the Eastern Türks, against another confederation, the Tuyuhun, who had a rather mixed history with the Chinese. The Tuyuhun were primarily horse breeders who roamed from the steppes to the borders of Tibet. Their relations with the Chinese pin-ponged between trade and raid depending on how active the Chinese were in attempting to control the important east-west trade routes that the Tuyuhun considered to be in their domain. The Tuyuhun alternated between helping to defend Chinese interests in the Tarim Basin, always for hefty payments in silk, and imposing their own monopoly over the region by force. The Chinese were not always the victims in this struggle for commercial advantage, nor did they always follow what may be considered as licit conduct. In one instance during a campaign the Northern Zhou (557–81 CE) were waging against the Tuyuhun, a Zhou force captured 240 merchants and 600 camels and mules carrying tens of thousands of rolls of silk. The merchants were summarily charged as being "barbarians" in league with the Tuyuhun, and all their goods were confiscated.[13] As for the Sui-Eastern Türk alliance, they were able to dislodge the Tuyuhun and take control of the trade routes, but the Tuyuhun later gained back some of their territory.

When the Tang replaced the Sui, matters did not improve on the steppe frontier. In 627 CE a rebellion broke out in the Eastern Türk Confederation, which the Chinese surreptitiously supported. When the confederation appeared to be on the verge of collapse, the Chinese invaded, ending the Eastern Türk Confederation. Meanwhile rebellions and assassinations shook the Western Türk Confederation, leading to two Chinese invasions between 639 and 648 CE. This ended Türkic power until the 680s when the Türks rose and created the Second Türk Empire. Once again, however, dissention fanned by the Chinese undermined the attempt to build a new empire. In 716 the ruling *qaghan* was assassinated and his head sent to China. A later *qaghan* was poisoned by one of his own officials, and by 740 the Second Türk Empire had collapsed.[14]

Diplomacy, for the Chinese, was based on the adage of "using barbarians to fight barbarians". The transport of goods was used to engender violence beyond their own borders. Such a policy was sometimes equated with weakness or even cowardice by the more martial faction in a court, a humiliating option for a proud people or a pretentious ruler. Nevertheless, despite its shortcomings, diplomacy was almost always cheaper for settled folk than the next two alternatives. For nomads, diplomacy might likewise have been seen as unheroic, but bribes, tribute and the rivalry for power among tribal elites were often stronger motivating forces. This was clearly expressed on what is known as the Orkhon Inscription left by the Türks, lamenting the downfall of their empire:

> Because of the disorders between nobles and their subjects, because of ruse and deceit, Chinese set younger brother against elder brother, nobles against those without rank; the people caused the disintegration of the empire that had been its own, precipitating the ruin of the *qaghans*.[15]

A second strategy was the aggressive and violent one: to match might with might and launch punitive campaigns against tribes that were perceived as a threat. Sometimes this would be to impose control over existing borders and secure territory, but it was also a useful justification for territorial expansion and the imposition of a state's rule on populations that had previously lived beyond their control. The rationale for this approach was neatly summed up by an Imperial Secretary in China in a memorial he presented to the Han emperor in 123 CE. After a long discourse on what emperors had done in the past, he reminded his sovereign that "the Classics clearly forbid advocating the reduction of the Empire", which somehow implied that they should expand the empire "and thus control all the western kingdoms, so as to smash the enemy's offensive over 10,000 li, and terrorize the Xiongnu".[16]

Most settled peoples could not hope to challenge the nomads in cavalry warfare but rather relied more on infantry massed in close combat using stabbing spears and swords. The great states and other settled peoples commonly used auxiliaries and mercenaries drawn from nomadic populations as supplementary cavalry. When an imperial state invaded the steppes or desert, the most common reaction for nomads was to retreat, since land was what they had plenty of, rather than risk a winner-take-all confrontation. However, when they did stand and fight, as the Xiongnu and later the Mongols occasionally did against the Chinese or the Scythians and later the Hephthalites against the Persians, it could turn out to be a disaster for the invading imperial force as a few slain or captured Chinese, Persian, and other emperors found out. Often, the most sensible objective for the invader was to threaten the nomads' resources, the key to power on the steppes, by disrupting their centers of supply, and by capturing or killing their people and animals.[17]

If occasionally the army of some powerful state did score a victory that would have lasting consequences as in causing a confederation to break up or ejecting it from its traditional pasturelands, most of the time successful invasions did little more than temporarily drive away the nomads who then returned later. The costs, given the need to supply the invading army and the losses in men, animals, and equipment, were always enormous. Occupying the entire steppes indefinitely was so unrealistic even the most egomaniacal of rulers did not set this as their goal. Occupying the choicer parts of Central Asia, on the other hand, did not appear to be nearly as foolish as it really was, and many of the great empires of the settled peoples tried it at one time or another. At best this gave them some control over particular sections of key trading routes or allowed them to block particular territories that had been used by migrating herders. However, even as a purely economic venture this proved to be no bargain.[18]

Beyond employing diplomacy or violence, a third strategy relied on building walls, ramparts, watchtowers, and various types of fortresses that could become elaborate systems of defensive fortifications. To some advocates, the wall was a symbol marking the line between savagery and barbarism on one side and order and civilization on the other. Walls ranged from encircling small areas like a town to barriers reaching across many miles. Wall-building could have a negative effect. Walls could become barriers to peaceful exchange, dislocate trade routes, and disrupt established migration patterns. By destabilizing local conditions, walls in themselves could become the underlying cause of war.

The greatest of all great walls runs across northern China; tourists by the droves stroll along it today. It is a wall of stone built by the Ming dynasty (1368–1644 CE) in the sixteenth century to keep out the Mongols. It did not, however, keep out the Manchus. An earlier Great Wall from the third century BCE also existed as did strings of fortified posts the Chinese established in passes and other strategic locales as they expanded westward under the Han and Tang. Settlements developed around them populated by exiles, among others. The Great Wall of China has become such a historical icon that the importance of other, if smaller walls, are often overlooked.

Some walls protected entire oases as in Samarkand (originally Afrasiab) and Bukhara. Samarkand was inhabited from at least the seventh or sixth century BCE and from a very early time had a strong perimeter wall five and a half miles long that was rebuilt at least twice.[19] A more impressive feat is credited to one of Alexander the Great's successors, the Hellenistic monarch Antiochus I Seleucid (r. 281–261 BCE), who ordered a wall to be built to protect from nomadic attack the city of Merv and the fertile oasis around it: according to Strabo, this reached 1,500 stadia (about 172 miles).[20]

Farther still to the west, the peoples on the other side of Eurasia had their own prominent barrier erected against the fearsome steppe people to their north and east. Over time this wall in the West came to have a good deal of mystery and mythology attached to it although it was not nearly as long or in most other measurable ways as great as the Chinese Great Walls. The mystery begins with the name and location of the wall. It was most commonly referred to as either the "Gates of Alexander" or the "Caspian Gates". Later it became associated with the historical Gates of Derbent (Dagestan) or the fortress at Dariali Gorge (Georgia). Both were in the Caucasus Mountains, which Alexander never crossed, and both were built centuries after Alexander and by Persians not Macedonians. Nevertheless, Alexander was said to have built gates of bronze there. Subsequently, this was also described as a wall made of iron. It was constructed to keep out a reported twenty-two "unclean nations", led by the notorious Gog and Magog.[21]

If northward-looking walls were built to keep out raiding or invading nomadic tribesmen, were Gog and Magog names given to actual tribes? Or were they generic terms for "barbarian" tribesmen bent on destruction? Or did they represent something more metaphorical? Who were Gog and Magog? Magog was first mentioned in the Bible, initially in passing in Genesis and later in the Book of Ezekiel. Biblically, Gog was described as a prince from a place called Magog who posed a threat to Israel. Finally, they are seen as allies of Satan in the final showdown between good and evil in the Book of Revelations, "When fire came down from heaven and consumed them".[22] The Jewish historian Flavius Josephus in the first century CE maintained that Gog and Magog were Scythians, whom the Jews referred to as Magogites, and that Alexander had built a wall with an iron gate in the Caucasus Mountains and locked them behind it.[23] But in the early centuries of the first millennium CE after the Scythians faded from history, a new, more aggressive, more frightening steppe invader appeared, the Huns. In 395 CE they moved through the Caucasus, penetrating far into both the Eastern Roman and Persian empires plundering, sacking, and wreaking havoc. It is at this time that the historical fortress of Dariali was built.[24] Nevertheless, the Byzantine historian Procopius, who wrote in the sixth century, insisted that "almost all the nations of the Huns" were still living north of the mountain range.[25]

It should be noted that the term "Hun" was by now a label used indiscriminately by settled peoples from Europe to India to refer to various nomadic pastoralist groups from the steppes. Procopius's Huns were not the Huns of Attila fame. In his time the major steppe powers were the Hephthalites and subsequently the Türks, who destroyed the Hephthalites in 560. In Procopius's description:

> As one passes beyond the boundary of Iberia [Georgia] there is a sort of path in a very narrow passage, extending for a distance of fifty stades. This path terminates in a place cut off by cliffs and, as it seems, is absolutely impossible to pass through. For from there no way out appears, except indeed a small gate set there by nature.[26]

Here, Alexander made a grand reappearance in the story, according to Procopius, by adding his own man-made gate and a fortress to the site. Whether or not this gate existed, it reflected an enduring fear of how to control the steppe frontier in the Caucasus. Although a great deal of enmity existed between the Byzantines and Persians, when the Persian emperor Khusraw I Anushiruwan (531–579 CE) requested an annual subsidy in gold to help support the Persian garrison at the gates against a potential invasion by the Huns, the Byzantine emperor Justinian (482–565 CE) agreed to it.[27]

In subsequent centuries peoples of the Islamic world still thought this wall protected them from evil forces. Scythians and Huns had been real people, but Gog and Magog did not have to be. The wall was also expected to keep out monsters of various sorts and cannibals, some of whom were said to eat cadavers and fetuses.[28] Islamic images of Gog and Magog emphasized their huge numbers as well as their physical hideousness, as in having claws, hairy tails, and ears so large they could sleep on them.[29] In 842 CE the Abbasid caliph al-Wathiq (842–7 CE) is said to have had a dream that cannibals had breached the wall, so he sent an expedition led by a man named Sallam. When Sallam returned, more than two years later, he reported that the wall and a tower were intact and still guarded by a family charged with that responsibility, who routinely checked the wall by striking it with a hammer. Scary noises could reportedly be heard coming from the other side.[30]

Somewhat later, in 921 CE, another expedition set out to make contact with a people beyond the wall, the Bulghurs, who lived up the Volga River, with whom the Arabs traded and knew to be a real people. This was led by Ibn Fadlan and did not go through the Caucasus but followed trade routes that started between the Caspian and Aral seas. On his return he wrote an account of his journey that included a report from the Bulghurs about a giant who had been found alive floating in the Volga and measured twelve cubits (a cubit ranged from eighteen to twenty-one inches). The Bulghur king wrote to the people of Wisu, who lived three months journey farther north and whom the king knew to be a real people, again through trade contacts: "They wrote informing me that this man was from Gog and Magog [a people] who are three months distant from us [that is, from the people of Wisu]. They are naked, and the sea forms a barrier between them and us, for they are located on its shore." They subsisted, Fadlan was told, on a diet of fish, and spent their time copulating with each other. Despite the distance, he still reassured his reader that "the wall lies as a barrier between them and the gate through which they were wont to pass".[31]

While the report of the giant may be a tad far-fetched, the connection between the Abbasid Empire, the Bulghurs on the Volga, and the people of Wisu probably represents a trade system long in effect before Fadlan's official mission. Rather than come from Gog and Magog, the supposed giant may have represented a people who lived on the shores of the White Sea or the Gulf of Finland.[32] A north-south trade system, one of several that have been dubbed as the "Fur Road", did operate between the late eighth and early eleventh centuries CE and appears to have been built on an earlier Persian system. It funneled a huge quantity of furs and other northern products, including walrus ivory, honey, and enslaved people to the Abbasid Empire in return largely for silver.[33]

If the giant in Ibn Fadlan's story did come from Gog and Magog, he was unique in that he did not represent the pastoral nomads of the steppes. The much feared and imagined apocalyptic hordes behind the wall reportedly included at different times a tribe of Amazons and, more historically, the Sarmatians and the Alans, successors of the Scythians and, like them, Iranian speakers. Subsequently, the Goths defeated the Alans and were in turn defeated by the Huns. Ultimately the Mongols arrived, who Christians and Muslims alike agreed had to be Gog and Magog. According to travelers who brought back information from the Mongol Empire, some Mongols themselves agreed that they descended from Gog and Magog, noting that "Mongol" was a corruption of "Magogites".[34] Arab writers often put Gog and Magog as living directly north of China and in the process jumbled together the wall in the Caucasus with what was left of the old Qin-Han wall.[35]

That the great wall of the Caucasus was not all myth or misinformation is evidenced by archaeological remains at two sites, both of which could claim to be the real Caspian Gates, both of which were probably blended together into the story of the gates. The Gates of Derbent, now consisting of thirty towers, stretched twenty-five miles between the eastern edge of the Caucasus and the Caspian Sea. In its time the wall may have reached up to sixty-five feet high and was ten feet thick at its base. It was likely built during the reign of the Persian emperor Khusraw I Anushiruwan, possibly as part of plans laid with his Byzantine partners mentioned above. Derbent and the fortifications in the Dariali Gorge, as described by Procopius, made up the cornerstones of the Persian and later the Abbasid Caliphate's defense system against a northern invasion.

When comparing the Great Wall of China with the Caspian Gates, it is easy to conclude that, when seeking to control the steppe frontier, short walls were more effective than long ones. Perhaps more pertinent still, it was helpful to have a major mountain range separating your cities from the steppe. Walls may have made those behind them feel more secure, and they may have intimidated those outside the walls who would have plundered whatever was inside had there been no walls. But if they are not maintained over the years and if, as was often the case, the essential building material in them was some form of pounded soil, they slowly disappeared, especially if nearby peasants came to realize that such soil might have been a good source of compost. Even stone can wear away, become buried, or be carted off for new projects. Once majestic watchtowers retained their usefulness only as convenient landmarks for passing caravans, a sad example being the once storied Jade Gate, of which only the ruins of a single beacon tower remain; nothing remains of its companion, the Yang Barrier. In the end, not even the greatest of walls could keep out a major invasion by a large, determined force. Fortunately for those behind the walls, this was not common, and most raids were small-scale events.

Crossing Borders

When invasion bent on conquest did come, the perpetrators were more likely to be a version of pastoralist who had some familiarity with settled peoples and hence some indication of the potential wealth they represented, rather than to come from distant nomadic pastoralists, who would more likely be prone to plunder but had no inclination to stay. Nevertheless, image and reality did not have to synchronize. The image of thundering hordes pouring out of Inner Asia into China, India, Persia, the Mediterranean Basin, or Europe was so frightening when it did happen, it left an impression that could linger indefinitely. What frightened settled folk did not realize was that nomads bent on conquest and imposing their rule was not a common event before Chinggis and his Mongols. Pastoral peoples who had long-standing contact with settled peoples risked being gradually absorbed sometimes piece by piece with the elite going first. This could happen culturally before it happened physically as witnessed by those nomads who roamed too close to the borderlands of China and were well on the way to being Sinocized by the time they actually crossed into China.

No matter how large the invading horde may have been, it would always be vastly outnumbered by the conquered people. Keeping their identity from disappearing into the mass they now ruled over prompted some conquerors to establish themselves in new, fortified places of power separate from the old capitals and major cities. To no avail. Sooner or later, usually within a few generations, conquerors became one with the conquered. Given the choice, most nomads did not see sedentarization as a happy alternative to their own lifestyle unless it was as a privileged ruling elite. Those at the lower end of the social scale usually had little desire to become cultivators unless life on the steppes had simply become too precarious. Most of the time nomads were satisfied with trading, collecting tribute, or just being paid off to go away. If that was not working, then raiding was usually the preferred option to outright conquest and permanent occupation.

On occasion a large, aggressive confederation could be tempted to conquest in order to take advantage of an unusual situation in which some great state or the ruling dynasty therein was in decline. No doubt waves of pastoral invasions damaged infrastructure and disrupted the interlinkages that held trade together. But just as extorters had no incentive to undermine those they extorted from, invaders usually did not set out to destroy the places they invaded. And in the main, what was considered as "barbarian invasion" was not the culprit in initiating the processes of deurbanization and economic downturn, leave aside the collapse of long-established states. Those processes were usually well under way internally; at most, the invaders just hastened or finished off the decline. Greed and aggression did not have to be the only catalysis. What was deemed invasion was more often migration, a movement of whole peoples driven by some ecological or human-induced disaster. The movement from steppe into settled, generally a north-to-south shift, could be paralleled farther north where the foraging peoples of the taiga forestland moved onto the steppes, trading their hunting-gathering-fishing lifestyle for that of the nomadic pastoralist. Both the Türks and the Mongols were thought to have been forest folk before moving onto the steppes and adapting to life on horseback.[36]

Steppe warfare, when tribes began the billiard-ball effect, could produce unexpected results. During the second century BCE the Xiongnu dislodged the Yuezhi, making their ruler's skull into a drinking vessel. The Yuezhi, in turn, slammed into the Saka, who then fled south to Kashmir and northwest India to be followed later by the Yuezhi after they were defeated by the Wusan. All of this must have involved desperate fighting since the Saka are reported to have retreated across the Suspended Crossings, a seemingly impossible feat for an army.[37] When the dust finally settled, out of all of this a great state was born, the Kushan Empire, which brought stability and economic growth to the region it controlled for several centuries. Generally, however, tribal chieftains, even the leaders of great confederations, often did not prove to be very competent rulers over the settled lands they conquered. The best strategy was often to employ the elite of the people they conquered to do the administering for them, assuming they had not been so foolish as to have completely wiped out the old governing class. The Yuan, that is the Chinggisid dynasty that ruled China (1271–1368), did not trust the Chinese, so often they used people like the Khitans and the Uyghurs, who themselves descended from steppe peoples but had long experience with Chinese society and the way government worked there.[38] The Yuan also hired professional bureaucrats and traders from the Islamic world or farther afield as in the case of Marco Polo.

Established states sought to protect themselves against further movement across their steppe borders by managing crossing points. Along frontiers where exchange had freely taken place, trade would become focused at those points where there were crossings were established. Under peaceful conditions, markets grew up sometimes followed by towns. Fan Ye noted: "Hu [Western] merchants coming to trade, and travelers, arrived at the frontier regions every day."[39] Engaging in frontier trade was part of still another strategy the Chinese used in dealing with their northern and western neighbors, often in conjunction with the diplomacy strategy. Frontier trade at border markets, along with what has come to be known as the tributary system, constituted the official machinery of Chinese foreign trade and became China's most regular form of exchange with the rest of the world. Frontier trade handled a much larger quantity of goods than did caravan-based long-distance trade, which tended to emphasize value rather than volume. The system was officially predicated on the belief that the Chinese didn't need to trade, but the people who lived on the other side of the walls did. Thus, trade took place only because of the gracious magnanimity of the Chinese emperor.

The reality was much different depending on the relative strength of the two sides. In periods of nomadic military superiority, more often than not the case, the Chinese were at a disadvantage. Chinese ideology placed much importance on precedent, especially when it was based on the dealings of previously successful dynasties. The Han and the Tang were usually held up as the exemplars of China's strength, yet both ended up striking bargains that were much to the benefit of their nomadic adversaries. The Tang, for example, had to deal with two formidable confederations in succession, the Türks and the Uyghurs. They did this by trading rolls of silk for horses but at greatly inflated prices, in effect, providing subsidies for the nomads. In return the confederations agreed to maintain peace, sometimes to ally with the Chinese against other enemies, and to accept the fiction that they were officially tributaries of China.

On the positive side, trade, under whatever conditions, was the most effective way of stabilizing the frontier and ensuring peace along the borders. Contrary to what they officially told themselves, the Chinese benefited much from it. They regulated the markets, which helped them to control their sometimes unruly neighbors. Only on rare occasion were markets open to all who wanted to come and trade, so the Chinese could open markets to some but not others, a good way to stoke resentments. Putting restrictions on trade or, worse, threatening to close markets was a way to reign in any potential misbehavior brewing across the border. If not, almost always war was the consequence. Negotiating over markets dominated diplomatic interaction between the Chinese and the various confederations and nomadic-based empires that came and went to the north and west for more than a millennium and a half.

An incident that occurred during the Northern Wei period (386–534 CE) was not easily forgotten by subsequent Chinese courts. The Rouran (or Juan-juans, a pejorative term given to them by the Chinese, which meant something like "unpleasant wriggling worms"; their real name is lost) constituted the most powerful nomadic confederation on the northern Chinese border between the end of the Xiongnu and the rise of the Türks. Their homeland was Mongolia, but at their height their sway extended from the Tarim Basin almost to Korea. Throughout most of their history, the Rouran and the Northern Wei dynasty were enemies. Finally, in 520, the Northern Wei, anxious to end the drain their never-ending war was putting on resources, offered the Rouran a bounty of gifts, including elite items such as finely crafted ceremonial weapons and clothing plus 200,000 bushels of grain, 1,000 bushels of cooked rice, 80 bushels of fried wheat, 50 bushels of fried nuts, 5,000 sheep, and 100 cattle.[40] But good deeds are quickly forgotten. Three years later, when the Rouran suffered a famine, they raided and plundered the Chinese.

Border exchanges faced some fundamental challenges. Both sides came into the relationship burdened with underlying mistrust, prejudice, and hostility toward the other. Both sides held resentment based on the firm belief that they were being cheated, and on the nomad side this was compounded by the common tribesman's observation that he was not getting enough compared to tribal leaders.[41] The borderlands were dangerous places; as a matter of policy the Chinese government exiled to the borderlands convicts, desperados, and others deemed as undesirables of every sort, including merchants. Illegal activity was rife. One of the main arguments that opponents of border markets pressed was that they promoted inefficiency and corruption, and, unfortunately, they were right. The whole system was at best slightly better than ineffective. Decisions were made at court, not on the frontier, and could be based on incomplete, faulty, or intentionally misleading information. The frontier was too far away from the capital for effective oversight. Both nomads and Chinese merchants often found it difficult to navigate through the bureaucracy and to deal with incompetent, arbitrary, and too often corrupt local officials. At times they were in collusion with the nomads, accepting bribes to allow tribute missions to cross the border without court approval or to trade in contraband. At other times they cheated the nomads, who they considered to be uncivilized, and their own government alike. Both sides traded inferior products from horses to silk when they thought they could get away with it.

Under the Ming there was a problem with revenge-minded border officials and their military counterparts, who lured unsuspecting Mongols to border markets and arbitrarily slaughtered them. For their part, nomads were known to come to border markets on the pretext of trade and plundering them instead. Of course, Chinese did have some effective, honest officials, but their pleas had little impact on an always very conservative court too indifferent to bother changing anything to improve the situation. Even progressive-minded emperors, and they were few and far between, often had their own bureaucracies, intentionally or just through lethargy, undermine attempts at reform. Nor were merchants and nomads always victims of the system. Government policies that were considered to be of vital strategic importance, foremost of which was maintaining the monopoly over the horse trade, were openly flouted by entrepreneurs who made fortunes from illicit horse rearing and trade. Even tribal leaders could not guarantee good behavior by their fellow tribesmen. Large tribute missions going to and from the capital to offer submission were known to terrorize the lands they passed through; sometimes Chinese officials looked the other way for a share of the loot.

That spying, trading, and politics were intimately connected and complicate our notion of borders as boundaries in the premodern world can be seen in an account of the kingdom of Kroraina, known to the Chinese originally as Loulan and later Shanshan, which existed astride the southern branch of the Silk Roads south of the Taklamakan Desert between Lop Nor and the Kunlun Mountains. Kroraina had a sometimes strained relationship with China. According to Ban Gu, it harassed and robbed Han delegations going westward, but at the same time he admitted, it "was frequently robbed, reprimanded or harmed by officials or conscripts and found it inexpedient to keep in contact with Han. Later the state again conducted espionage for the Xiongnu". The King of Kroraina had crossed the line: "This was highly contrary to the rules of Heaven." The Han Emperor sent a mission directly to the Krorainan ruler, bringing gold and other presents to clear matters up. In the celebration that followed, the king became intoxicated, and a member of the Chinese mission then stabbed him to death. His head was sent back to the Chinese capital, where it was hung at the North Palace gate.[42]

Joining corruption, mismanagement, and general misconduct as insoluble problems in border trade was smuggling. This is a special kind of trade that relates to the particular conditions under which a commodity is exchanged. Selling an iron plow or even a knife or arrowhead may be perfectly legal when done from one location in China to another, but such a transaction became illegal when crossing a border unless it received some kind of official sanction. Smuggling was a crime against the state because the state was eliminated from controlling the transaction and benefiting from it. Thus, in the eyes of the government, smuggling was a crime like treason, meaning it was worse than a crime against a mere individual. The state was shown not to be in control of its own territory.[43] Despite strict regulation, clandestine exchange was a problem even when the frontier markets were open and doing business, and the tribute missions were arriving. When the frontier markets were closed, smuggling became rampant. Smuggling also increased when the Chinese government, as under the Ming, offered prices that were unreasonably low or tilted the market some other way the nomads thought was unfair.

Some goods were not supposed to be traded at all, including strategic material that could be used for military purposes. At times this could become rather stretched as under the Song when the list of prohibited goods included books, maps, copper cash, silver, salt, and rice;[44] under the Ming it included the broader categories of grain and textiles. If caught, the least a transgressor could expect was confiscation of his merchandise and likely imprisonment. In 121 BCE the Han emperor, Wudi, had 500 merchants executed for selling contraband to members of a Xiongnu mission in Chang'an.[45] Under the Song a smuggler from the other side of the border, if caught, was beheaded on the spot, and the Ming executed tea smugglers. Nevertheless, laws against the private exchange of goods across the border were commonly ignored due to the substantial profits that could be realized. Contraband trade was carried on along the entire frontier. High ranking officials on the spot and back in the capital reaching into high ranking circles became involved even in the weapons-for-horses exchange. In Chang'an, Manichaean priests appear to have operated their own smuggling ring from the Western Market under the Tang.[46]

Smuggling may not have been the most serious transgression. Chinese control over border commerce was partly out of concern that the nomads would use merchants to spy with the intention of scouting out potential weak points in Chinese defenses. This was not a case of unfounded paranoia. By its secretive nature, espionage history is difficult to ferret out even if hints of it appear in many contexts, but there can be no doubt that merchants were used as spies in many places.[47] The sixth-century historian Procopius, in his discussion of war and trade between the Byzantine and Sasanian empires, provides the most straightforward description of this widespread practice:

> It has been customary from ancient times both among the Romans and the Persians to maintain spies at public expense; these men are accustomed to go secretly among the enemy, in order that they may investigate accurately what is going on, and may then return and report to the rulers.[48]

Procopius believed such people "act in a spirit of loyalty to their nation", but then he warns of double agents, including a Persian who flipped sides and provided the emperor Justinian with valuable information.

For traders the gathering of cloak-and-dagger intelligence has to be put in a mercantile context: this was a valuable commodity from which to garner the best price from the most appreciative customer. In another of his writings, Procopius claims that a merchant, or perhaps a spy disguised as a merchant who was working for the Byzantines, made it all the way to the Persian palace at Ctesiphon.[49] In an attempt to counter such threats, it was not uncommon for states to prohibit the merchants of a potential or current enemy from penetrating past their border. The Chinese tried several strategies. Under the Han, envoys were sent out "to escort merchants of the barbarians".[50] This was probably to ensure than no shenanigans, including spying as well as thieving and marauding, took place. In Song trade with the Jin, traders on both sides of the border did not deal directly with each other but turned their merchandise over to officials. They, in turn, sent the merchandise to officials on the other side of the border, who sold the goods to their own traders at a standard price plus tax.

The other mechanism in Chinese overland trade was the tributary system, which was supposed to be more political in its intent than economic. From one perspective, it can be seen as a continuation of royal gift exchange that went back to the Bronze Age. The Chinese the tributary system had been in operation at least since the Han. At that time in the late first century CE, as the Chinese were extending their power into the Tarim Basin and enjoying a certain measure of success against the Xiongnu, "Kingdoms such as Tiaozhi [Characene and Suisiana], Anxi [Parthian Persia] and all the kingdoms as far as the shores of the [Western] sea more than 40,000 li away offered tribute".[51] States in faraway Iran and Mesopotamia may have sent congratulatory messages to the Han accompanied by appropriate gifts, but it is not likely they interpreted this as having voluntarily become tributaries of China. Rather, this interpretation was based on the ideology that proclaimed China as being at the center of the universe represented by the imperial court in the person of the emperor. He maintained this position above all other peoples of inferior culture by reason of his virtue. The Chinese considered the tributary system as a moral matter, even as it carried considerable material baggage with it.

The traditional Chinese attitude regarding hierarchy is best seen in a memorial presented to the Emperor Wen in the mid-first century CE:

> The situation of the empire may be described as like that of a person hanging upside down. The Son of Heaven is the head of the empire. Why? Because he should remain on the top. The barbarians are the feet of the empire. Why? Because they should be placed at the bottom ... Yet each year Ha provides them with money, silk floss and fabrics. To command the barbarians is the power vested in the Emperor on the top, and to present tribute to the Son of Heaven is a ritual to be performed by the vassals at the bottom.[52]

According to what the Chinese told themselves: "With bared heads, they [emissaries from countries in the West] walked toward the east on their [knees and] elbows before the Imperial Court and the Son of Heaven."[53]

In this Sinocentric world order all other peoples, whether in states large or small or tribes near or far, were obligated to show their subservience by an act of ritual subordination that would ensure the proper functioning of the cosmic order. This was expressed through the periodic sending of official missions to perform required rituals and present tribute to the Chinese court consisting of "the most marvelous products of their countries".[54] According to protocol, once the tribute was received, the emperor then bestowed what was deemed to be "gifts" or "presents" on the visiting delegation, not necessarily rare but valuable. Indeed, while the tribute was sometimes little more than a token, the gifts, often in the form of silk, were much more valuable. This was interpreted on the Chinese side as the emperor being magnanimous to his dependents for recognizing his superiority. The emperor could also confer certain rights to those who offered tribute, the most important being the right to trade at border markets. The Chinese had to provide food and accommodations for each member of the tribute mission, and each was also entitled to a gift depending on his standing. Also, each was allowed to engage in private trade with Chinese merchants in the capital at a designated place for a specified period of time.

Neighboring states and tribal confederations typically accepted the system, ignoring the theoretical humiliation even when they were notably stronger than the Chinese. Not surprisingly, members of a tribe vied to be appointed to a tributary mission, and often merchants who were not even part of the tribe, were able to attach themselves to reap the benefits. The size of the missions grew as did the expectations for additional gifts. The Chinese tried to restrict the times such delegations could show up and the numbers in their entourages. Nevertheless, nomadic leaders continued to demand the "right to petition for presenting tribute" even as the Chinese court continued to dissuade them from doing so. If the petition was rejected, it could lead to war.

Tribute was usually in the form of horses, other domestic animals such as sheep and Bactrian camels, and products obtained through hunting, such as furs and skins. Most of the time the Chinese determined the value of the goods and the rate of exchange, which was usually based more on political than purely commercial considerations. The Türks, however, specified the gifts they were to receive and the amounts they expected, while the Ming converted tribute to a price equivalent from which the gifts were then determined.[55] Although the system was not, in theory, based on supply and demand, if those forces became too disrespected, the exchange could become very out-of-whack. During the period of the Five Dynasties (907–60 CE), a time of Chinese weakness between the end of the Tang and the establishment of the Song dynasty, trade to the west came under control of one group of Uyghurs whose tribute missions grew larger each year. The Uyghurs did bring tribute in the form of jade, the major source of which was under their control. The Chinese cherished jade, but too much, even of a good thing, can be too much. Jade piled up in the Chinese treasury. A solution was worked out under the transient Later Zhou dynasty (951–60 CE) in which the Uyghurs were allowed to sell their jade on the open market instead of handing over all of it to the court as tribute. The value of jade eventually stabilized, and the court was able to sell off some of its stockpile. The Uyghurs continued to send tribute missions, but they were unlikely to have included jade.[56]

The decision to maintain border markets and the tribute system had its detractors at the Chinese court, which from time to time was able to appeal to the underlying Confucianist bias against commerce in general and trade with these customers in particular. Their basic argument was that exchanging goods with nomads enhanced the strength of people they had a good chance of facing as enemies sooner or later by providing those people with grain and metal products. Secondarily, the costs of maintaining and protecting border markets, leaving aside underwriting the expenses associated with visiting tribute missions, was too high for what the Chinese got back. Economically it was a bad deal. As one official pointed out to a Ming emperor, the whole matter was rather illogical: "The horses are purchased only for expeditions against the barbarians. If the markets lead to peace, then where are the horses to be used? Moreover, why should the barbarians give us good horses?"[57]

The horse argument was, ironically, true for both sides. The Chinese had learned back in the Warring States era (476–221 BCE) that cavalry had an advantage over infantry and chariotry. Since much of China was not suitable for breeding horses and nomads fought as cavalry, the Chinese needed to obtain horses from somewhere to have a chance at defending themselves. Horses were plentiful on much of the steppes. During the Han period, among the Wusan Confederation, "the state owned numerous horses and rich persons may own as many as four or five thousand".[58] Conversely, land in China that could have become pasture was used to grow human food, so border markets were also a key source for other livestock, including cattle, sheep, Bactrian camels, and donkeys. Recognition of the benefits of this exchange sometimes made its way into the imperial court, but the argument most often heard there in support of trade was that it would win over the nomads, who would as a result want to pay homage to the emperor. Although this was little more than Sinocentric self-flattery, it often carried the day.

The Chinese horse trade with nomadic pastoralists went back long before the Qin unification. The trading partners were a very early confederation known as the Yuezhi, who lived to the west and traded horses and jade for silk. In the mid-second century BCE, the Yuezhi were replaced by the Xiongnu, with whom the Chinese had a more contentious relationship, one result of which was the building of the first Great Wall. The Han did carry on trade with the Xiongnu, including the opening of border markets as stipulated by treaties the two made during their on-and-off conflicts with each other. Chinese assumptions were correct in one central way. The nomadic peoples needed trade on an even more basic level than the Chinese, at times driving their animals to the borders in the hope of making some transaction. But always, demand for Chinese products, subsistence and luxury, exceeded supply. It was not unheard of for trade to be carried on during open hostilities. The Song regularly traded with the Jurchens when the two were at war, and the Uriyangkha Mongols sent tribute delegations when they were openly at war with the Ming.

If in the long run of almost two millennia, border trade proved to be a positive experience for nomads because it allowed them access to products they needed and for the Chinese because it helped to promote peace with their neighbors, it was a very imperfect mechanism. A totally peaceful border lasting indefinitely may not have been possible: there were too many unsolvable issues, too many unpredictable variables, too many things that could go wrong. But misunderstandings leading to violence could have been lessened through well-thought-out and disciplined policies at the Chinese court and among the tribal peoples. Sometimes this was the case, but too often it was not.

Throughout the complicated history of border relations on the Eurasian steppe, there were few periods where trade ceased to take place. The borderlands between steppe and sedentary state represented too many opportunities, either for trading in products that were valued across this border, or because the steppe represented a route through which these commodities carried might be carried to more distant markets. Border markets were located in the borderlands, at the edge of the state, which by their nature were precarious, hazardous places where space was often contested, places that could easily degenerate into no-man's land. Being important points of contact, yet fraught with uncertainty, these markets offer a useful example for understanding more deeply both the dynamics of trade on the steppe frontier, but also for structures of trade that were common across the premodern world. The Chinese placed their markets with both security and commercial matters in mind. They were typically located near fortified strongholds on natural corridors for overland transport often in passes or astride water routes. They were not permanent, open-daily marketplaces but are probably best characterized as annual livestock or sometimes just horse fairs.[59] A similar dynamic shaped markets on China's maritime border, where port towns were simultaneously points of cross-cultural and commercial exchange as well as secured sites.[60]

In administering border markets and the tribute system, the major Chinese dynasties – Han, Tang, Song, and Ming – all faced the same problems; sometimes they responded in very similar ways, at other times quite differently. Even over the lifetime of a single dynasty as in the early period in contrast to the later period, the temper of the court often changed. The Chinese tried and retried a hodgepodge of basic strategies sometimes more or less successful than at earlier or later times, but no institutionalized system was maintained over the centuries, although they did seek to uphold the same basic principle: the Chinese would be in control. However, that was not always the case.

Under the Tang each border market was controlled by a high-ranking official who was under the Directorate of Imperial Workshops, which was under the Department of Treasury, which was part of the Board of Finance.[61] His staff consisted of a number of assistants, including several who were responsible for fixing prices. Brokers who specialized in frontier markets were also used as they were under the Song. Strict rules governed the proceedings, and all dealings were conducted by officials. According to the *Regulations of the Department of Treasury*, "The common people must not be allowed by have free intercourse with them",[62] referring to the tribesmen. On the day designated for the market, there was a set period to trade.

The government prohibited private trade outside of the established border market system. When private Chinese merchants were allowed to participate in border trade, they did so under many restrictions and were rigidly controlled. Policies under the early Ming were designed to stifle competition from private traders, allowing the government to set lower prices in its trade with the nomads. Private traders had to be registered and pay a tax; under the Song they also had to pay a brokerage fee to the government. The Song maintained a rigid distinction between official and private trade; official trade dealt with commodities that were under government monopoly, foremost of which were horses. Goods prohibited from trading always included weapons and sometimes other metal products, especially those made of iron. Private individuals might be forbidden to trade in luxury goods such as silk and gold and silver items. Commodities could change in status. Tea from Sichuan had been free of government control, but as demand for it grew north of the border, the government assumed a monopoly over its supply and export.

The Yuan dynasty was established by Khubilai (1260–94) in 1271 following the Mongol victory over the Southern Song. As nomadic pastoralists from the northern steppes, the Mongols had limited experience in dealing with sedentary folk and before Khubilai, little idea as to what to do with a place like China. So, they recklessly pillaged and devastated the part that came under their initial control, northern China. Influential people at the Mongol court actually proposed to Ogodei, Chinggis' son and the ruling khan at the time, that the Mongols exterminate all the Chinese peasants and turn their agricultural land into pasture. Ogodei was finally talked out of this horrific act of genocide by one of his advisors, Yelu Qucai, a Sinocized Khitan, who argued the obvious: that more wealth could be had for the Mongols by setting up an efficient tax system. But it was a close call.

During the period of empire building, the Mongols raged tremendous destruction on trade routes, cities, and infrastructure across Eurasia. But unlike some Chinese rulers and like other steppe peoples, the Mongols, in the form of the Yuan dynasty, appreciated the role of trade. Once in power they encouraged and supported it at all levels from local to long distance caravan traffic. The result was a huge upsurge that eventually linked China with the Mediterranean world in the last great transcontinental land route system before railroads. The Mongols reaped the benefits from taxes, commercial fees, profits, support costs, and especially protective services in this Via Mongolia (*c.*1250–1350 CE).[63] Unlike in the north of China, the conquest of the south did little damage, and Khubilai set about revitalizing the Chinese economy. His success was noted by the historian Hayton the Armenian writing in 1307: "The empire of Cathay is the greatest that you will find on the face of the earth, and it abounds with population, and has wealth without end."[64]

In 1368 the Yuan court, including the emperor, and most of the other Mongols left in China, packed up and rode back to Mongolia. Matters had gone awry in China. In the countryside natural disasters, especially floods, led to famine and soon thereafter widespread social collapse. Chinese bandit gangs transitioned to rebel armies; the Yuan's response was to engage in its own orgy of self-destructive fratricidal wars. The retreat to Mongolia was more a strategic withdrawal than an outright defeat and escape, and the Mongols probably intended to regroup, reconquer, and return to rule again. But this did not happen. Instead, Zhu Yuanzhang, better known by his imperial temple name of Taizu (1328–98), the leader of the most successful bandit gang turned revolutionaries, established the Ming dynasty. He was a ruthless man and established a despotic regime. From a peasant background, he was also suspicious of trade and commerce and forbade private foreign trade. The result on the northern frontier was another bout of rampant smuggling, the most manifest of the culprits being poorly paid Chinese soldiers.

The third Ming emperor, Chengzu (1360–1424), better known as the Yongle Emperor, understood tribal politics better than any ruler in his dynasty and was the most successful in dealing with the Mongols. He used diplomacy, trade, and, when necessary, warfare to dominate the frontier, fighting those tribes that appeared most likely to unite the steppes into one powerful confederation, sending gifts and opening border markets to allies or others he was courting. Unfortunately for the Chinese, his successors were less visionary and much less capable. They were haunted by the specter of a Mongol reconquest. The memory of the invasion and domination by a people they considered to be the foulest of barbarians proved so traumatic for the Chinese of the time, it distorted Ming relations with its northern neighbors for the life of the dynasty. Long after the Mongols had ceased dreaming of reestablishing their empire in China, the Ming continued to interpret every raid, every border incident, as the prelude to a new invasion.[65]

The core of Ming foreign policy became a revived version of the tribute system. This had worked well under the Han and Tang, particularly in the later periods of these dynasties when both benefited from friendly nomadic military support, internally and externally, in return for Chinese subsidies usually in the form of an unbalanced trade relationship. The Song, militarily the weakest if economically the most powerful of the great Chinese dynasties, could not impose this fiction on its more powerful neighbors that came to control parts of northern China: the Khitans from the fringes of the steppes in Manchuria; the Jurchens from farther east in the mountains of Manchuria; and the Xixia Tangats from north of Tibet centered in Gansu. So, the Song made what they bald-facedly admitted to as "yearly payments" in silk and silver to all three and allowed the opening of border markets. The result was a generally stable frontier, and the Song easily recovered their yearly payments in the profits they made in the border markets. Obviously, the Yuan were a special case since they were the nomads themselves; they were able to control Mongolia and the tribes of the steppes but again by using the resources of China.

Under the Ming, the Mongols were willing to go back to participating in the tribute system if the Ming insisted, however humbling it was supposed to be, as long as it brought the nomads the goods they needed. After the Yongle Emperor died in 1424, however, the Ming did not operate the border market and tribute mission policies on a consistent basis. The Ming wanted to have as little to do with the nomads as possible and, if possible, to have nothing to do with them at all except to get horses from them to fight them when necessary. This policy featured strategies of non-intercourse, non-accommodation, non-appeasement, retrenchment, and exclusion. When border markets had to be opened, both sides tried to cheat the other, and the Ming sometimes tried to get the nomads to accept Chinese cash coins and even paper money instead of the silk, other textiles, and grain they wanted. Mongol groups were only occasionally allowed to send tribute missions when the Ming determined it would be a convenient device for turning one tribe or faction against another. An important part of the strategy of exclusion was the reinstation of major wall building projects, which began in 1474. Initially, these were constructed of pounded earth as in the past, but stone soon replaced earth and simple walls became elaborate fortifications.[66] In effect, the Ming established a new frontier that was much less porous than the old one that went back to before the Qin. In the process, Ming policy severed the eastern end of the network of connections that had culminated in the Mongol Empire linking China and western Eurasia via the steppes.

Unfortunately, Ming policy ran head on into how the Mongols thought their relationship with the Chinese should be conducted. After a generation or so, the Mongols settled back into life on the steppes and had no plan to reconquer China and rule over it. Instead, they returned to the traditional practices of the pre-Chinggisid nomads from the Xiongnu to the Uyghurs: raid and harass the Chinese until at minimum they agreed to open trade or at best they agreed to trade on terms that favored the Mongols thus, in effect, providing subsidies. They did not understand why the Ming did not allow open trade, even the kind that both sides benefited from, thus maintaining peace.

In particular, the Ming feared the coming together of the separate tribes to form an effective confederation, which in turn could create an empire. But the Mongols were divided. Theoretically, they comprised a confederation; in fact, they were split into factions. At the top were supposed to be the Chinggisid descendants who had comprised the Yuan dynasty; they still claimed the title of Great Khan. To the west were the Oirats; their rivals and sometimes bitter enemies were the Three Eastern Commanderies of the Uriyangkhad, with whom the Yongle Emperor had formed alliances. This was also the case with some scattered groups of Jurchens in Manchuria. The Chinese granted their leaders impressive sounding titles and used them as a counterbalance to more hostile Mongols. Through the Ming period, the Uriyangkhad maintained the status of "most favored barbarians",[67] and they were often rewarded with the establishment of border markets and the right to submit tribute and receive gifts. Other tribes were usually denied such perks, causing envy, friction, and war. But even here the road could be bumpy. The Uriyangkhad began to abuse their prerogatives and came so frequently to present tribute, receive gifts, and live off the largess of the imperial court, the Ming had to restrict the number and size of their missions. When the Ming closed the horse markets to the Uriyangkhad, they flew into an eight-year revolt (1436–44 CE). When the Uriyangkhad finally relented, presented tribute, and tried to make up, the Ming snubbed them. But only for a while; they had too many common enemies among the other Mongols.

The overall lack of success the Ming had in its relations with neighboring pastoralists was rooted in a dysfunctional court where decisions were often made based on very misconstrued conceptions of steppe peoples. A highly factionalized court of bureaucrats and military officers together with too many mediocre or subpar emperors devolved into a collective state of inertia. Border officials often advised the court to make peace and open trade, and at the court some high-ranking officials took this up. In the backbiting atmosphere that prevailed, however, they were accused of cowardice or of being too sympathetic to the barbarians. Even when a policy turned out to be an unmitigated disaster, the main movers and doers at court were incapable of accepting responsibility. Scapegoats, usually in the form of border officials or military officers not currently present at the court, were found to take the blame. The Chinese hid behind their walls.

Ming strategy proved successful in one crucial way. Because the Ming refused to subsidize the Mongols whether directly or through trade, no Mongol leader was able to accumulate enough wealth to unite all the tribes into a steppe empire. For this success the Chinese paid a high price in the form of chronic border raids. Twice the Mongols came close to threatening the Chinese heartland itself, and in both instances this was because they were led by extraordinary men. The Oirats were pastoral nomads who roamed western Mongolia and Dzungaria (northern Xinjiang) and in the past had sometimes raided the states of the Tarim Basin and Central Asia. In the mid-fifteenth century the Chinese attempted to keep the Oirat from allying with the Chinggisid Great Khan by opening horse markets for them and allowing them to send tribute missions. However, this soon got out of hand, the Oirats greatly increasing the size of the missions from less than 100 to a whopping 1,000. Under the Oirat leader, Esen Taishi (r. 1438–55), this jumped to 2,000 in 1444; even so Esen inflated the numbers he reported to the Chinese to 3,000 to obtain more gifts. On his side, Esen complained that Chinese officials had treated his entourage rudely and that the Chinese had cut the prices they were paying for his horses. When the Oirat moved into territory the Chinese considered as belonging to them, the war party at the Chinese court carried the day.

In September 1449, the emperor Yingzong led an army reportedly a half million men strong northward. After marching first through soaking rainstorms and somehow later managing to run out of drinking water, after sixteen fruitless days the Chinese decided to retreat. Near a postal station named Tumu, about sixty miles northwest of Beijing, the Oirats ambushed them. Rank and file soldiers panicked and attempted to surrender but were massacred. The emperor was captured and led away, while back at court officials proclaimed a new emperor. Esen was unable to press forward after his principal ally made a separate peace, so the Oirats contented themselves with devastating the northern Chinese frontier. However, beginning in 1450 and lasting into the 1470s, the Oirats became involved in a series of Mongol civil wars, featuring frequent assassinations, largely against Esen's nominal overlord, the Great Khan, and the Eastern Mongols, during which, in sequence, both the Great Khan and Esen were killed. The wars frequently spilled over into northern China, bringing further ruin. In the chaos the market system collapsed. Nevertheless, all the Mongol factions involved demanded at one time or another that the Chinese trade with them, and all were turned down. Each time the respective Mongols retaliated with renewed raiding.

In the century after Esen Taishi, Altan ("Golden") Khan (1507–82) became leader of the Tumed Mongols, rivals of the Oirats. He led raids into China in 1529 and 1530, but in 1541 he offered to make peace if the Ming would open border markets. When he was rebuffed, he launched a cataclysmic attack the following year, which in one month reportedly killed or captured 200,000 Chinese people.[68] In a subsequent raid in 1550 he reached Beijing. The Chinese finally agreed to open a market in which the Mongols would trade horses for cloth. When the Mongols requested that grain also be included, the Chinese promptly closed the market. In 1552 the Mongols made eight major raids on China.

For forty years the Mongols raided China annually. Altan Khan's objective was not the conquest of China or even parts of it; it was to force the Chinese to trade. This was following the traditional strategy that steppe nomads had practiced for centuries: trade or we will raid. The difference was in the obstinacy of the Ming, who refused to follow the traditional strategy of previous dynasties and allow for border trade lubricated by just enough subsidies to keep peace on the frontier. In the end, the exhausted Ming finally gave in and negotiated a peace treaty in April 1571. Border markets were opened, and tribute was allowed to be given. On his side, Altan Khan kept those tribes that were under him from misbehaving by threatening to cut off their trading privileges. While the Ming were unsuccessful in striking a similar deal with the Great Khan, in general peace finally came to China's northern frontier. It lasted until the end of Ming rule.

Trade wars were not uncommon in history although commercial considerations were usually combined with other motivating factors, be they geopolitical, dynastic, religious, or just stark aggression. What is different in the Ming-Mongol situation is that the central issue was whether or not to trade, with one side fighting for the right to do so and the other side equally determined not to trade. The reluctance of the latter was not essentially a matter of whether this was fair and equitable trade as opposed to piratical trade carried out under duress, in which one side reaped all the benefits. When they did trade with the Mongols, the Ming could be as shrewd, cunning, calculating, and at times deceptive as any private merchant. The reluctance to trade was one element of the larger "Policy of No". In the long run the "Policy of No" did not work well: China under the Ming suffered from more attacks than any other dynasty in Chinese history.[69] In the hands of an adroit statesman, trade could become an effective instrument of statecraft. However, to weaponize trade by refusing to engage in it was an experiment that floundered somewhere along the border between the Great Wall and the steppes.

Notes

1 James Belich, John Darwin, and Chris Wickham, "Introduction" in James Belich, John Darwin, and Chris Wickham (eds.), *The Prospect of Global History* (Oxford, 2016) ; Jan de Vries, "The Limits of Globalization in the Early Modern World", *The Economic History Review* 63:3 (2010), pp. 710–33.
2 For a debate of this control, see Frederick Cooper, "What Is the Concept of Globalization Good for? An African historian's perspective", *African Affairs* 100:399 (2001), pp. 189–213.
3 Jessica Wang, "Reckoning with the Spatial Turn: Cartography, territoriality, and international history", *Diplomatic History* 41:5 (2017), pp. 1010–18.
4 Edmond Smith, "Commercial Culture in Contested Spaces" in Cátia A. P. Antunes and Francisco Bethencourt (eds.), *Merchant Cultures: A global approach to spaces, representations and worlds of trade, 1500–1800* (Brill, 2022).
5 Michael Khodarkovsky, *Russia's Steppe Frontier: The making of a colonial empire, 1500–1800* (Bloomington, 2002), pp. 5–8.
6 Eric Tagliacozzo, Helen F. Siu, and Peter C. Perdue, "Introduction: Spatial assemblages" in Eric Tagliacozzo, Helen F. Siu, and Peter C. Perdue (eds.), *Asia Inside Out: Connected places* (Cambridge, MA, 2015), p. 12.
7 Jeremy Adelman and Stephen Aron, "From Borderlands to Borders: Empires, nation-states, and the peoples in between in North American history", *The American Historical Review* 104:3 (1999), pp. 814–41.
8 Gary Seaman and Daniel Marks (eds.), *Rulers from the Steppe: State formation on the Eurasian periphery* (Los Angeles, CA, 1991), p. 35; Frederick Mote, *Imperial China, 900–1800* (Cambridge, MA, 2003), p. 26; Patricia Ebrey, *Chinese Civilisation and Society: A sourcebook* (London, 1981), p. 184.
9 Fan Ye, *Hou Hanshou*, trans. John Hill, *Through the Jade Gate to Rome: A study of the Silk Roads during the later Han Dynasty 1st to 2nd centuries* (2009), pp. 217–19.
10 Ban Gu, *Han Shu*, trans. Anthony François Paulus Hulsewé and M. A. N. Loewe (eds.), *China in Central Asia: The Early Stage: 125 BC–AD 23; an Annotated Translation of Chapters 61 and 96 of the History of the Former Han Dynasty* (Leiden, 1979), p. 126.
11 Fan Ye, *Hou Hanshou*, trans. John Hill, *Through the Jade Gate to Rome: A study of the Silk Roads during the later Han Dynasty 1st to 2nd centuries* (2009), p. 27.
12 Carter Vaughan, *The Turks in World History* (Oxford, 2005).
13 Sechin Jagchid and Van Jay Symons, *Peace, War, and Trade along the Great Wall: Nomadic-Chinese interaction through two millennia* (Bloomington, IN, 1989), p. 184.
14 Luc Kwanten, *Imperial Nomads: A history of central Asia, 500–1500* (Leicester, 1979), pp. 37–40; Denis Sinor, "The Establishment and Dissolution of the Türk Empire" in Denis Sinor (ed.), *The Cambridge History of Early Inner Asia* (Cambridge, 1990), pp. 310–13.

15 Citation from Denis Sinor, "The Establishment and Dissolution of the Türk Empire" in Denis Sinor (ed.), *The Cambridge History of Early Inner Asia* (Cambridge, 1990), p. 310. See also Gerard Chaliand, trans. A. M. Berrett, *Nomadic Empires: From Mongolia to the Danube* (London, 2003), p. 30.
16 Fan Ye, *Hou Hanshou*, trans. John Hill, *Through the Jade Gate to Rome: A study of the Silk Roads during the later Han Dynasty 1st to 2nd centuries* (2009), p. 11.
17 Fan Ye, *Hou Hanshou*, trans. John Hill, *Through the Jade Gate to Rome: A study of the Silk Roads during the later Han Dynasty 1st to 2nd centuries* (2009), p. 51.
18 Valerie Hansen, *The Silk Road: A New History* (Oxford, 2012), pp. 99–102, 107, 237.
19 John Hill, *Through the Jade Gate to Rome: A study of the Silk Roads during the later Han Dynasty 1st to 2nd centuries* (2009), p. 383.
20 Strabo, *Geographica*, vol. 11, book 10, part 2.
21 Sauer Eberhard, *Dariali: The "Caspian Gates" in the Caucasus from antiquity to the Age of the Huns and Middle Ages* (Oxford, 2020); Runni Andrew Anderson, *Alexander's Gate, Gog and Magog, and the Inclosed Nations* (Cambridge, MA, 1932).
22 Revelations 20:7.
23 Flavius Josephus, *De Bello Judaico*, trans. H. Thackery, *The Jewish War* (Cambridge, MA, 1927–8), pp. 244–51. See also Emeri J. Van Donzel and Andrea Schmidt, *Gog and Magog in Early Syriac and Islamic Sources: Sallam's quest for Alexander's wall* (Leiden, 2009); Peter Bietenholz, *Historia and Fabula: Myths and legends in historical thought from Antiquity to the Modern Age* (Leiden, 1994), pp. 122–3.
24 John Andrew Boyle, "Alexander and the Mongols" in *The Journal of the Royal Asiatic Society* 2 (1979), pp. 123–36.
25 Procopius, *Hypèr tōn Polémon Lógoi*, trans. Henry Bronson Dewing, *History of the Wars* (Cambridge, MA, 1914–40), vol. 1, book 10, part 6.
26 Procopius, *Hypèr tōn Polémon Lógoi*, trans. Henry Bronson Dewing, *History of the Wars* (Cambridge, MA, 1914–40), vol. 1, book 10, parts 3–5.
27 Procopius, *Hypèr tōn Polémon Lógoi*, trans. Henry Bronson Dewing, *History of the Wars* (Cambridge, MA, 1914–40), vol. 1, book 10, parts 8–11; vol. 2, book 10, part 21.
28 Richard Stoneman (ed.), *The Greek Alexander Romance* (London, 1991), pp. 185–7.
29 Zakariyya' al-Qazwini, *Āthār al-bilād wa-akhbār al-ʿibād* [Monuments of the Lands and Historical Traditions about Their Peoples], quoted in Van Donzel and Schmidt, *Gog and Madog*, pp. 65–74.
30 Ibn Khurradādhbih, *Kitāb al Masālik w'al Mamālik*, trans. Michael Jan de Goeje, *Ibn Khurradādhbih's Kitāb Al-Masālik Wa L-Mamālik and Part of the Kitāb Al-Kharāj by Qudāma Ibn Jaʿfar* (Leiden, 1889), pp. 125–31.
31 Ibn Faḍlān, *Risāla*, trans. Richard Frye, *Ibd Fadlan's Journey to Russia: A tenth-century traveler from Bagdad to the Volga* (Princeton, NJ, 2005), pp. 58–9.
32 Marius Canard, "La relation du voyage d'Ibn Fadlân chez les Bulgares de la Volga", *Annales* 16 (1958), pp. 41–145.
33 James Howard-Johnston, "The Fur Trade in the Early Middle Ages" in Jacek Gruszczyński, Marek Jankowiak and Jonathan Shepard (eds.), *Viking-Age Trade: Silver, slaves and Gotland* (London, 2020), pp. 57–74; Melanie Michailidis, "Samanid Silver and Trade along the Fur Route", *Medieval Encounters* 18:4–5 (2012), pp. 315–38.
34 David Cook, *Contemporary Muslim Apocalyptic Literature* (Syracuse, 2005), pp. 12, 47, 206.
35 Ibn Battuta, *The Rihla*, trans. H. A. R. Gibb and C. F. Beckingham (eds.), *The Travels of Ibn Battuta, AD 1325–54*, 4 vols. (London, 1994), pp. 896–7; Henry Yule, *Cathay and the Way Thither: Being a collection of medieval notices of China, vol. 3* (London, 1914), p. 255.

36 Denis Sinor, "The Establishment and Dissolution of the Türk Empire" in Denis Sinor (ed.), *The Cambridge History of Early Inner Asia* (Cambridge, 1990), pp. 289, 313.
37 Ban Gu, *Han Shu*, trans. Anthony François Paulus Hulsewé and M. A. N. Loewe (eds.), *China in Central Asia: The Early Stage: 125 BC–AD 23; an Annotated Translation of Chapters 61 and 96 of the History of the Former Han Dynasty* (Leiden, 1979), pp. 104–5, 120–1.
38 Shiba Yoshinobu, "Sung Foreign Trade: Its scope and organization" in Morris Rossabi (ed.), *China Among Equals: The Middle Kingdom and its neighbors, 10th–14th centuries* (California, 1983), p. 245, pp. 89–115.
39 Fan Ye, *Hou Hanshou*, trans. John Hill, *Through the Jade Gate to Rome: A study of the Silk Roads during the later Han Dynasty 1st to 2nd centuries* (2009), p. 55.
40 Sechin Jagchid and Van Jay Symons, *Peace, War, and Trade along the Great Wall: Nomadic-Chinese interaction through two millennia* (Bloomington, IN, 1989), p. 121.
41 Jonathan Karam Skaff, "Survival in the Frontier Zone: Comparative perspectives on identity and political allegiance in China's inner Asian borderlands during the Sui-Tang Dynastic transition (617–630)", *Journal of World History* 15:2 (2004), pp. 117–53.
42 Henry Yule, *Cathay and the Way Thither: Being a collection of medieval notices of China, vol. 3* (London, 1914), p. 258.
43 Willem Van Schendel and Itty Abraham, *Illicit Flows and Criminal Things: States, borders, and the other side of globalization* (Bloomington, IN, 2005), p. 14.
44 Shiba Yoshinobu, "Sung Foreign Trade: Its scope and organization" in Morris Rossabi (ed.), *China Among Equals: The Middle Kingdom and its neighbors, 10th–14th centuries* (California, 1983), p. 98.
45 Sechin Jagchid and Van Jay Symons, *Peace, War, and Trade along the Great Wall: Nomadic-Chinese interaction through two millennia* (Bloomington, IN, 1989), p. 183.
46 Sechin Jagchid and Van Jay Symons, *Peace, War, and Trade along the Great Wall: Nomadic-Chinese interaction through two millennia* (Bloomington, IN, 1989), p. 184.
47 Étienne de la Vaissière, trans. James Ward, *Sogdian Traders: A history* (Leiden, 2005), p. 230.
48 Procopius, *Hypèr tōn Polémon Lógoi*, trans. Henry Bronson Dewing, *History of the Wars* (Cambridge, MA, 1914–40), vol. 1, book 22, parts 11–12.
49 Étienne de la Vaissière, trans. James Ward, *Sogdian Traders: A history* (Leiden, 2005), p. 230.
50 Ban Gu, *Han Shu*, trans. Anthony François Paulus Hulsewé and M. A. N. Loewe (eds.), *China in Central Asia: The Early Stage: 125 BC–AD 23; an Annotated Translation of Chapters 61 and 96 of the History of the Former Han Dynasty* (Leiden, 1979), p. 111.
51 Ban Gu, *Han Shu*, trans. Anthony François Paulus Hulsewé and M. A. N. Loewe (eds.), *China in Central Asia: The Early Stage: 125 BC–AD 23; an Annotated Translation of Chapters 61 and 96 of the History of the Former Han Dynasty* (Leiden, 1979), p. 5.
52 Arthur Waldron, *The Great Wall of China: From history to myth* (Cambridge, 1990), p. 41.
53 Fan Ye, *Hou Hanshou*, trans. John Hill, *Through the Jade Gate to Rome: A study of the Silk Roads during the later Han Dynasty 1st to 2nd centuries* (2009), p. 55.
54 Fan Ye, *Hou Hanshou*, trans. John Hill, *Through the Jade Gate to Rome: A study of the Silk Roads during the later Han Dynasty 1st to 2nd centuries* (2009), p. 55.
55 Gary Seaman and Daniel Marks (eds.), *Rulers from the Steppe: State formation on the Eurasian periphery* (Los Angeles, CA, 1991), p. 67.

56 Luc Kwanten, *Imperial Nomads: A history of central Asia, 500–1500* (Leicester, 1979), p. 54.
57 Quoted in Sechin Jagchid and Van Jay Symons, *Peace, War, and Trade along the Great Wall: Nomadic-Chinese interaction through two millennia* (Bloomington, IN, 1989), p. 90.
58 Ban Gu, *Han Shu*, trans. Anthony François Paulus Hulsewé and M. A. N. Loewe (eds.), *China in Central Asia: The Early Stage: 125 BC–AD 23; an Annotated Translation of Chapters 61 and 96 of the History of the Former Han Dynasty* (Leiden, 1979), p. 144.
59 Xinru Liu, "Silk Road Trade and Foreign Economic Influences" in Debin Ma and Richard von Glahn (eds.), *The Cambridge Economic History of China, vol. 1, to 1800* (Cambridge, 2022), pp. 203–40.
60 Adam Fong, "Together They Might Make Trouble': Cross-Cultural Interactions in Tang Dynasty Guangzhou, 618–907 C.E.", *Journal of World History 25:4* (2014), pp. 475–92.
61 Denis Twitchett, "The T'ang Market System", *Asia Major* 12:2 (1966), p. 223, pp. 202–48.
62 Denis Twitchett, "The T'ang Market System", *Asia Major* 12:2 (1966), p. 224.
63 Colleen Ho, "Overland Trade in the Mongol World" in Michael Hope and Timothy May (eds.), *The Mongol World* (New York, 2022), pp. 484–504.
64 Ban Gu, *Han Shu*, trans. Anthony François Paulus Hulsewé and M. A. N. Loewe (eds.), *China in Central Asia: The Early Stage: 125 BC–AD 23; an Annotated Translation of Chapters 61 and 96 of the History of the Former Han Dynasty* (Leiden, 1979), pp. 85, 89–91.
65 Thomas Barfield, *The Perilous Frontier: Nomadic empires and China* (Oxford, 1989), p. 230.
66 Arthur Waldron, *The Great Wall of China: From history to myth* (Cambridge, 1990), p. 57.
67 Thomas Barfield, *The Perilous Frontier: Nomadic empires and China* (Oxford, 1989), p. 235.
68 Patricia Ebrey, *Chinese Civilisation and Society: A sourcebook* (London, 1981), p. 210.
69 Thomas Barfield, *The Perilous Frontier: Nomadic empires and China* (Oxford, 1989), p. 248.

4 Travel and Transport

In the previous three chapters, premodern trade has been approached, predominantly, from the perspective of the Eurasian steppe. The focus has been on understanding how the particular structure of steppe society, the mobility of nomadic populations, and the incentive to trade goods with sedentary peoples beyond the steppe all contributed to shape and structure of exchange. In some respects, these chapters have all approached premodern trade from a starting point according to which the largest scales, that is to say the impact of the environment or geography, have been predominant. This has helped expose common features in trade across broad regions, societies and cultures. In the second half of the book, the focus shifts towards an opposing starting point. These chapters consider the impact of local conditions on the way in which long-distance trade was conducted. While the Eurasian steppe remains an important geography in this discussion, it is now joined more by a multitude of other sites of exchange that were part of a wider web of trade that included but also moved far beyond the steppe frontier. That being said, some of the same themes occur again and again throughout this discussion: trade incentives; geography and the environment; mobility and borders; the role of states; and the importance of intersecting networks of local, regional, and long-distance exchange.

Mapping and Measuring

As the focus shifts towards smaller geographies of analysis and the experience of traversing them, it is worth asking how historical actors conceived of space themselves? How did they comprehend the vast distances over which goods and people traveled in the premodern trading world? How did their understanding of how the world fit together change how they approached travel and trade?

Of course, no one in the premodern world had any idea as to the length or overall size of what are now called the Silk Roads. To understand travel at that time, it is important to remember that people did use units of measurement for distance but did not rely on them for the exactness that came to be expected in the modern world. Units of measurement for weights and

DOI: 10.4324/9781003052890-5

volumes were taken more seriously and were more likely to be standardized, especially in the marketplace to ensure reliable commercial transactions.[1] However, for distances, no universal standards had to be recognized, and efforts to measure and record journeys and geographies across Eurasia were stymied by technology available. Overland, this was easier, especially when authors described familiar and well-trodden territories. In the Chinese tradition, the standard measure of distance was the *li*, put at 0.36 of a mile under the Han, but varying widely later under the Tang.[2] At times, this allowed a high degree of precision among Chinese geographers. Ban Gu's *Han Shu* (32–92 CE) gave accurate distances between Tashkurghan and both Yarḳand and Kashgar, both about 140 miles.[3] A somewhat later official history, the *Hou Hanshu*, compiled by Fan Ye (398–446 CE), provides measurements for the distances between Uch (Indus Valley) and the caravan city of Herat (northwest Afghanistan) and from Herat to Susa (southwest Iran), both of which are remarkably almost exactly correct at about 900 miles.[4] This proved, however, to be something of an anomaly.

The Greeks used the *stade*, which was based on the distance normally covered in a footrace around a stadium, and the Romans picked this up, adding a bit to it (from 600 to 625 feet, with approximately eight stadia to the mile). However, the measurement of distance could be a rather subjective matter, as the geographer Strabo (64 BCE–24 CE) notes:

> Every writer does not agree with every other, particularly about the distances as I often say. As for myself, where it is possible to reach a decision I set forth my opinion, but where it is not, I think I should make known the opinions of others.[5]

The challenge of gauging distance accurately was even more difficult when trying to measure distances by sea, and the figures that were available were often wildly inaccurate – as contemporaries readily recognized. For example, Diodorus Siculus (c. 60-30 BCE) estimated that the circumference of Britain was approximately 4842 miles, which is more than double the island's actual coastline.[6] Even when the underlying measurements could be agreed upon, obtaining accurate information that used a common methodology for understanding distance was not always forthcoming. The exacting standards of Ptolemy were frustrated when he sought to trace the journey between the Golden Chersonesus and Cattigara (peninsular and insular Southeast Asia) as relayed to him by Marinus of Tyre, who, to the Greek geographer's chagrin "lengthens the distance, interpreting some days to mean many days and believing (ridiculously it seems to me) that the expression 'some days' was used because the days were too many to be counted". In concluding his discussion, Ptolemy could not hide a hint of sarcasm: "Now let us, as Marius did, agree that some days and many days correspond in meaning."[7] A millienia later, Abu Rayhan al-Biruni (973–1050 CE) was similarly frustrated by the lack of clear distances available for measuring India, and was forced to "rely upon tradition", which "is of such a nature that already Ptolemy incessantly complains of its transmitters and their bias towards storytelling". Dismissing both Hindu accounts of how much an oxen could carry, and the value of measuring distance by the time it took for oxen to carry goods between locations, he begged "the readers pardon" as he sought to "correct the statements of the Hindus" and present his readers with a geography of India carefully packaged into *farsakh*.[8]

In Persianate and Arabic geographies, the measurement of distance often depended on the time taken to travel across a particular region. Under the Abbasid Empire a major unit of distance was the *parasang*, an old Persian measurement that was approximately 3-and-a-half miles, but in practice anywhere between three and four miles, representing the distance a unit of infantry could march in an hour rather than a precise delineation of space. Ibn Khurradādhbih uses the *parasang* throughout his book, and doubtless Ptolemy would have applauded his attempt at exactitude in informing his readers, for example, that the distance between Baghdad and Mecca was 275¾ *parasangs*.[9] Nevertheless, al-Idrisi, who served as the official court geographer for King Roger II of Sicily and was the best known in Europe of all Arab geographers, used no uniform scale for measuring distances in his cartography. He did, however, use an array of measurements in common usage during his period of writing – including the classical Arabic *mīl* (mile), *farsakh* (3 *mīls*) and *majrā* (one days sailing), the "Frank *mīl*" from Christian Europe, and the *marḥalah* (one days march, approximately 30 miles) that he noted was used in the mountainous regions of India, among other terms – when describing distances in his writing.[10] In a similar vein was the *kôs*, used in parts of Central Asia, which varied in distance from 1 to 2.5 miles depending on the hardships encountered along the way.[11]

On occasion, these distances were laid out for travelers in the form of manmade signs and markers. The Romans, in their obsessively practical ways, put milestones on their roads. This was more to measure distance and thus allow the traveler some degree of predictability in timing a journey than to guide the way since the road itself did that. Under the Umayyad Empire (661–750) mile markers were placed at appropriate locations as part of an overall project to improve the empire's road system.[12] In his travels through India, the wide-ranging Moroccan traveler Ibn Battuta (1304–69) reported that on the road between Zihar, "the chief city of Malwa", and Delhi, there were "pillars on which is engraved the number of miles from each pillar to the next" as well as information about the nearest post-station or town.[13] That Ibn Battuta makes a point to mention this, however, is a good indication of how extraordinary it was. Landmarks were more likely to be unintended. In well-populated places, tombs and cemeteries often lined the way that caravans moved across while in more remote areas travelers had to rely on old watchtowers, the remains of abandoned forts, and ghost towns to ensure they were going the right way. Along especially barren wastelands, cairns, pyramidal or rounded heaps of stones, were piled up to guide travelers. Most disconcerting were paths marked by the remains of earlier travelers as noted in one Chinese chronicle for a route that threaded between the Taklamakan to the west and the Gobi Desert to the northeast:

> All the way from Tun-huang [Dunhuang] to that country [Turfan], sand and rocks abound, so that neither the road nor the mileage can be exactly marked. Only the skeletons of men and animals and by the droppings of camels and horses can one verify [which is the way].[14]

If measuring units of distance was confusing, judging direction was baffling. The most advanced instrument available was the astrolabe, invented in the Hellenistic period but improved on by Islamic scholars during the eighth century CE. Geographers, scientists, and mathematicians sometimes had access to such instruments, but common travelers, including merchants, usually did not. Consequently, even large geographical features like mountain chains, deserts, major rivers, and inland seas were often thought to run east to west or north to south when in fact they ran vice versa.[15] Even for the best of the ancients, the great ranges could be dazingly muddled. Long before modern geology showed that the Pamir Knot tied separate but related ranges together, classical authors believed there was a series of connected ranges or one vast range that ran across Asia. Strabo tried to connect these ranges running west to east beginning in eastern Asia Minor through the Caucasus, then below the Caspian Sea all the way to the Indian Ocean in a range the Greeks named "Taurus" (today a range only in southern Turkey).[16]

Pliny begins from the eastern side with the "immense range" of the Taurus rising out of the Indian Ocean, stretching westward and northward, "forming a curve", being deflected by various seas including the "Phoenician Sea" (Eastern Mediterranean), Black, Hyrcanian (Caspian or possibly the Aral), and the Sea of Azov until it reaches "the kindred range of the Ripaean Mountains". This was a name vaguely applied to all mountain ranges to the north of Europe and Asia in "the region called Pterophorus, because of the feather-like snow continually falling there; it is a part of the world that lies under the condemnation of nature and is plunged in dense darkness, and occupied only by the work of frost and the chilly lurking-places of the north wind".[17] Ptolemy did tidy up some of the muddle left by Strabo and Pliny, but in his endearing way creates all new muddles, much of which modern historians are still trying to figure out. After passing the Stone Tower, "from there you come to the mountains which run in an easterly direction, ending at Imao which is north of Palimbothris".[18] This last place is apparently a reference to the Pataliputra, the metropolis on the Ganges River far to the south, the former capital of the Mauryan Empire (323–184 BCE), the first great empire of India, which collapsed several centuries before Ptolemy wrote.

Rather than precise cartography, for travelers in the premodern world, it was often more useful to have the spaces between locations broken down into the amount of time that it would take to cross them. In caravan travel the most used unit of measurement was the "stage" although it is best not to consider it as an exact indicator of distance. Stage seems to have meant different things to different caravanners as well as to different geographers. Under the Abbasid Empire, the latter generally used the term to mark journeys between towns. In crossing deserts and other wastelands, stages were often referred to travel between wells and other water sources. In other places stages meant how far pack animals could cover in a day even though different pack animals moved at different speeds. The most reliable use of the term comes from Pliny the Elder in his examination of the "Incense Road" that ran across southern and western Arabia from Tumna to Gaza. According to him, this was a trip of 1487.5 miles, which he divides into sixty-nine stages with halts for camels.[19] It appears that each stage represents one day's travel, but with watering stations likely spread inconsistently across the region, some were likely short or longer days of travel apart or requiring multiple days of travel to reach. In a similar vein, in a collection of travel accounts known as the *Akhbar al-Sin wa-al-Hind* (The Book of the Wonders of India) (851 CE), the maritime route from Muscat to China was divided into four stages that each took a month at sea.[20]

Ambiguity in the meaning of "stages" as a measure of distance is more pronounced in other accounts. The anonymous Persian geography known as the *Hudūd al-Ālam* (982 CE) provided a detailed route for travelling across the Toghuzghuz region (Türkic lands west of China) stage by stage:

1 an earthen mountain and a stage for the merchants
2 a stage at which a big river and plenty of grass are found
3 a stage where formerly lived the Toghuzghuz and which is now desolate
4 a stage at which it snows and rains constantly
5 a stage … [?]
6 a stage with pasture lands and springs
7 a stage which is never free from snow[21]

The changes here from stage to stage here are far too stark to be moving from one day to the next; it is as if this author is moving across whole ecozones.

At the other end of the spectrum, multiple stages are passed through each day in the best surviving examination of the trans-Saharan routes by al-Bakrī, who provides a description of the route between the cities of Sijilmasa and its neighbor, Tamdult (Morocco), and Awdaghust (Mauritania) northwest of Timbuktu. This is a very detailed and helpful account except that he includes both stages, of which he concludes there were 51, and days, of which he seems to indicate there were 29.[22] He also describes a second route that ran from the Dar'a River valley, south of the Anti-Atlas Mountains, across the Sahara to the land of the Sudan (black people). Here he mentions stages only twice, initially in the beginning when going from the Dar'a to the Sahara (five stages) and at the end between the territory of the last major Saharan tribe, the Lamtuna, and the land of the Sudan (ten stages). All other passages are given in days. In some places he states the distance between watering places in stages, but in other places he states the distance in days.[23] Clearly for al-Bakri a stage is neither the equivalent of a day nor the distance between watering places. Likely it does signify a place of rest, perhaps in measured distance coming closest to a *marhala*.[24] Apparently al-Bakrī assumed his readers knew the difference between stages and days, and there was no need for him to reconcile the two.

Finally, to put the whole matter of stages within a larger setting, Cosmas Indicopleustes, the sixth-century Greco-Egyptian merchant turned monk, who made an attempt to explain world geography in the context of Christian theology, came to the conclusion that the earth consisted of about 400 stages in length and 200 stages in breadth, each stage at 30 miles. A footnote from his editor clarified that "the Greek word used here can also mean 'mansions' or 'halting places'".[25] In any case, crossing a region from point A to point B was usually calculated by merchants and other travelers in time, as in so many days, weeks, months, or sometimes years rather than in measurements of distance like *stadia*, *parasanges*, or *li*. This held true for describing geographical size as well. In his discussion of the Lamtuna, al-Bakrī mentions that their territory "extends for a distance of two months' traveling in breadth by the same in length between the land of Islam and the land of the Sudan".[26]

Measuring distances based on how long it took to travel between two locations, whether in stages or days, did require a dependable average for the speed of travel. On the earliest of roads, many of which were essentially little more than well-trod paths, an average day's march might be ten to twelve miles.[27] Much depended on the condition of what was being traveled over and the method of travel. On the slow side, according to the Persian scholar al-Biruni, distances between places in India were judged by the rate a caravan of oxen traveled.[28] This was a common means of transportation in much of India, but since a pair of bullocks traveled at about two miles per hour and normally moved only about twelve miles per day, this was an excruciatingly slow rate of travel in comparison to almost any other way of getting around. On the subject of oxen travel, a handbook by Florentine Francesco Balducci Pegolotti (1290–1347) used by European merchants in the early fourteenth century adds that in moving across relatively flat land between the cities of Tana (Azov) near the mouth of the Don River and the fair at Gintarchan (near Astrakhan) on the Volga, it took twenty-five days by ox wagon and from ten to twelve by horse wagon.[29]

The Persian geographer Sharaf Al-Zamān Ṭāhir Marvazī (1120 CE), in tracing the distance from Kashgar across the Tarim Basin to the border of China, reckoned 19.2 miles travel per day across 600 miles, around one month of travel.[30] However, two centuries later Marco Polo (1254–1324 CE) heard that it took a year to get from one side to the other of the Taklamakan desert, that is, roughly the same trip as Marvazī describes.[31] This rate of travel was certainly not at a hasty pace and must have included lengthy stopovers along the way, although to travelers who straggled out of the Taklamakan on one side or the other it probably seemed at least that long. Ibn Khurradādhbih also provides some interesting contrasts. Coming from Nouschadjan in Central Asia to the frontier of China was a fifteen-day trip by caravan, but the government postal service using Türkish horsemen could make it in three.[32] Another government official, Qudāma ibn Ja'far, agreed, but going in a different direction adds: "The distance that separates Nouschadjan from Schâscb is passed over by caravans in a forty days' march, but traveling quickly, one can make it in thirty days."[33] In other words caravans, even when intentionally traveling at full speed, could move only so fast.

During the period when the Mongols had unified much of Eurasia, people from westernmost Eurasia, including Europeans, could travel directly to China. Under normal conditions, merchants did not bother to keep records of how far they traveled or other matters relating to distance, but official embassies sometimes did. In 1339, for example, an official embassy took nine to ten months to travel between Constantinople and Central Asia. A later embassy from Herat to Beijing took about a year.[34] But the most useful information on trans-Eurasian long-distance trade comes from Francesco Balducci Pegolotti, a Florentine merchant who never went to China himself. He did, however, meticulously gather information from other merchants who had made the trip, which allowed him to write a guidebook, the *Libro di Divisamenti di Paesi* (The Book of the Descriptions of Countries) sometime around 1340. This offered a remarkably precise set of instructions for travelers seeking to traverse the wide expanse of Eurasia from Tana to China. Pegolotti concluded that the trip took two hundred days of actual travel time, not counting delays for whatever reason including stopping to rest. This meant that the entire trip would have taken about one and a half years.[35]

Traversing the Land

The long route that carried traders and others across the breadth of Eurasia as detailed in Pegolotti was, of course, just one part of the vast and interconnecting trade routes through which premodern goods were carried and exchanged. Across these routes, travelers had to contend with an array of challenges, and premodern trade depended on the successful navigation of spaces that ranged from well laid roads to fierce deserts, frozen mountains, and treacherous seas.

The ideal route was the most direct, quickest, easiest, and least hazardous. It might pass through fertile areas in rich valleys where fields were cultivated or in drier areas where palm groves were plenteous. Here resources, foremost of which were food, fodder, and potable water, were abundant and available. Unfortunately, however, this was some merchant's pipe dream. If he wanted the easiest and least hazardous, he usually had to forego the most direct and quickest. The shortest route could be the most arduous and risky; the most direct route could be waterless or lack staging posts. A long route through

rough hills may have been more secure than one across open plains where wars were raging or robbers and roaming bands of bandits were set to plunder passersby. Even traveling over the best of grounds, animals had to be fed, which meant that caravans had to travel from pasture to pasture as well as from water source to water source. In places like the Sahara, pools and even wells often proved to be temporary and were not where they had been the year before, or they had become inadequate to handle several dozen or several hundred thirsty beasts. If on a map it appeared that routes should run in straight lines, on ground level, obstacles were more often the rule. Navigating through dense forests, strenuous climbs in barren mountains over narrow, rocky, precipitous cliffs, and lower down traversing marshlands and swamps over waterlogged roads were all part of overland travel as was finding suitable places to cross broad, deep rivers.

Regional and interregional routes that had been developing on their own before fusing became the components of an expanding system of relays. Even when the great Eurasian system was considered as being completed, individual traders worked their own section of the circuits. No one was likely to have set out in the year 1 CE or the year 1000 CE from the shores of the Mediterranean with a pack of goods, crossed the wide expanse of the Eurasian steppes, negotiated the Pamir Mountains at the highland knot of Inner Asia, and come out in the Hwang He River valley of western China. This came later and lasted for about a century during the time of the Mongol Empire – the era of Marco Polo – using the normally under-traveled system known as the Steppe Road that ran north of the basic Silk Roads system. Even then, merchants traversing the whole route were only a small fraction of the travelers that interacted with part of it. At other times, but under unusual circumstances, rare, precious, or exotic goods would have had a better chance of making such a transcontinental trip, but this would have involved the changing of hands numerous times. The connections were there as they were in other north-to-south and west-to-east systems.

Pinpointing the opening of a long-distance trade system is usually a vain endeavor. Suffice to say that the creation of such a system was always a process rather than an event. A system-in-the-making became a recognized system when it qualifies as having "sustained trade", or is referred to as an "organized network", or is composed of "integrated land (or maritime) routes". Unfortunately, such terms do not come with universally accepted definitions. The demand for precious commodities such as frankincense and myrrh for the Incense Road, gold for the Trans-Saharan, and silk for the Silk Roads would often serve as a catalyst linking otherwise distinct routes together or consolidating smaller systems into a larger one. Parts of what became larger systems crossing Eurasia were under construction by the third millennium BCE although the grand opening of the Silk Roads according to traditional Chinese historiography, which tends to favor events over processes, doesn't come until the time of the Han dynasty emperor Wudi (r. 141–87 BCE). His actions in sending commercial, diplomatic, and military missions deep into Central Asia were important in fusing China formally and firmly into the system.[36]

China had never really been completely cut off from the lands to its west. An ancient if ill-defined commercial tie referred to as the Jade Road brought jade from the Tarim Basin to northern China and a variety of other products, some of which likely came from farther west. A whole mythology had evolved from tidbits of information brought back by Chinese merchant-adventurers who had ventured into real and imagined places, the most important being the tales of the Emperor Mu. But the argument that Wudi's actions in thrusting China into Central Asia suddenly opened the Silk Roads is based on the idea that only powerful states had the economic and military resources to sustain sophisticated trade networks across enormous distances. They provided the anchors at each end of a system. In the case of the Silk Roads, this began with Achaemenid Persia and its successors, the empire of Alexander the Great and the Roman Empire in the West, the Mauryan and Kushan empires in the South, and finally Han China in the East. Actually, all of these great states were connecting into something that at least in part was already there. Nevertheless, they brought stability and provided markets luring people who lived in between and who had something to sell. The state officially became part of the process by formalizing its role in encouraging, sponsoring, and in some instances taking control over commerce. In this line of thinking, the official opening of cross-Eurasian long-distance trade can be set at between the second century BCE and the first century CE. It may be said to have culminated under the Abbasid Empire (750–1258), which witnessed a great expansion of trade due in part to its enormous size that wove together hundreds of points of supply and demand into a single system.

In looking at the origins of trade routes, one misconception should be addressed. When invading someone else's territory, armies generally used the same routes long followed by merchants, not vice versa. When Arab armies invaded Central Asia, they followed the Silk Roads, specifically to capture the cities and caravan routes of that system. Armies invading India from Central Asia via Afghanistan took the same passes through the mountains that goods had been shipped across for centuries. In 1590–1 the Moroccan army of Judar Pasha followed the ancient gold route from Marrakech to the Niger River, not the easiest way to cross the Sahara but shorter than alternatives. Judar lost about half his men, but when the remaining half emerged from the desert, it came as a complete surprise to an enemy that had not adequately prepared, and the Moroccans won a great victory.[37] In instances when armies went their own ways seeking short cuts over little traveled roads to take their victims by surprise, suddenly appearing out of what was thought to be an uncrossable desert or an impassable snowbound mountain range, they took a great risk.

There were good reasons why a trade route traversed a particular landscape. Whoever was responsible for pioneering it, be that Neolithic and Bronze Age herdsmen, early salt or obsidian traders, or someone else, if such a route survived into later periods, it must have offered the optimum conditions of travel from one particular place to another. At the same time, regular use meant that routes were more likely to obtain and maintain human alterations to the landscape, such as wells or bridges. The parameters of a route were set by natural features and environmental conditions. Topography channeled trade. Weather, determined by season, circumscribed the choice of routes, as noted by the geographer Ptolemy, in his examination of the road between the Pamir Mountains and China. Being exposed to "winter tempests ... there must have been many deviations in that journey, especially since it was undertaken for the purpose of carrying merchandise".[38] Weather was not the only factor: in some places at certain times swarms of biting insects could rule out passage. Dependable sources of drinking water had to be available at suitable intervals for man and beast. At least for major routes over which a lot of traffic passed, it was simply not practical to travel over long distances that were waterless. Human factors, including the economic and political situation, security or the lack thereof, and the level of transport technology also played roles as did the demand for particular goods in particular places. And human factors were highly variable; conditions could change with little or no warning.

A trip had to be practicable for laden transport, which meant plenty of places to forage. Early routes often followed river valleys that served as natural corridors. The same streams could be crossed and recrossed multiple times according to the lay of the land. Overland routes across grasslands connected river systems so goods could be carried by land and boat. Even wadis, the beds of seasonal or dead rivers that crossed the deserts of Arabia and western Iraq, became integrated into major route systems if water was available from springs or other local sources. Routes ran between revictualling places and in time these often became centers of human habitation that depended on or benefited from their position on the route. These could be way stations around which caravanserais and other facilities serving traveling merchants were often located, around which markets grew up. In desert areas oases provided fresh supplies of food and fodder along with replacement pack animals and guides if necessary. Facilities increased in availability as caravans passed through more fertile and populated areas. The belly of the Silk Roads system went through Central Asia, a land of valleys and alluvial plains where people clustered along complexes of rivers and a sprinkling of oases. Outside of these favored regions, however, it was mostly a land of sparsely inhabited elevated steppe and often uninhabited desert. Ibn Khurradādhbih provides an interesting contrast in describing the region lying between Tibet and Ferghana. The march from Atbâsch to Nouschadjan supérieure, which he considered to be "the Center of the Orient", was "a six-day trip across a country where there is not a single village". However, from Nouschadjan to the capital city of the Toghozghor (Uyghur) Türks took three months "across a country of pasturage covered with many market towns".[39]

The major natural challenges for long-distance travel overland across Eurasia came from mountains and deserts. Whether high mountains, scorching deserts, extortionate taxes, or lurking brigands, as Ptolemy reminded his reader, "journeys very rarely are made in a straight line".[40] He provided an interesting example of a trip from Antioch Margiana (Merv in modern Turkmenistan) to the Stone Tower located between the Pamir Mountains and the Tarim Basin on the western edge of China:

> From Antioch to Bactria, the journey deviates to the east, and after ascending the Comedon mountains it bends to the north. From the mountains, where it comes to the plain at their base, it inclines to the south [and finally] ... the journey for fifty schena [150 miles] before coming to the Stone Tower, deviates to the north.[41]

The most extraordinary range of mountains a merchant had to cross came in an enormous clump that divided Central, South, and East Asia. At its heart is a convergence zone, sometimes referred to as the "Pamir Knot", tying together the highest and most massive mountain chains in the world, starting at the Pamirs, then radiating clockwise through the Tian Shan, Kunlun, Karakorums, Himalayas, and Hindu Kush. These ranges fan out spokelike, overlapping with each other at some points. They are young ranges in geological time, the children of crustal tectonics. Once a part of the super continent Gondwanaland, the Indian continental plate broke away and headed northeast across what would become the Indian Ocean, ultimately slamming into the Eurasian plate about sixty million years ago. The uplift that resulted from this collision rippled from south to north, creating a series of folds in the earth that became the great mountain ranges of today. Statistics speak to this greatness. The thirteen highest peaks in the world are here. Over thirty peaks are in excess of twenty-five thousand feet, and some are still growing. The mountains became a world of ice and snow, whose cloud-scraping peaks were at the same time lofty and awe-inspiring but treacherous and forbidding. The ancient Persians coined the epithet "Roof of the World", which was picked up by nineteenth century Victorian travel writers and later plagiarized to describe next-door Tibet.

Although the Pamirs are not the highest or most massive of these mountain chains, an argument could be made that for the history of long-distance trade, they played a role unequalled by the other ranges with the exception at various times of the Hindu Kush. Overland traffic going between China and Central Asia, West Asia, Europe, and the Mediterranean Basin most likely would have gone through the Pamirs. Traffic going between China and India that chose to avoid the higher and riskier Karakorums could take a more circuitous if less problematic route through the Pamirs and down across the Hindu Kush. The Pamirs, featuring bitterly cold peaks of over 20,000 feet, were touted as the "Watershed of Asia" or even "the Spine of Asia". The Chinese author Ban Gu (32–92 CE), who was the brother of Ban Chao, one of the most noted of early Chinese explorers of Central Asia, mentions two mountain ranges he refers to as the Greater and the Lesser Headaches, which seem to correspond to the eastern Pamirs along with other "obstacles" beginning with the Dragon Mounds and farther on the Slopes of the Red Earth and the Fever of the Body.[42] In reality these headaches were, of course, caused by altitude sickness. The Portuguese Jesuit-explorer Bento de Gois, who in 1603 became the first European to travel from India to China via the Pamirs in his search for Prester John, reported that the men in his caravan ate large quantities of garlic, leeks, and dried apples and rubbed the gums of their horses with garlic to help them breathe.[43]

From a very early period, merchants and Buddhist pilgrims found ways to cross the breaks in the crest lines, the gaps and gorges that slashed through the highlands, to access and traverse the plateaus lying between the peaks. This is not to imply that going through a range like the Hindu Kush was like eating a piece of cake. The Chinese monk Faxian (337–422 CE), coming from the north, passed into the Hindu Kush, which he refers to as the Snowy Mountains:

> There is snow both in winter and summer. Moreover, there are poison-dragons, who when evil-purposed spit poisons, winds, rain, snow, drifting sand, and gravel stones; not one of ten thousand [people] meeting these calamities escapes ... The mountainside is simply a stone wall standing up to 10,000 feet.[44]

A later Chinese pilgrim, Xuanzang (602–64), held much the same opinion of the Snowy Mountains: "These mountains are high and the valleys deep; the precipices and crevasses are very dangerous. The wind and snow keep on without intermission; the ice remains through the full summer; the snowdrifts fall into the valleys and block the roads." Xuanzang, like Faxian, had come through the Taklamakan Desert and over the Pamirs. He offers an interesting contrast: "The road [over the Hindu Kush] is twice as difficult and dangerous as in the desert and among the glaciers. The sky is continually overcast with frozen clouds."[45]

There were some advantages in traveling through mountains (one did not travel over mountains): the ground was usually firm; in the summer mountain travel was cooler than travel in the lowlands; and access to water from springs, creeks, and other sources was generally not a problem. Gradient was important, ranging from easy to steep to nearly impossible. On the best of ground, carts had the advantage over pack animals, but where even pack animals could not go, as in, for example, the high places of the Hindu Kush, human porterage had to be used, the most inefficient method of moving goods. The season determined the passages. During the summer, mountain passes were preferable since the river valleys below were often impassable due to flooding. In the winter when passes were full of snow and inclement weather made them impassable, travelers hugged the sides of the now tame or sometimes frozen rivers. The Broghil Pass in the Wakhan Corridor of the Hindu Kush was so frigid and snowbound it was closed three months of the year. When open, however, it was the only pass in the area suitable not only for pack animals but carts as well. Some very barren regions in the Pamirs were void of human habitation over substantial distances, meaning that merchants had to devote much of the valuable space on the backs of their animals to carrying their own supplies. However, if a route saw significant traffic, facilities were often available even high in the mountains.

Unless they had to cross somewhere in the Pamir Knot set of ranges, or smaller clumps of mountains like the Alps in Europe, the Altai in Siberia, or the various branches of the Atlas in North Africa, most trade caravans were more likely to encounter challenges from deserts than from mountains. One advantage in moving over a desert was that the ground was usually level and soft, good for camels. The disadvantage centered on the availability of water or lack thereof. Deserts across Afro-Eurasia ran in an east-west belt beginning with the Alashan, Ordos, and Gobi in the east through the Taklamakan, then splitting into the Kyzul Kum (Qizil Qum) and the Kara Kum (Qara Qum) to the north and the Thar farther south, coming back together in the Dash-e-Kavir (Great Salt Desert) of the Iranian Plateau to the Syrian and Arabian deserts, leaping the Red Sea, and culminating in the Sahara. The Roman naturalist Pliny the Elder (23–79 CE) described Inner Asia as a mixture of landscapes, although he thought it to be rather heavy on deserts. First, there was a region uninhabitable due to snow, followed by a land where the inhabitants were so savage no agriculture could be practiced:

> This is the country of the Cannibal Scythians who eat human bodies; consequently, the adjacent districts are waste deserts thronging with wild beasts lying in wait for human beings as savage as themselves. Then we come to more Scythians and to more deserts inhabited by wild beasts, until we reach a mountain range called Tabis which forms a cliff over the sea.[46]

To the south was China.

Somewhere in Pliny's sequence of deserts were the Gobi and the Taklamakan although neither can be said to have been thronging with wild beasts since there was not much to eat in such places even for wild beasts. The Gobi is the second largest desert in Asia, behind the Arabian, and third in the world. It is a vast succession of waterless, stony plains and small depressions more pebbly and gravelly than sandy and swept by icy winds. Going through it was a north-south passage tying northern China to the steppes and northward to the taiga forest. In terms of long-distance trade, the considerably smaller and somewhat more severe desert directly to the west of China, the Taklamakan, had more historical impact on trade than its larger neighbor. The Taklamakan itself comprises about 125,000 square miles. The Silk Roads pretty well required a trip across the Taklamakan unlike the Gobi, which was more connected into the eastern end of the Steppe Roads. Crossing the Taklamakan was done by going around its edges since most of the time heading straight across its breadth would have been suicidal. Even going around its edges, winter crossings were at best uncomfortable and often dangerous, and summer crossings were to be avoided if possible.

Huge expanses of the Taklamakan were sparsely inhabited or not habitable at all. Winter was long and bitterly cold, summer much shorter and scorchingly hot. It was a harsh and lifeless place comprised of pulverized miniscule rock particles, much of it devoid of vegetation, a true wasteland. Winds blew throughout the year from both the northeast and northwest often at the same time, producing some of the world's weirdest sand dunes that can be extraordinarily high and stretch into the horizon. Caravans usually traveled at night to avoid the heat, following established routes in stages representing a day of travel. But they did not move in straight lines, avoiding especially dry areas, hopping from water source to water source. Even so, ferocious sandstorms were known to have overwhelmed caravans, suffocating men and camels. The most chilling description of crossing the Taklamakan may come from Faxian, who passed through in the year 400:

> There are evil spirits and hot winds that kill every man who encounters them. There are no flying birds above, no roaming beasts below, but everywhere gazing as far as the eye can reach in search of the onward route, it would be impossible to know the way but for dead men's decaying bones, who have perished there to serve to mark the way.[47]

Not all parts of the desert were entirely dismal. In his discussion of the western route of the Trans-Saharan trade, the Andalusian geographer al-Bakrī (1040–94) included a description of a spot known as "the place where the waters collect, where there are many kinds of trees and henna and basil". On the other side of some hills was "a sandy but wooded region" followed by "the land of the Sanhaja [a tribal confederation], where there is plenty of water in the wells".[48] Other geographers describe trips crossing deserts that, if not delightful, were better than tolerable in places. Ibn Khurradādhbih, in tracing the route between Mecca and Yemen, mentions wells and springs, palm groves, and several large market towns.[49] From Merv to Koschmehan, Qudāma ibn Ja'far found "great villages on the route of the desert that continued until the territory of the Ghoz" (Türks). He also describes desert regions into which flowed great rivers.[50] Ibn Jubayr traveled in Egypt's Eastern Desert across the

"Road of the Two Slaves", where "no one will journey save on camel by reason of their endurance of thirst ... Most travelers ride their camels on top of their baggage and so painfully endure the rigors of the burning heat." Nevertheless, the trip was adequately supplied with watering holes including one at Amtan, "a spring which God has blessed in particular, for its water is the best and sweetest of the way. Water buckets beyond counting will be found there, and these will water the many caravans that descend upon it."[51]

Vast and very dry deserts – the Sahara, Taklamakan, Gobi, Kavir (Iranian), and others – had to be negotiated under the threat of dehydration, dried up and polluted wells, sandstorms, and even flash floods. Freezing to death, being buried in a snowstorm, or becoming disoriented from altitude sickness was more likely to happen in the vast mountain ranges – Pamirs, Tian Shan, Hindu Kush, and Alps. In forests and jungles attacks by wild animals were common. Passage on narrow paths across precipitous landscapes combined with the need to traverse torrential rivers added to the challenges of traveling overland.

Routes existed to help traders navigate these troubling regions, but passes too could present special problems. Local traders used little-known passes, and taking an occasional short cut through a mountain spur could save long-distance pack animals the challenge of a burdensome trip through a mountain chain. But major caravan traffic had to stick to main routes. Taking high passes, often over ten thousand feet, could result in much shorter trips except that many passes remained jammed with snow as late as June. In great ranges like the Karakoram, high passes had to be cleared by driving herds of yaks over them.[52] Individual mountains and even some mountain chains could present such challenges that routes simply went around them. And there were always tradeoffs. Of the three major routes that crossed the Hindu Kush, the longest, which included eight passes, half of which were over ten thousand feet high, was the most used because it had the easiest gradient and forage was available. Seemingly wherever merchants traveled, danger lurked.

Some passages were not practical for caravan traffic. The Salang Pass was the shortest but highest passage between two of the most important river basins in Asia, the Indus and Oxus (Amu Darya), separating Central Asia from South Asia. Nevertheless, it seems likely that it was usually avoided by caravans because of its steepness. One route that was impossible for baggage animals was the Xuandu, the "Hanging Passages" in Upper Hunza in the gorges of the Indus River. It was by far the shortest overland course on the direct route between China and India, and it could connect westward to Kabul, Merv, the Iranian Plateau, and ultimately the Persian Gulf. It was open most of the year and provided rapid communications for people in a great hurry like official couriers and other messengers for whom time was of the essence. Sometimes it was used by Buddhist pilgrims. But the Xuandu were man-made pathways built on stakes driven into bare cliffsides as narrow as eighteen inches in some places. Several descriptions of these passages survive, one of the best coming from Ban Gu:

> Furthermore, there are the Three Pools (in which lived a dragon who sent snowstorms if not offered a sacrifice) and the Great-Rock Slopes with a path that is a foot and six or seven inches wide, but leads forward for a length of thirty *li*, overlooking a precipice whose depth is unfathomed. Travelers passing on horse or foot hold on to one another and pull each other along with ropes: and only after a journey of more than two thousand *li* [this is probably a copyist error and should read twenty *li*] do they reach the Suspended Crossing. When animals fall, before they have dropped half-way down the chasm they are shattered in pieces and when men fall, the situation is such that they are unable to rescue one another. The danger of these precipices beggars description.[53]

For merchants the most important considerations were safety and profit; usually they were willing to pay for both with time.[54] Their routes they followed could meander with long detours following riverbeds, going along the base of mountains, taking lower but more out-of-the-way passes. Time was a consideration, but it was not always of the essence. There was, however, a limit, so if a course proved too roundabout, other options had to be considered. Most of the time there was a multitude of variables to be factored in. A narrow path with a 200-foot fall may have been the best choice given the alternatives. On the other hand, traveling through well populated, fertile farming areas was usually desirable but not if caravans had to navigate through extensive irrigation works, canal systems, or a variety of construction projects. Caravans could deviate from main routes when they determined that some benefit was to be gained.

In the trade-off between safety and profit, the pendulum could swing both ways. The Trans-Saharan system consisted of parallel routes used to get from North Africa to sub-Saharan West Africa. In all respects, the western route was much more traveler-friendly than the central route, which is why it was the predominant way to get from Morocco to the Western Sudan region in the early centuries of the Trans-Saharan trade. In fact, it was easier, if much longer, for a caravan from as far west as Tlemcen (Algeria) to go directly east, then pick up a route to the south terminating at the city of Gao on the easternmost point of the Niger River bend. From Gao the caravan would then head west to its final destination at the Kingdom of Ancient Ghana. All of this circumambiency was to avoid the central route, which cut straight across the gruesome stretch of land lying directly north of the Niger bend. Here the dead zones became wider, wells were farther apart, the temperature was higher, and life became more precarious.

Nevertheless, despite the hardships, the central route ultimately emerged as the busiest with the rise of the empires of Mali and Songhay, which succeeded Ghana and came to control, in sequence, much of the Western Sudan.

The growth of the city of Timbuktu with its position near the western point of the Niger bend, which could be used as an avenue into the interior, was a crucial factor. But the determining consideration lay in the middle of the desert itself: the development of a great salt mine at Taghaza, which was on the central route. Caravans stopped there on their way south to load up since there was a great demand in the Western Sudan for the high-quality rock salt that Taghaza produced.

In places like the Sahara, routes were often little more than a general direction of travel over rocky surfaces or shifting, windswept sands. Trail markers and landmarks helped delineate the way. In dry and desert regions, they could consist of residual organic material such as wood, textiles, and skeletal and fecal matter. Great trees, live and petrified, often marked a boundary or where a road split and caravans went in separate directions. Kodâma ibn Dja'far mentions one called the Talhat al-Malik (the Acacia of the King) on the border between Yemen and al-Hijaz (west central Arabia).[55] The western route of the Trans-Saharan network had its own famous tree overlooking a great well that marked the end of a five-day trip across sand dunes in the region of Wārān.[56]

Traversing the Seas

One alternative to these arduous overland journeys was for merchants to travel by sea instead, although this option carried its own challenges. For the vast majority of premodern trade, merchants travelling by sea were almost as unlikely as their overland rivals to traverse the length of Eurasia. Instead, a similar pattern of multiple interlinking exchanges that carried goods from one emporium to another, where they changed hands and continued their journey, was typical. Through this process, commodities could find their way from the easternmost to the westernmost markets available. The Mediterranean and Indian Ocean were both home to heavy maritime traffic that shuttled goods between continents by the first millennium BCE, and sites across the Black Sea, the Red Sea, the Persian Gulf, and the South China Sea, among others, were all beneficiaries of seaborne trade. On many of the world's coastlines, the possibilities of maritime trade and production nudged coastal populations towards the sea as an "obvious topography of interaction and recourse for livelihoods".[57]

Humans have been using boats for thousands of years: whether making boats from animal skins, hollowed out tree trunks, bundled of branches lashed together, or other suitable material, they have been paddling and punting their way across the water. Probably first used for fishing, boats quickly became useful for an array of activities and appear to have been used for trade by at least the seventh millennium BCE, when obsidian was traded by boat in the Aegean Sea.[58]

Using boats and ships to traverse maritime spaces allowed humans to cross distances far more quickly than other transport options, and to do so over areas that were, of course, otherwise impassable. Travelling by sea could be faster and more reliable for longer-distance voyages and could provide easier and sometimes direct access to exotic goods of low bulk but high value. Alternatively, the greater transportation capacity it offered meant that bulky commodities – especially mineral resources and agricultural staples – could be carried much greater distances despite their relatively lower value. In the premodern world, both options offered opportunities for traders, and seaborne exchange was carried out over short, medium and long distances. Such connectivity along coastlines and across seas transformed how certain people were able to interact with each other. In the Bronze Age Mediterranean, maritime travel meant that an island like Crete could be an emporium for goods carried from as far as Britain and Egypt, while the Peloponnese took on features similar to an archipelago of connected islands rather than a landmass where difficult overland travel separated its regions from each other.[59] Likewise, on Eurasia's eastern coast, the Austronesian expansion connected islands across Micronesia, Polynesia and Southeast Asia from the third millennium BCE, a maritime expansion that laid webs of contact and communication that provided important structure for a nascent maritime trading system.[60]

The traditional method of navigation was to sail within eyeshot of the coast, but coastal sailing lengthened most trips and could be dangerous since many hazards were concealed near the coastline, and pirates could be lurking. The earliest ships that used mast and sail to capture the power of the wind and push further and faster than human effort would allow were also prehistorical. It is likely that their planks were not nailed together but stitched or held together with twine; their sails would have been simple until slow and incremental improvements led to more advanced craft.[61] Maritime travel had its own risks and required specialist knowledge about the natural environment to traverse safely. Whether tides, currents, winds, or weather, the conditions of specific localities, and the wider ocean contained powerful forces that needed to be understood to be navigated safely. Technological progress as well as increasing knowledge about travel by sea, meant that in time these risks were reduced, but there were never overcome entirely.

Natural features were not the only consideration in determining which road a merchant chose to take. Human factors played a central role, in particular, the related issues of security and protection costs. Security had to be bought, at least in theory, from official sources, that is, governments, in the form of taxes, transit duties, import and export levies, permit fees, and other imposts. Often unofficial costs in the form of bribery and extortion by government officials, as well as payment for immunity from attack by pirates, were as important for merchants traveling by sea as it was for those on land. Despite such payments, ships often carried armaments to protect themselves when passing through the most dangerous regions. Protection costs often exceeded the total of all other forms of transportation costs sometimes by a wide margin.[62] The availability of cheap transportation was not the main driving force in the creation of a trade route, but it was a crucial factor in determining which routes prospered and which withered. This was the case at sea as much as it was on land.

For states and merchants alike, maritime trade demanded different types of investment and presented different challenges for establishing or controlling routes. For starters, once they were at sea, controlling the movement of travelers was almost impossible. Some routes were monitored, but for the most part this movement could only be governed once a ship returned to shore, whether in a port city with a well-constructed harbor, a fishing village where locals could ferry goods ashore, or in a discreet bay far from the watchful eyes of any tax collectors. Maritime trade did not require any sunk costs in the form of road building or the clearing of passes, where costs could be recouped over long periods once a route was in place. However, it could benefit from investment in infrastructure ranging from safe harbors to lighthouses, which served not to open up routes but rather act as attractive end destinations for merchants.[63]

The overland "Silk Road" represents the most well-known example of long-distance trade in the premodern world. A comparable maritime route allowing for direct travel from Europe to eastern Asia was simply not possible – but that should not lead us to conclude that long-distance trade was not taking place. Goods were carried across this expanse by sea, but passed from trader to trader and ship to ship to do so. Simply, while deserts, steppes and mountains could be crossed by an enterprising traveler with the help of domesticated animals, using a boat to travel by land and sea together simply will not work. The lack of direct waterway between the Mediterranean and the Indian Ocean meant that goods had to be unloaded and reloaded after being carried overland at least once during the journey. Other challenges served to separate these two oceans, and "severe environmental and meteorological challenges shaped the transport systems between the Mediterranean and the Indian Ocean before the invention of steam power".[64] When these challenges had been overcome, it still made more sense for most traders to make shorter journeys between the numerous commercial emporium that emerged on coastlines across Eurasia, engaging as they went with regional trading networks that sought goods from near and far. There are examples of ships travelling from Arabia to China, but this was not typical.

While the sea provided a potential avenue for carrying good and people across the premodern world, traversing these spaces required more specialist gear than a simple journey by land. In Arabia, local geography should have favored the development of sailing to establish linkages between the Indian Ocean and Mediterranean. With a very long coastline on three sides of the peninsula, and a desert interior that could be difficult to cross, trade across the narrow seas to neighboring lands in Northeast Africa and Persia, offered opportunities. Across the enclosed waters of the Persian Gulf and Red Sea, Arabian seafarers were able to establish trade with two of the ancient centers of wealth in Egypt and Mesopotamia. Through them, a wide world of trade awaited.

More ambitious voyages could cross to East Africa easily and then follow the coast south, a pattern that later carried maritime traders eastward to India. In time, understanding of the monsoon winds and the skills to manage them aided voyages that circled between Arabia, India, and East Africa.[65]

Arabian seafarers, though, despite the geographical benefits of their peninsular position, had to overcome ecological and geological challenges to take advantage of the sea. Arabia did not produce wood suitable for building seafaring ships, nor does it contain iron from nailing them. In the earliest times, the 1200 mile stretch of the Red Sea served to isolate Arabia from Egypt, with the overland Incense Road providing only an intermittent means of exchange between the two regions. Vast coral reefs abounded that could scupper ships attempting the journey, there were hundreds of miles of coastal desert to pass that provided little means of sustenance along the way, available harbors were poor, and enterprising nomadic peoples saw little difference between raiding on land and turning to piracy. The Persian Gulf was more promising for early mariners, but not by much. It would not be until the latter half of the first millennium BCE that Arabia would be connected enough with wider trading worlds to provide access to the commodities and technologies that they needed to brave these waters on scale.[66] Indeed, long-distance trade created the conditions for more long-distance trade, a virtuous cycle that would rapidly lead in the first millennium CE to an Arab maritime trading expansion that traversed the Indian Ocean World.

Evidence of the early Egyptian trade on the Red Sea, from as early as the reign of Sahure (c. 2470 BCE) provides some hints about how ship building technology was transferred from one society to another. Journeys to the country of Punt used ships built in the Gulf of Suez that passed the whole length of the Red Sea before returning home against head winds – a task that would have represented quite the challenge with technology available. In Egyptian texts this voyage was undertaken using "ships of Gebal", a reference to the Phoenician city of Byblos, because the design was from this port or that the same type of ships were used the trade thither. Essentially, the Egyptians were able to obtain the pine wood and resin from Byblos that was needed to establish their own shipbuilding industry. As Egyptian power in the Red Sea declined, Phoenician's appeared as the main maritime power in the Red Sea, with voyages to the Kingdom of Ophir (probably in India) carrying back gold, silver, jewels, ivory, apes, and peacocks via the Red Sea and into the Mediterranean. Phoenicians, too, were active on the Persian Gulf side of the peninsular, and were employed by the Assyrian ruler Sennacherib (705–681 BCE) to build powerful ships that could be manned by sailors brought from the Mediterranean, intended to impose his power on the maritime provinces beyond the Euphrates. An explosion of maritime activity followed the Persian conquest of much of Western Asia and Egypt under Darius (521–483 BCE), and there are numerous accounts of fleets deployed on the Indian Ocean and Mediterranean borders of the empire.[67]

As connectivity increased, knowledge of different maritime systems began to filter through. In the Indian Ocean, Malay and Indian sailors had ridden the monsoon winds from an early time, but the first European recorded experience of these systems was from Eudoxus of Cyzicus around the turn of the millennium. In this account, which was described by Strabo, Eudoxus was in Egypt when an "Indian was brought to the king by the coast-guards of the recess of the Arabian Gulf, who said that they had found him half-dead and alone on a stranded ship". Because "they did not know who he was or where he came from, since they did not understand his language", the man was taught Greek and in time came to describe how he had sailed from India. Eudoxus would, according to Strabo, go on to complete two voyages in the Indian Ocean, returning with a cargo of precious stones and aromatics, as well as further information about the seas learned from pilots met along the way.[68] Probably referring to the final decades of the later Ptolomies rule in Egypt, Strabo noted that "not even twenty ships [per year] dared to traverse the Arabian Gulf so as to come out beyond the straits" and into the Indian Ocean.[69] Trade was taking place, routes were becoming more familiar, but links between the Mediterranean and Asian maritime world were still intermittent and uncertain.

During the Roman period, the Red Sea took on a much greater role as a space for maritime trade, and it was during the early centuries of the first millennium that Arab seafarers, and others, honed skills and technologies necessary for traversing the wide expanse of the Indian Ocean beyond.[70] A Greek merchant who was resident in Egypt wrote the *Periplus Maris Erythraei* (Periplus of the Erythraean Sea), probably in the first century CE, in which they described in detail both the Red Sea and its maritime traffic but also the lands of western India and eastern Africa. The text described lands including the Horn of Africa known as the "the Cape of Spices", Yemen or "Frankincense Country", the Kingdom of Aksum and its important market for ivory, and further south on the African coast to sites that may have been Tanzania or Mozambique – both of which remained important east African emporiums over the consequent centuries. In India, it described Bharuch on the Gulf of Khambhat, which already in the first century CE was a source of "cotton and the Indian cloths made therefrom", as well as silk, pepper, ivory, agate and other goods. In return, local traders were keen to obtain Italian wine, copper, tin, lead, coral, gold, silver, and various other commodities. Greek traders were known even in the Chola regions of southern India, where they obtained even rarer items like diamonds, sapphires, and spices. The *Periplus* also detailed the journey of the mariner Hippalus, who was knowledgeable about the monsoon winds.[71]

Archaeological evidence and recent research using the fragmentary surviving texts known as the *Muziris Papyrus* have done much to expose the practices and wider maritime trading networks that tied the Indian and Roman trading worlds.[72] Arab seafarers had, by the early centuries of the first millennium, overcome many of the challenges that faced them in the Red Sea and beyond, and were active throughout the routes that carried a busy trade between the Arabia and across the western Indian Ocean. At Muza, "a market town established by law", on the Arabian Red Sea coast near Mokha, "the whole place is crowded with Arab ship owners and seafaring men, and is busy with the affairs of commerce; for they carry on trade with the far-side coast [the Horn of Africa] and with Bharuch [in India], sending their own ships there".[73] Nearby Socotra was home to Arab, Greek, and Indian traders, and large Indian ships known as *sangara* on the Malabar coast, and others called *colandia,* carried Indian merchants throughout the Indian Ocean world.[74] On the African coast, Arab traders had traveled alongside colonists, and the important trading cities of Aksum and Zanzibar, as well as states in Somaliland, all had Arab rulers.[75] Over the following centuries, Aksum would grow into the powerful Aksumite empire, a state that bridged the Red Sea with territories in East Africa and Arabia: alongside China, Rome, and Persia, it was considered one of the great empires of the world by the Persian author Mani.[76]

In East Africa, this maritime trade contributed to the establishment of an enduring trading system built on the Indian Ocean's monsoons to sustain a mercantile society of independent or autonomous port states scattered along the African coast from Mogadishu in the north to Sofala in the south with trading posts in Madagascar and elsewhere. Its exports included ivory and tortoise shell, and Sofala was a major gold exporter for a while. Among its imports were iron products and even Chinese ceramics. Arab traders from the north joined an African coastal environment where rich Swahili towns were already connecting the littoral with the continental interior. Maritime trade represented a clear incentive for local Swahili to adopt Islam. The risks presented by slave raiding, piracy and warfare meant that it benefited all parties to establish a common legal and commercial system, and Islam facilitated this development. Consequently, Islamic traders arriving in the region could enjoy some degree of security and safety while they waited for the seasonal monsoon winds. The growth and wealth of settlements like Manda, Pate, and Kilwa attest to East Africa's integration into wider regional and long-distance trading networks, as well as the economic and political power of these cities. The presence of Chinese ceramics and silks, Indo-Pacific beads, pottery, cloth, jewelry, and Islamic pottery, among other commodities, in sites on the coast attests to complexity of material culture that tied the coast to far flung trading partners across western and eastern Asia.[77]

In the Indian Ocean World, Islam similarly helped generate institutions that provided security and stability for merchants taking advantage of the monsoon to traverse the region: although, notably, other religious and political structures supported an array of trading partners and competitors across the region too. Persian traders travelling from ports in the Persian Gulf, were traversing this expanse of ocean at a very early date, possibly going even further and travelling to China directly by sea. This was quite the remarkable feat: the sea route from Basra to Guangzhou was over 6000 miles in length, complex and treacherous.[78] The ports of Male in Malabar and Calliana (near modern Mumbai) were home to Persian communities, who built churches in each.[79] It is likely that they were drawn to both emporium that held goods from across Eurasia and the opportunity to access commodities produced locally – especially black pepper. One classical Tamil poem offered a succinct analysis of the trade dynamics of the region, describing how foreign traders "arrive with gold and leave with pepper". The Malabar Coast had a near monopoly on the production of black pepper and there were eager consumers across Eurasia. Demand was rarely met and despite a sense of superabundance – accounts talk about pepper being poured as plentifully as corn – there were rarely occasions when over supply caused prices to drop. Profits from trading pepper from Malabar to Aden, the first stage on which they might be carried to sale further north and west, were reportedly as high as 30 percent. By the twelfth century, the pepper trade had accrued mainly to Muslim merchants, who carried goods across the Indian Ocean and beyond, coming to dominate points of connection between regional networks that, together, linked Malabar to China.[80]

The western terminus for trade coming across the Indian Ocean was accessed through either the Red Sea or Persian Gulf – the first carrying goods through Egypt and into the Mediterranean and the latter into lands adjoining the Tigris and Euphrates rivers, with routes onwards connected them with the overland "Silk Roads". The Red Sea route had enjoyed a boom under the Roman Empire, but Byzantine naval power was concentrated in the Mediterranean, leaving the Red Sea largely unprotected. Under Sasanian Persia, trade had shifted to the Persian Gulf and southward towards Sri Lanka. The Sasanians were succeeded by the Umayyads and then the the Abbasids, during which time Persian Gulf and Indian Ocean trade grew exponentially. Due to links like these, Greek and Roman geographers often presented the Mediterranean as an inevitable concluding geography for trade routes from the east, and Arabic geographers presented their "land of Islam sandwiched between the 'Sea of the Romans' and the 'Sea of the Persians' (or the Ethiopians or the Chinese)".[81] However, for maritime actors across the Indian Ocean and beyond, the Red Sea and Persian Gulf links westward were an important but likely only peripheral point of interest. Certain goods were highly sought after through this route, notably including metals, but these were available elsewhere. Cornwall did not become a world-renowned land of wonder known as the "Tin Peninsular" in the way that the "Spice Islands" of the Banda Sea became almost mythologized in geographical accounts produced across Eurasia. Similarly, "Silk Roads" leading to China drew traders eastward in larger numbers from greater distances than British woolen cloths drew merchants westward (although these did, notably, attract many traders from Europe who stamped their mark on London's Italian-influenced "Lombard Street" or in the Hansa built Steelyard). Recognizing this direction of traffic across Eurasia does not diminish the role of maritime trade in western Eurasia, so much as to highlight that similar or even richer webs of exchange and interaction can be traced across maritime Asia too.

The eastern terminus for this maritime trade was across the South China Sea to Guangzhou, located where the wind pattern brought ships. From there, goods passed into the interior of China through the river system and the Grand Canal. Understanding in China of the long maritime routes that connected it with the Persian and Roman worlds to the west can be traced in early but detailed knowledge about the routes. A Chinese chronicle that spanned the period 386–556 CE detailed how a traveler, once in Persia, could "following the crooked shape of the sea coast, you can go to Ta-st'in [Syria], bending around over 10,000 *li*" of coastline. There was also interest in the linkages that made the route function: the emporium and ports along the way that merchants visited. Another Chinese source, from the fifth century, reported that sea trade took place between China, India, East Africa and Syria. Chinese ships and traders probably met their counterparts from the western Indian Ocean in ports in Sri Lanka, where a Chinese pilgrim noted there were "many Sabean [in Arabia] merchants" when he visited in 414.[82] European sources, likewise, highlighted the role of Sri Lanka as an emporium that connected Chinese and other traders from eastern Asia with the western Indian Ocean. However, rather than Arab traders, these accounts are more likely to note Persian, Aksumite or Greek traders as the key participants travelling from west to east on the monsoon winds.[83]

Transporting bulk items with low value relative to weight favored water transport. A single ship could carry many times the goods that an average caravan could carry at a fraction of the cost. As Abbasid-Tang trade increased, so did sea commerce. Bulk market products such as ceramics and cotton textiles began replacing luxury goods. In southeast Asia, Tang ships carrying up to 700 people were used, with trade to Korea, Japan, and westward through the Straits of Melaka all reported in contemporary sources.[84] Over the following centuries, examples of Arab or Persian traders traversing the entire length of maritime Eurasia become more common. Along the way, too, they intersected with a plethora of other maritime states and traders. As early as 617 CE, the Chinese pilgrim I-ching reported travelling on a *Po-sse*, that is Persian, ship from Guangzhou. In 717, an Indian traveler recounted a fleet of thirty-five Persian ships travelling to China via Sri Lanka and Sumatra, although it is unclear if the ships survived the journey. However, this was likely not a one-off event, and the same traveler noted that Persian's "sail in big craft to the country of China, straight to Guangzhou for silk piece goods and the like ware". By 748, a Persian village was reported on the Chinese island of Hainan, and in the same year they were listed alongside Brahman and Malayan ship owners in Guangzhou.

Under the Abbasid Empire (750–1258 CE), a new impetus to engage with the wider maritime world, coupled with the integration of the Euphrates and Tigris riverine systems with navigable canals, meant that the capital in Baghdad was practically and intellectually embedded into multi-directional long-distance trading networks. According to al-Tabari (839–923), the Abbasid Sultan al-Manṣūr (r. 754–75) was well aware of the potential scope of these links and reportedly described how "there is no obstacle between us and China; everything on the sea can come to us on it [the Tigris river]".[85] This was not always a peaceful exchange, and Arab merchants appear in Chinese accounts as a resident community in Guangzhou for the first time in 748, when they joined with their Persian counterparts to sack and burn the city. The city was re-opened only in 792 for western merchants, whose numbers grew in the city to as many as 120,000, before Huang Chao (835–84) attacked the city and massacred much of its population in 878.[86] As a frontier town for the Chinese state, Guangzhou could be a perilous place for merchants at the best of times, and there were repeated efforts to control the extent of cultural exchange that could take place within this border community.[87]

Despite violence playing an important role on the maritime border much as it did the steppe frontier, the arrival of goods from across maritime Eurasia into China was becoming more common throughout this period. Pepper was noted as originating in countries of "western barbarians" in the seventh century, when it was described as being carried predominantly by south Indian traders.[88] Wars in Central Asia made overland traffic increasingly problematic. At the same time, the rise of Srivijaya (670–1025 CE), a federation of ports centering on Palembang in southeast Sumatra, protected maritime commerce, provided a safe place for exchange and transshipment, and made available storage facilities and accommodations.[89] Powerful merchant guilds in south Asia were supported by the growth of the Chola (848–1279) and Srivijaya states, who together dominated much of the maritime route between southern India and the Straits of Melaka. Sustained and largely stable trade across the region enabled the establishment of trusted and familiar routes.[90] Srivijaya was attacked and plundered by the Chola navy in 1025. Thereafter a rival center emerged in east Java, which developed the rice-for-spice trade with the Maluku Islands to the east. By the late thirteenth century, a trade-based empire centered in Java, Majapahit, became the dominant power in this sector of the maritime Eurasian world.

As the Tang gave way to the trade-friendly Song dynasty (960–1279 CE), the growing role of Muslims in Chinese port cities was likely shaped by new practices of maritime transportation that facilitated direct voyages from India to China, rather than requiring stops along the way. At the same time, more Chinese junks were making the westward voyage to India themselves. Arabic sources describe Chinese ships in Malabari ports in the ninth century, but it was especially during the Song period that they became a regular feature on the coast.[91] Chinese merchants became more common features of trade across a wide geography of trade in eastern maritime Eurasia, forming diasporic networks that would survive the tumultuous political environment in China.[92] The final triumph of maritime routes came with a series of technological innovations including the magnetic compass. From the twelfth century on, China took the lead in building ever larger ships, and vessels carrying as many as 1000 people ceased to be a novelty.[93] Massive, government-funded voyages culminated in those of the Treasure Fleets in the early fifteenth century: which, not surprisingly, had the Indian coast as the primary destination for the first two voyages.[94] During the Yuan period (1271–1368), both Marco Polo and Ibn Battuta described the presence of huge Chinese ships in Malabar. According to Polo, for every basket of pepper exported westward ten more were sent to Quanzhou. China had become the largest market for pepper in the world: a long-distance maritime trading link that ensured the circulation of bulk goods as well as luxurious commodities.[95]

In the west the Abbasid Caliphate collapsed in the thirteenth century CE, and maritime traffic shifted to the Red Sea with the revival of Egypt under the Fatimids and later the Mamluks. Europe was re-energizing as a market, leading to the "Commercial Revolution" of the thirteenth century. Alexandria on the northern Egyptian coast was tied intimately with trading republics in Italy: a relationship grounded on the Egyptian port's connection to Malabar and the pepper trade.[96] The same chronology corresponded to the Asian sea trade boom, which saw a dramatic expansion of maritime trade between India, the Indonesian archipelago, and China. In southern India, the collapse of the Chola empire in the eleventh century had undercut the authority of local merchant guilds, presenting an opportunity for Muslim traders to establish themselves as key intermediaries in the region. Around the same time, the Mongol defeat of the Song and consequent establishment of the Yuan dynasty led to more and more of China's maritime trade also falling into the hands of Islamic traders who were resident in Guangzhou and Quanzhou. In time, these merchants would form a trading diaspora throughout maritime Asia.[97]

The maritime route between Arabia and China was a challenging proposition. Yet, maritime commerce was a defining feature of exchanges that meant that goods traveled across the Asian coastline via maritime trade long before direct voyages from the westernmost and easternmost ports of Eurasia were taking place. Long-distance trade was a familiar part of the commercial world of Eurasia. It sustained the movement of people, goods and ideas across vast geographic areas. While the overland "Silk Road" created a direct link by which some Europeans could reach China, the maritime routes that tied these same destinations together were responsible for carrying a dizzying array of commodities. Rather than a single route, the maritime world of Eurasia is better understood as a multiplicity of intersecting networks. No single state predominated or set the rules of travel and exchange across the region: though they did control and influence how ports and markets operated. Instead, mercantile communities that were able to operate across different spaces effectively were responsible for ordering and organizing the trade. Sometimes this was assisted with considerable state support, but this was not always the case. The major trading cities of maritime Eurasia were more likely to be described as hosting people from many different places, and it was their very value as points of contact that made them so valuable.

Notes

1 For a wide array of examples from across the world, see Jan Gyllenbok, *Encyclopaedia of Historical Metrology, Weights and Measures, vol. 1* (Switzerland, 2018).
2 John Hill, *Through the Jade Gate to Rome: A study of the Silk Roads during the later Han Dynasty 1st to 2nd centuries*, vol. 1 and 2 (2009), p. xxxii.
3 Ban Gu, *Han Shu*, trans. Anthony François Paulus Hulsewé and M. A. N. Loewe (eds.), *China in Central Asia: The Early Stage: 125 BC–AD 23; an Annotated Translation of Chapters 61 and 96 of the History of the Former Han Dynasty* (Leiden, 1979), pp. 404, 410.
4 Fan Ye, *Hou Hanshou*, trans. John Hill, *Through the Jade Gate to Rome: A study of the Silk Roads during the later Han Dynasty 1st to 2nd centuries* (2009), pp. 18–19.
5 Strabo, *Geographica*, vol. 6, book 3, part 10.
6 Diodorus Siculus, *Bibliotheca Historica*, vol. 3, book 5, part 21.
7 Claudius Ptolemy, *The Geography*, trans. Edward Stevenson (New York, 1932), p. 33.
8 Al-Biruni, *Taḥqīq mā li-al-Hind* [History of India], trans. Edward Sachau, *Beruni's India: Account of the religion, philosophy, literature, geography, chronology, astronomy, customs, laws, and astrology of India, about A.D. 1030* (London, 1888), pp. 199–200.
9 Ibn Khurradādhbih, *Kitāb al Masālik w'al Mamālik*, trans. Michael Jan de Goeje, *Ibn Khurradādhbih's Kitāb Al-Masālik Wa L-Mamālik and Part of the Kitāb Al-Kharāj by Qudāma Ibn Jaʿfar* (Leiden, 1889), pp. 2–3, 60.
10 S. Maqbul Ahmad, "Cartography of al-Sharīf al-Idrīsī" in J. B. Harley and D. Woodward (eds.), *The History of Cartography, vol. 2, book 1: Cartography in the traditional Islamic and South Asian societies* (Chicago, 1992), pp. 156–74.
11 John Hill, *Through the Jade Gate to Rome: A study of the Silk Roads during the later Han Dynasty 1st to 2nd centuries*, vol. 1 and 2 (2009), p. 339.
12 Ibn Khurradādhbih, *Kitāb al Masālik w'al Mamālik*, trans. Michael Jan de Goeje, *Ibn Khurradādhbih's Kitāb Al-Masālik Wa L-Mamālik and Part of the Kitāb Al-Kharāj by Qudāma Ibn Jaʿfar* (Leiden, 1889), p. 153.
13 Ibn Battuta, *The Rihla*, trans. H. A. R. Gibb and C. F. Beckingham (eds.), *The Travels of Ibn Battuta, AD 1325–54*, 4 vols. (London, 1994), pp. 791–2.
14 Ban Gu, *Han Shu*, trans. Anthony François Paulus Hulsewé and M. A. N. Loewe (eds.), *China in Central Asia: The Early Stage: 125 BC–AD 23; an Annotated Translation of Chapters 61 and 96 of the History of the Former Han Dynasty* (Leiden, 1979), pp. 189–90.
15 M. Cary and E. H. Warmington, *The Ancient Explorers* (London, 1929), p. 5.
16 Strabo, *Geographica*, vol. 5, p. 259.
17 Pliny, *Naturalis Historia*, book 4, chapter 12, trans. John Bostock, *The Natural History* (Perseus Digital Library: http://data.perseus.org/citations/urn:cts:latinLit:phi0978.phi001.perseus-eng1:12.32).
18 Claudius Ptolemy, trans. Edward Stevenson, *The Geography* (1932), p. 34.
19 Pliny, *Naturalis Historia*, book 12, chapter 32.
20 Anon., *Akhbar al-Sin wa-al-Hind* [The Book of the Wonders of India], quoted in George Hourani, *Arab Seafaring in the Indian Ocean in the Ancient and Early Medieval Times* (Princeton, NJ, 1995 [1963]), p. 74.
21 Anon., *Hudūd al-Ālam*, trans. Vladimir Minorsky, *A Persian Geography, 372 AD–982 AD* (London, 1970), p. 95.
22 Al-Bakrī, *Kitāb al-Masālik wa-al-Mamālik*, trans. Nehemiah Levtzion and J. F. P. Hopkins (eds.), *Corpus of Early Arabic Sources for West African History* (Cambridge, 1981), pp. 66–9.

23 Al-Bakrī, *Kitāb al-Masālik wa-al-Mamālik*, trans. Nehemiah Levtzion and J. F. P. Hopkins (eds.), *Corpus of Early Arabic Sources for West African History* (Cambridge, 1981), pp. 69–70.
24 Al-Bakrī, *Kitāb al-Masālik wa-al-Mamālik*, trans. Nehemiah Levtzion and J. F. P. Hopkins (eds.), *Corpus of Early Arabic Sources for West African History* (Cambridge, 1981), p. 482.
25 Cosmas Indicopleustes, *Topographia Christiana*, trans. J. W. M. Crindle, *The Christian Topography* (London, 1897), pp. 49–51.
26 Al-Bakrī, *Kitāb al-Masālik wa-al-Mamālik*, trans. Nehemiah Levtzion and J. F. P. Hopkins (eds.), *Corpus of Early Arabic Sources for West African History* (Cambridge, 1981), p. 70.
27 Geoffrey Hindley, *A History of Roads* (London, 1972), p. 9.
28 Al-Biruni, *Taḥqīq mā li-al-Hind*, trans. Edward Sachau, *Beruni's India: Account of the religion, philosophy, literature, geography, chronology, astronomy, customs, laws, and astrology of India, about AD 1030* (London, 1888), p. 199.
29 Francesco Balducci Pegolotti, *Libro di Divisamenti di Paesi* [The Book of the Descriptions of Countries], trans. Henry Yule, *Cathay and the Way Thither: Being a collection of medieval notices of China, vol. 3* (London, 1914), p. 146.
30 Sharaf Al-Zamān Ṭāhir Marvazī, trans. V. Minorsky, *Sharaf al-Zamān Ṭāhir Marvazī on China, the Turks, and India* (London, 1942), pp. 18, 70–1.
31 Marco Polo, *Il Libro di Marco Polo detto il Milione*, trans. Hugh Murray, *Travels of Marco Polo* (Edinburgh, 1845), p. 245.
32 Ibn Khurradādhbih, *Kitāb al Masālik w'al Mamālik*, trans. Michael Jan de Goeje, *Ibn Khurradādhbih's Kitāb Al-Masālik Wa L-Mamālik and Part of the Kitāb Al-Kharāj by Qudāma Ibn Jaʿfar* (Leiden, 1889), p. 21.
33 Qudāma ibn Ja'far, quoted in Ibn Khurradādhbih, *Kitāb al Masālik w'al Mamālik*, trans. Michael Jan de Goeje, *Ibn Khurradādhbih's Kitāb Al-Masālik Wa L-Mamālik and Part of the Kitāb Al-Kharāj by Qudāma Ibn Jaʿfar* (Leiden, 1889), p. 203.
34 Morris Rossabi, "The 'Decline' of the Central Asian Caravan Trade" in James Tracy (ed.), *The Rice of Merchant Empires: Long distance trade in the early modern world, 1350–1750* (Cambridge, 1990), p. 352, pp. 351–70.
35 Francesco Balducci Pegolotti, *Libro di Divisamenti di Paesi* [The Book of the Descriptions of Countries], trans. Henry Yule, *Cathay and the Way Thither: Being a collection of medieval notices of China, vol. 3* (London, 1914), pp. 137–69.
36 Craig Benjamin, *Empires of Ancient Eurasia: The first Silk Roads Era, 100 BCE–250 CE* (Cambridge, 2018), pp. 68–90.
37 Al-Sa'di, *Tarikh al-Sudan* [History of the Sudan], trans. John Hunwick, *Timbuktu and the Songhay Empire: Al-Sadi's Tarikh al-Sudan down to 1613 and other contemporary documents* (Leiden, 1999), pp. 217–19.
38 Claudius Ptolemy, *The Geography*, trans. Edward Stevenson (New York, 1932), p. 33.
39 Ibn Khurradādhbih, *Kitāb al Masālik w'al Mamālik*, trans. Michael Jan de Goeje, *Ibn Khurradādhbih's Kitāb Al-Masālik Wa L-Mamālik and Part of the Kitāb Al-Kharāj by Qudāma Ibn Jaʿfar* (Leiden, 1889), p. 22.
40 Claudius Ptolemy, *The Geography*, trans. Edward Stevenson (New York, 1932), p. 26.
41 Claudius Ptolemy, *The Geography*, trans. Edward Stevenson (New York, 1932), p. 34.
42 Ban Gu, *Han Shu*, trans. Anthony François Paulus Hulsewé and M. A. N. Loewe (eds.), *China in Central Asia: The Early Stage: 125 BC–AD 23; an Annotated Translation of Chapters 61 and 96 of the History of the Former Han Dynasty* (Leiden, 1979), pp. 97–111.

43 Bento de Gois, *De Christiana expeditione apud Sinas*, trans. Henry Yule, *Cathay and the Way Thither: Being a collection of medieval notices of China, vol. 4* (1916), p. 217.
44 Faxian, quoted in Irene Franck and David Brownstone, *The Silk Road: A history* (New York, 1986), p. 151.
45 Xuanzang, quoted in Irene Franck and David Brownstone, *The Silk Road: A history* (New York, 1986), p. 178.
46 Pliny, *Naturalis Historia*, vol. 2, book vi, pp. 377–9.
47 Faxian, quoted in Irene Franck and David Brownstone, *The Silk Road: A history* (New York, 1986), p. 199.
48 Al-Bakrī, *Kitāb al-Masālik wa-al-Mamālik*, trans. Nehemiah Levtzion and J. F. P. Hopkins (eds.), *Corpus of Early Arabic Sources for West African History* (Cambridge, 1981), pp. 62–87.
49 Ibn Khurradādhbih, *Kitāb al Masālik w'al Mamālik*, trans. Michael Jan de Goeje, *Ibn Khurradādhbih's Kitāb Al-Masālik Wa L-Mamālik and Part of the Kitāb Al-Kharāj by Qudāma Ibn Jaᶜfar* (Leiden, 1889), pp. 103–4.
50 Qudāma ibn Ja'far, quoted in Ibn Khurradādhbih, *Kitāb al Masālik w'al Mamālik*, trans. Michael Jan de Goeje, *Ibn Khurradādhbih's Kitāb Al-Masālik Wa L-Mamālik and Part of the Kitāb Al-Kharāj by Qudāma Ibn Jaᶜfar* (Leiden, 1889), pp. 156–7.
51 Ibn Jubayr, *Rihla*, trans. Ronald Broadhurst (ed.), *The Travels of Ibn Jubayr: Being the chronicle of a medieval Spanish Moor concerning his journey to the Egypt of Saladin, the holy cities of Arabia, Baghdad the city of the Caliphs, the Latin kingdom of Jerusalem, and the Norman kingdom of Sicily* (London, 1952), pp. 60–1.
52 Janet Rizvi, *Trans-Himalayan Caravans: Merchant princes and peasant traders in Ladakh* (Oxford, 1999), p. 42.
53 Ban Gu, *Han Shu*, trans. Anthony François Paulus Hulsewé and M. A. N. Loewe (eds.), *China in Central Asia: The Early Stage: 125 BC–AD 23; an Annotated Translation of Chapters 61 and 96 of the History of the Former Han Dynasty* (Leiden, 1979), pp. 97–111.
54 Bin Yang, "Horses, Silver and Cowries: Yunnan in global perspective", *Journal of World History* 15:3 (2004), pp. 281–322.
55 Kodâma ibn Dja'far, quoted in Ibn Khurradādhbih, *Kitāb al Masālik w'al Mamālik*, trans. Michael Jan de Goeje, *Ibn Khurradādhbih's Kitāb Al-Masālik Wa L-Mamālik and Part of the Kitāb Al-Kharāj by Qudāma Ibn Jaᶜfar* (Leiden, 1889), pp. 148.
56 Al-Bakrī, quoted in Ibn Khurradādhbih, *Kitāb al Masālik w'al Mamālik*, trans. Michael Jan de Goeje, *Ibn Khurradādhbih's Kitāb Al-Masālik Wa L-Mamālik and Part of the Kitāb Al-Kharāj by Qudāma Ibn Jaᶜfar* (Leiden, 1889), pp. 62–87.
57 Justin Leidwanger and Carl Knappett, "Maritime Networks, Connectivity, and Mobility in the Ancient Mediterranean" in Justin Leidwanger and Carl Knappett (eds.), *Maritime Networks in the Ancient Mediterranean World* (Cambridge, 2018), pp. 1–21.
58 B. Horejs et al., "The Aegean in the Early 7th Millennium BC: Maritime networks and colonisation", *Journal of World Prehistory* 28 (2015), pp. 289–330.
59 Justin Leidwanger and Carl Knappett, "Maritime Networks, Connectivity, and Mobility in the Ancient Mediterranean" in Justin Leidwanger and Carl Knappett (eds.), *Maritime Networks in the Ancient Mediterranean World* (Cambridge, 2018), pp. 1–21.
60 Jiun-Yu Liu, "Intertwined Maritime Silk Road and Austronesian Routes: A Taiwanese archaeological perspective", *Journal of Global History* 18:3 (2023), pp. 384–400.

61 George Hourani, *Arab Seafaring in the Indian Ocean in the Ancient and Early Medieval Times* (Princeton, NJ, 1995 [1963]), pp. 3–5.
62 Janet Abu Lughod, *Before European Hegemony: The world system AD 1250–1350* (1989), p. 177.
63 Justin Leidwanger and Carl Knappett, "Maritime Networks, Connectivity, and Mobility in the Ancient Mediterranean" in Justin Leidwanger and Carl Knappett (eds.), *Maritime Networks in the Ancient Mediterranean World* (Cambridge, 2018), p. 6.
64 Federico De Romanis, *The Indo-Roman Pepper Trade and the Muziris Papyrus* (Oxford, 2020), pp. 32–5.
65 George Hourani, *Arab Seafaring in the Indian Ocean in the Ancient and Early Medieval Times* (Princeton, NJ, 1995 [1963]), pp. 4–5.
66 George Hourani, *Arab Seafaring in the Indian Ocean in the Ancient and Early Medieval Times* (Princeton, NJ, 1995 [1963]), pp. 5–6.
67 George Hourani, *Arab Seafaring in the Indian Ocean in the Ancient and Early Medieval Times* (Princeton, NJ, 1995 [1963]), pp. 7–11.
68 Strabo, *Geographica*, book 2, chapter 3.
69 Strabo, *Geographica*, book 17, chapter 1.
70 Kasper Grønlund Evers, *Worlds Apart Trading Together: The organisation of long-distance trade between Rome and India in Antiquity* (Bicester, 2017).
71 Anon., *Periplus Maris Erythraei* [*Periplus of the Erythraean Sea*], trans. Lionel Casson (ed.), *The Periplus Maris Erythraei: Text with introduction, translation, and commentary* (Princeton, NJ, 1989). The Periplus and the maritime links therein are discussed in Xinru Liu, *The Silk Road in World History* (New York, 2010), pp. 34–7.
72 Federico De Romanis, *The Indo-Roman Pepper Trade and the Muziris Papyrus* (Oxford, 2020).
73 Anon., *Periplus*, quoted in George Hourani, *Arab Seafaring in the Indian Ocean in the Ancient and Early Medieval Times* (Princeton, NJ, 1995 [1963]), p. 32.
74 George Hourani, *Arab Seafaring in the Indian Ocean in the Ancient and Early Medieval Times* (Princeton, NJ, 1995 [1963]), p. 33.
75 George Hourani, *Arab Seafaring in the Indian Ocean in the Ancient and Early Medieval Times* (Princeton, NJ, 1995 [1963]), p. 33.
76 Stuart Munro-Hay, *Aksum: An African civilisation of late Antiquity* (Edinburgh, 1991), p. 17.
77 Stephanie Wynne-Jones and Adria LaViolette, *The Swahili World* (London, 2017), pp. 133–62.
78 John W. Chaffee, *The Muslim Merchants of Premodern China: The history of a maritime Asian trade diaspora, 750–1400* (Cambridge, 2018), pp. 12–50.
79 George Hourani, *Arab Seafaring in the Indian Ocean in the Ancient and Early Medieval Times* (Princeton, NJ, 1995 [1963]), p. 41.
80 Sebastian Prange, *Monsoon Islam: Trade and faith on the medieval Malabar coast* (Cambridge, 2018), pp. 207–10.
81 Federico De Romanis, *The Indo-Roman Pepper Trade and the Muziris Papyrus* (Oxford, 2020), p. 31.
82 All quoted in George Hourani, *Arab Seafaring in the Indian Ocean in the Ancient and Early Medieval Times* (Princeton, NJ, 1995 [1963]), p. 38.
83 George Hourani, *Arab Seafaring in the Indian Ocean in the Ancient and Early Medieval Times* (Princeton, NJ, 1995 [1963]), pp. 40–1.
84 Mei-Ling Hsu, "Chinese Maritime Cartography: Sea charts of pre-modern China", *Imago Mundi* 40 (1988), p. 96, pp. 96–112.
85 Quoted in George Hourani, *Arab Seafaring in the Indian Ocean in the Ancient and Early Medieval Times* (Princeton, NJ, 1995 [1963]), p. 64.

86 George Hourani, *Arab Seafaring in the Indian Ocean in the Ancient and Early Medieval Times* (Princeton, NJ, 1995 [1963]), pp. 62–3, 77.
87 Adam Fong, "Together They Might Make Trouble': Cross-Cultural Interactions in Tang Dynasty Guangzhou, 618–907 CE", *Journal of World History* 25:4 (2014), pp. 475–92.
88 Sebastian Prange, *Monsoon Islam: Trade and faith on the medieval Malabar coast* (Cambridge, 2018), p. 217.
89 Hermann Kulke, "The Naval Expeditions of the Cholas in the Context of Asian History" in Hermann Kulke, K. Kesavapany, and Vijay Sekhuja (eds.), *Nagapattinam to Suvarnadwipa: Reflections on the Chola naval expeditions to Southeast Asia* (Singapore, 2009), pp. 1–19.
90 Sebastian Prange, *Monsoon Islam: Trade and faith on the medieval Malabar coast* (Cambridge, 2018), pp. 216–18.
91 Sebastian Prange, *Monsoon Islam: Trade and faith on the medieval Malabar coast* (Cambridge, 2018), pp. 217–18.
92 T. Sen, "The Formation of Chinese Maritime Networks to Southern Asia, 1200–1450", *Journal of the Economic and Social History of the Orient* 49:4 (2006), pp. 421–53.
93 Mei-Ling Hsu, "Chinese Maritime Cartography: Sea charts of pre-modern China", *Imago Mundi* 40 (1988), p. 96.
94 T. Sen, "The Formation of Chinese Maritime Networks to Southern Asia, 1200–1450", *Journal of the Economic and Social History of the Orient* 49:4 (2006), p. 422.
95 Sebastian Prange, *Monsoon Islam: Trade and faith on the medieval Malabar coast* (Cambridge, 2018), pp. 218–19.
96 Georg Christ, *Trading Conflicts: Venetian merchants and Mamluk officials in late medieval Alexandria* (Leiden, 2012), pp. 19–35.
97 Sebastian Prange, *Monsoon Islam: Trade and faith on the medieval Malabar coast* (Cambridge, 2018), pp. 208–10.

5 Merchants and Networks

Making Trade Work

Originally written around 1340 for the ruler of the Ilkhanate, Abu Sa'id Bahadur Khan, Hamdallah Mustawfi's (1281–1340s) *Nuzhat al-Qulub* was part of a literary tradition common across the Arab and Persianate worlds that blended histories of key people and events with geographical materials, maps, and guides.[1] The *Nuzhat al-Qulūb* was an important text within the corpus of Persian material about the world and was reproduced repeatedly over the following centuries. Although dominated by detailed overviews of the key cities, towns, ports, and regions of the Ilkhanate world of the fourteenth century, mainly in Iran, Mustawfi's text did seek to present its readers with information related to the very edges of their known world – and to interrogate the commercial links that had brought these places into the Persianate world's orbit.

Readers of the *Nuzhat al-Qulūb* learned about places ranging from the Wāqwāq Islands, where pure gold was so plentiful it was used for making dog collars, to garnets from the far west of "Frank country", and the "land of the blacks" in West Africa.[2] As well as information about where commodities came from, for one island in particular, Mustawfi thought it important to clarify precisely how merchants travelling to the fringes of the world were able to do business with people so distant. Here, on the Island of Bartayil, foreign merchants sought to purchase spices through a process of silent barter. They landed during the day, laid out their goods separately on the coast, and left. At night, the local inhabitants would come down to the coast and leave a quantity of aromatics they believed equal. If the amount was deemed sufficient the aromatics were taken and the imported products left behind, if not, they would wait a further night to see if more goods were forthcoming in exchange.[3] Through works like the *Nuzhat al-Qulūb,* readers in the Persianate world could experience the challenges global trades presented to traders, and perhaps gain a better understanding of the challenges implicit in so much cross-cultural exchange.

The inhabitants of Bartayil were not the only people who were reported to undertake silent trading practices: such traditions can be traced as far back

DOI: 10.4324/9781003052890-6

as Herodotus, who recounted a "silent trade" between Carthaginian merchants and traders on the Northwest African coast.[4] Likewise, according to the Arabic writer, Ibrāhīm Ibn Wasīf Shāh, spices were purchased through a similar process on the edges of the Valley of Cloves, where they were sold by genies resident on the island.[5] Abu Rayhan al-Biruni, another Persian author, maintained that trade in "a country called Laṅga" followed the same pattern. Here, "merchandise is placed beside the sea on leather mats marked with the owners name" and left. The "next day they find cloves on the mats as payment".[6] The Chinese historian Zhao Rukuo's *Zhu Fan Zhi*, a geographical description of the world and catalogue of trade goods, presented a similar account where "in the Western Sea there is a market where a silent agreement exists between buyer and seller ... the seller first spreads out his goods; afterwards the purchaser spreads out the equivalent, which must lie by the side of the articles for sale till taken by seller, when the objects purchased may be carried off".[7] Ibn Battuta, the fourteenth-century Arab traveler, described a similar practice by traders on the Volga River, where "skins of sable, miniver, and ermine" were obtained by leaving goods on the river's banks.[8] While in West Africa, similar accounts were passed by Arab traders to European travelers to the region. The Venetian traveler Alvise da Cadamosto, for instance, recounted how he had received "information from many merchants, Arab as well as Sanhaja, and also from persons in whom faith can be placed" about how gold was obtained from the lands south of Timbuktu. Travelling south, Arab merchants piled salt, mined further north at Taghaza, on the banks of a river before withdrawing, allowing local traders to leave gold in return. The barter continued until an acceptable exchange was agreed and "in this way, by long and ancient custom, they carry on their trade without seeing or speaking to each other".[9]

Descriptions of silent trade like these may identify common tropes adopted by authors across the world, represent archetypes used to comprehend the unknown, or even represent accurate descriptions of commercial encounters. Perhaps what is most useful about them, however, is what they reveal about their authors' understanding of the world. In each case, trade on the edges of their known worlds necessitated an interaction that broke the usual rules and practices.[10] On the frontiers of the familiar, doing business meant losing the social and cultural baggage that underpinned trade in more familiar markets.

Most of the time, though, traders could be confident in whom they were doing business with and that the profits from carrying commodities here and there for sale would more than make up for the risk and cost of travel. In an odd etymological twist, the word "trade" originates from the Old Saxon "trada", meaning "to tread", from which in Middle Low German came to mean path or track. Eventually this evolved through a series of steps to signify exchange, and particularly the exchange of commodities.[11] Long-distance trade was not only defined by or valued because of its geographical reach; matters of value and quantity were important considerations. Transporting goods over distance needed at least some assurances of safety, reliability, and predictability, and the market to which these goods were headed must have exhibited some degree of stability and permanency. Merchants had to have a reasonable presumption that there was a demand for what they were bringing and that they could make a profit from their efforts and the risks they were taking. The price differential between where a commodity originated and where it ended up must have at least matched the original cost of that commodity, plus transportation, handling, and other expenses in addition to expected profit.

The were never any guarantees. For merchants who were careless, injudicious, or just unlucky, sometimes the system did not operate in their favor. To help address this, a crucial step for participants in a system was to cultivate a set of trading partners with whom they were connected through a system of communications. Trade was not a one-off occasion, but a structured process sustained by various types of intermediaries, including transporters and other support personnel. It was essential for merchants to be able to undertake business in overseas markets that lay within and without the familiar confines of their home markets. In these many of these spaces, frequent interaction and the prevalence of common legal norms and customary practices across different national and cultural boundaries helped create some form of what's been called *lex mercatoria* – the law merchant.[12] Where this happened, the shared behaviors of all merchants – in spite of linguistic, religious, and legal different – facilitated the efficient and secure operation of trade.

Traders or merchants were commercial specialists. They were the link between the producers of something and the consumers of that something. They served as the agents of exchange. Within this occupational group there was tremendous gradation beginning at the bottom with hawkers who sold their goods out of sacks and peddlers who used wagons and carts. In villages small scale merchants collected peasant surpluses while in more urban areas, retailers rented stalls or, if they were more fortunate, owned their own shops. In some regions, particularly in Southeast Asia, West Africa, and parts of the eastern Mediterranean, women often controlled the retail market. Far above, at the pinnacle of this occupational group, were the merchant bankers and wholesale operators who owned ships and warehouses. Among the most notable of these were the Persian Gulf merchants who operated the maritime trade with China through the port of Guangzhou and became immortalized for their proverbial wealth.

In many of the most active commercial sectors, the mercantile classes at all levels were often professionalized as trade became more regular. Nevertheless, individuals who were engaged principally in other occupations but who were able to engage in trade on the side or part-time often played an important commercial role. This ranged from artisans and craftsmen who sold their products directly to the public to nomadic pastoralists on the Eurasian steppes who picked up and exchanged items during their annual cycles to pilgrims on their way to and back from Islamic, Christian, and Buddhist holy sites. On a more elevated level, diplomats and other government officials who traveled to foreign courts to represent the geopolitical and dynastic interests of their states and rulers often used the opportunity to do some private wheeling and dealing. Finally, the rulers themselves sent each other "gifts" that, in effect, amounted to high level trade in luxury items. Added to these were the collateral and support groups of agents, brokers, professional shippers, guides, translators, and caravaneers. Mercantile groups can be categorized in ways other than just full- or part-time. Full-timers could be itinerant or resident; they could deal only in specific items like silk or woolen textiles, incense or wine, or gems or grain designed for specific markets; or they could constitute what has been called a "traveling bazaar", picking up whatever was cheap in one place and selling whatever was dear in another, a practice at sea known as tramping. They could deal in local, regional, inter-regional, or long-distance trade in luxury or bulk commodities according to weight, value, and distance.

The classic analysis of commercial "institutions" (that is, the rules and practices that underpinned trade and other economic activities) presupposes that, "the development of long-distance trade, perhaps through caravans or lengthy ship voyages, requires a sharp break in the characteristics of an economic structure". Long-distance trade required something different to more familiar and local types of exchange. This literature that global trade developed through "largely a story of institutional evolution" driven, in a large part, by state-backed initiatives.[13] However, this interpretation has been challenged by more recent scholarship. Not only does it too often sideline the role of diasporic trading communities, which are now understood as essential parts of the premodern trading system, but it also unevenly distributes the facility to trade towards the transporters of goods like ship owners or caravan masters. In sites of production and distribution of goods for the global market – whether gold mining regions in West Africa, ceramic manufactories in China, or silk producers in Persia – local economic cultures retained great influence over how goods were traded throughout.[14] Institutional evolution on the part of states was all well and good, but the support of your monarch at home meant often meant little if your factors are unable to do business thousands of miles away where their power meant little.

From this perspective, it is not surprising that traders found such fruitful opportunities in the spaces lying between "formal institutions" of premodern states. Indeed, "jurisdictional conflicts were ubiquitous" in the premodern world, and would remain so even in places where imperial powers sought to establish control over trade, like on China's steppe frontier or in the Indian Ocean.[15] Merchants operating in cross-cultural marketplaces could not depend on presumed customary norms that they carried with them as a stable foundation for their business affairs. To make trade work, merchants had to establish relationships with new trading partners, either as customers and suppliers or as full-fledged trading partners. In these conditions, commercial actors' pre-existing expectations of commercial culture were not always a useful starting point when engaging with potential trading partners with their own established outlook on the conduct of trade. Akan merchants in West Africa simultaneously adapted to Arabic and Portuguese commercial engagement by altering the region's agricultural and salt-production output, the physical spaces of local markets, and the process by which deals were struck.[16] In turn, the Portuguese and Arab traders were expected to alter their own behavior to operate within this environment.[17] In local contexts like these, where traders from cross-cultural backgrounds interacted, new forms of commercial practice emerged in response to long-distance trading intersections. Trade, then, often needed premodern merchants who "worked across geopolitical, linguistic, and religious boundaries", as well as different economic cultures, customs and jurisdictions.[18] Understanding premodern long-distance trade requires doing "global history on a small scale" that "responds to the desire to understand the inner workings of cross-cultural trade as well as the structural relations of political and economic power within which it took place".[19] In places of exchange, whether in a port, an oasis, or a well regulated market, trade in the premodern world was undertaken by people whose lives and experiences were shaped by the local conditions of places they traveled and the people they met. Their lives and the trade routes that they navigated were precarious and they adopted strategies intended to make them safer.

A common premodern solution to this challenge was the trade diaspora, where members of the same commercial community – typical tied by familial, religious, and cultural links – would live in different locations across a trading system, working with and for each other as agents. Merchants were commonly operating as "trans-imperial subjects", "men and women who straddled and brokered political, linguistic, and religious boundaries between" different imperial and cultural regimes, and this reliable community of partners could be the difference between poverty and profit.[20] Trade diasporas go far back in history, the most noted in the ancient period being the Old Assyrian-Cappadocian system of the early second millennium BCE. During the period under study, diasporas extended across the settled world.[21] Often, as in Guangzhou, local host communities designated certain quarters as compounds for resident foreign merchants, most of whom were sojourners.[22] They served as intermediaries and agents for arriving merchants belonging to the same socio-ethnic or religious community. Elsewhere in Asia, Gujarati merchants, for instance, were long accustomed to operating in contested imperial spaces, while in Africa, Wangara traders facilitated exchange across an array of different cultural, religious and linguistic regions.[23] Diaspora communities like these were often granted some degree of autonomy, and their leaders were charged with facilitating relations with the host community. The arrangement was intended to guarantee security and predictability, and thus promote efficiency.

In these circumstances, the strength and success of any particular merchant community depended on all of its members, and groups that had means of internally regulating the trustworthiness of members were more often more successful than those without. When this worked well, the effect was spectacular, and "trade diasporas remained the most efficient way of organizing commerce across much of Afro-Eurasia until the nineteenth century".[24] This was, in part, because "trust was an essential component of early modern long-distance trade".[25] Yet, this essential component for merchant communities to operate effectively was not guaranteed – trust was generated through communal forms of governance and reciprocal behaviors.[26] Rather than seeing trust as a natural by-product of diasporas forming "closely knit communities", historians should instead interrogate how "communities of mercantile trust" were carefully formulated and maintained.[27] Trust in historical communities was not an inevitable consequence of familial, national, or religious ties, and the formation of stable international networks "developed where channels of communication were numerous enough to permit the diffusion of information about a merchant's conduct and the enforcement of collective boycotts against those who proved untrustworthy".[28] Because of the great distances and travel time involved, global trade was undertaken in circumstances where "the *quid* was separated from the *quo* over time and space".[29] Concepts like "social capital", "creditability", or "communal governance" help frame the institutions generated within these communities, and through them it becomes clear how global trade depended on merchant networks developing and maintaining economic cultures that both strengthened internal ties and remaining externally adaptive. For many merchant networks in the early modern world, spreading outward to enter new markets, encounter new peoples, and establish new trades was an essential part of business. Those who succeeded were commercial communities whose economic cultures and institutional frameworks were most suitable to adapting to changing conditions as they crossed imperial and jurisdictional boundaries.

Many of these practices can be traced in Egypt, which functioned as something of a crossroads for Eurasian trade in the early centuries of the second millennium CE. The inception of Fatimid rule in 914 CE led to growing connections between Egypt and the Indian Ocean World, with the capital at Fustat the "initiator of international trade".[30] These links were sustained despite the region changing dynastic hands multiple times, first with the ascension of the Ayyubid dynasty (1171–1260) and then the Mamluk Bahrite dynasty (1260–1382). After a long period of relative decline, Egypt was increasingly prosperous following reforms that restored agricultural production around the Nile as well as supporting existing industries producing sugar, paper, glass, and textiles that were sought after exports. Fatimid rule also left a lasting legacy on the commercial landscape, having signed treaties with the Byzantine Empire that secured Egyptian control in the eastern Mediterranean, efforts were made to impose their control in the Red Sea, as part of efforts to wrest command of trade with India away from the rival Abbasid state in Bagdad. Fatimid governors and the state at large made considerable investments in these activities, owning fleets of trading vessels and shops that were "among the largest capitalistic undertakings of their time".[31]

Around 1052, the *matjar,* or Trade Office, was founded, managing a state monopoly on silk, olive oil, lead, and other products, through which it controlled prices and oversaw trade with foreign merchants for these commodities.[32] However, while the *matjar* served the interests of the state, it's management was not monopolised by members of the Fatimid dynasty or a local Islamic elite. Local merchants, too, were able to obtain influential positions within the organisation, up to and including the leading position of vizier. Merchants also took a key role in collecting taxes. Vitally, the role of *wakīl al-tujjār* was created to serve as a representative for foreign merchants in each city, who took on responsibilities that included reimbursing debts, storing merchandise, and overseeing the purchase and sale of goods. As an arbitrator between merchants, the *wakīl al-tujjār* was an important mediator in the cross-cultural trade that was common in Egypt.[33]

Under the Fatimids, Jewish merchants were particularly prominent in trades that bridged the Mediterranean and Indian Ocean, and oversaw the movement of trade goods that linked sites as far flung as East Africa, India, and Russia. In twelfth-century Aden, Madmūn ben Hasan served as an intermediary between merchants operating across the two regions, and was recognised as "leader of the Jewish community of the Indian Ocean" by both the Jewish Exilarch of Baghdad, then under Seljukid rule, and by the chief of the Jewish community in Egypt. Among his correspondents were the Tunisian Jewish merchant Abraham ben Yijū, who had settled on the Malabar Coast between 1132 and 1149, where he served as Madmūn's agent as well as running a metallurgical workshop that used copper and tin he imported from Aden. Another member of the same network, Makhlūf ben Mūsā, operated between Spain and India.[34]

The activities of this mercantile network were not just geographical expansive, they were also complex and underpinned with clear institutional structures designed to facilitate trade. Transactions were conducted through partnerships, in which each party was responsible for a particular locality and the particular commodity exchanges that passed through it. In practice, this meant that the Jewish merchant Isḥāq b. Makhlūf could send goods to Aden for storage in Madmūn ben Hasan's warehouse to wait for favorable prices, while Abraham ben Yijū had an Indian servant who served as his agent in Aden. The "interfaith character of some networks or enterprises was remarkable". Madmūn partnered with Yemeni Bilāl ben Jarīr, the commander of the troops of the sultan of Aden, who together owned a ship that sailed between Aden and Sri Lanka. Other business relationships included a Nestorian Christian and numerous Muslims, and he described people bearing Hindu names as "brothers and friends". To strengthen them further, partnerships sometimes overlapped with familial ties. Madmūn was linked to the representative of Cairo's merchants, Abū Zikrī Kohen Judah, who was married to his cousin. As well as representing his community, Abū Zikrī Kohen

Judah also had his own trading interests between India, where he stayed for long periods, and Morocco.[35]

The Ayyūbids dynasty altered these dynamics somewhat in favor of Muslim merchants, the *kārimī*, who came to dominate Indian Ocean trade through their influence in Yemen and Gujarat. The *kārimī* included traders already active in the Egypt-Yemen trade, as well as new arrivals, such as Sunni merchants from Iraq who had migrated when Saladin took power in Egypt.

However, the *kārimī* did not hold a monopoly over trade, and safe passage was offered to any merchant traveling in the same region, irrespective of whether they were carrying "spices or other goods that the merchants of the Kārim usually import".[36]

Premodern commercial networks like these could be expansive, effective, and contributed to the transportation and exchange of large quantities of luxury and non-luxury goods across the world. Networks like that of the Jewish community in Aden were only part of overlapping networks that, in this geographical space, also included parallel networks of Indian and Hindu merchants, whose interests intersected with each other in certain spaces while also spreading beyond them into different hinterlands. This meant that traders operating in major markets like Aden and others were never far from merchants with interests across Afro-Eurasia. In Aden, merchants were linked as far as China to the east, and into Spain, Morocco, and the trans-Saharan trade to the west.

Merchants taking part in long-distance trade in the premodern world conducted their business in places that might be less well known to themselves, but were usually already home to an array of economic cultures and possessing their own laws, customs, and behaviors. Through merchants, goods ranging from Akan gold to Japanese silver, Indian cottons, Chinese ceramics, Venetian glassware and Indonesian spices were traded across common networks of exchange that crisscrossed the globe. This trade did not run through sites of perfectly balanced exchange, where price alone drove decisions. Commerce in the early modern world instead took place in spaces where the processes of exchange were contested. Personal relationships, communal governance, local institutions, and international politics were all at play and influenced how, where, what, and with whom people could do business. Rather than "instantaneous transaction between two strangers", global, cross-cultural trade depended on "prolonged credit relations and business cooperation between merchants who shared implicit and explicit agreements about the rules of exchange".[37] New-entrants to established markets sought to integrate global commercial practices with established and locally recognized "rules of recognition".[38] This meant that to undertake commercial activities, traders depended on cultural and social intuitions, in one form or other, to provide structure for the practice of exchange. The practice of trade in contested spaces created hybridized commercial cultures wherein economic actors' behaviors were influenced through their participation in cross-cultural exchange rather than being imposed by powerful states or empires.[39]

Routes and Systems

The reports of silent trade described at the start of the chapter joined places like Timbuktu (when presented as a mythical city of gold), "Ultima Thule", "Hyperborea", the "Land of Darkness", and the "Land of Gog and Magog" to become as much a metaphor for the global interactions than real places. They represented a means to bundle together the snippets of information about distant lands and repackage them as conceptualizing systems that imposed some structure over what would be a chaos of disjointed facts.[40]

In a similar vein, the "Silk Roads" is a modern scholarly construct that does represent reality on a certain level as it was a thousand or two thousand years ago, even if it smooths out some of the complexities that shaped all ancient and medieval trade systems. In a rough sort of way, caravans laden with trade goods did traverse the particular space now recognized as the Silk Roads as well as other similar trade routes. Aside from an occasional river valley and some lush pastureland, much of the Silk Roads ran across wasteland: deserts in the lowlands broken in the middle by frigid heights, not a part of the world that would attract a lot of attention except that it lay between large clumps of humanity at both ends. In the best of times, the Silk Roads was the way people, goods, ideas, religions, and technologies traveled between east and west across Eurasia. In the broadest sense of the word, it can be thought of as a system, hence the plural "Roads", parts of which reached back into the second millennium BCE but most of which did not survive into the late second millennium CE. Its halcyon days came at the very end of the first millennium BCE and lasted with much waxing and waning through the first millennium CE, although an argument can be made that its peak came later under the Mongol Empire. The Mongol Empire, however, lasted only a short time and was essentially a military and political entity that commerce piggybacked on. For the Silk Roads trading system, the period of the Mongol Empire is best thought of as a last gasping hurrah.

Different systems have been assigned their own names usually according to their most important or noted commodity except in a few instances when geography was the prevailing feature as in the Trans-Saharan or Steppe Roads systems. The term "Silk Roads" should not imply that the whole system was built on the trade of one commodity. Silk was indeed a major trade commodity that, for a while, had only one source, China, with an insatiable demand for it elsewhere as a glamor product and status symbol. Other luxuries also headed to and from China, including gems, furs, and precious metal objects, as did more mundane products like glass items, medicines, aromatics, leather goods, cotton textiles, ceramics, paper, comestibles, carpets, and horses. Nor were all trade goods intended to make the whole trip. Virtually all the mundane and many of the luxuries could be traded off along the way in the cities of the Tarim Basin, Central Asia, and Persia or sent over connector roads to India in the south and the steppes and forest lands in the north. Rather than a single, clear pathway across Eurasia, the Silk Roads were a bundle of intersecting networks.

The people who resided along a particular road likely knew only that they were living along the way to whatever the next major city or notable place happened to be. Their economic lives were defined by their own local systems, even as these fed into larger webs of exchange that took place at regional or even global scales. In Iranian and Central Asian areas, cities and whole regions were often just referred to by the name of their major river. Merchants and other travelers were avid in assigning their own names to geographical and human features. These could be colorful, descriptive, or sometimes foreboding as in the Mountain of Hell or the Poisonous Mountain (both in Tibet). The Tooth Breaker Pass (in Afghanistan between Zuhak and Balkh) was not intended to be inviting while the Pass of the Ass (Hindu Kush, Afghanistan) was somewhat less intimidating provided travelers had the right animals. Castle of the Wind (Northeast Iran near Nishapur) evoked an aura of mystery while there were at least three major Iron Gates (one between Samarkand and Balkh, another on the Danube, and the third on the northeast corner of the Tarim Basin near the oasis of Korla). On a less somber note was the town of Happy on the Volga River along with more neutral sounding urban centers including Black Town (on the Yulduz near Turfan), Brown City (Ujjain in west central India), Fire City (south of the Tian Shan Mountains on the eastern border of China), several Towns of the Grape, a Town of the Jujube (in Quhistan), and a City of Pots (in Burma). On the road between Baghdad and Mecca was the Pool of the Stoned One.

Roads were not named to express their economic role. The Romans named the roads they built starting with the Via Appian in 312 BCE, later using their emperors' names as in the Via Augusta. Important roads that tied together great empires were usually referred to by grandiose titles such as the Royal Road and the Imperial Highway, going back to the time of the Assyrians and continuing to be prominent in Persia and India. The Chinese version ran from the city of Chang'an (now Xian), capital under the Han and Tang and various other dynasties in between, across the westernmost province of Gansu to the Yumen Guan, better known as the Jade Gate Frontier Post about fifty miles (80 kilometers) northwest of Dunhuang ("Blazing Beacon"). It was erected by the Han emperor Wudi around 121 BCE, and together with its companion to the south, the Yang Barrier in the Nanhu oasis, marked the end of official China and the beginning of the "Western Regions".[41] Caravans were required to pass through one of these frontier gates that concluded a defensive line. When the Han extended Chinese control far into Central Asia, the road was extended to Kashgar and was referred to as the Road South of the Tian Shan (Celestial Mountains).[42] Eventually, however, trade routes shifted to the north, and the Jade Gate and Yang Barrier fell into disuse in the sixth and seventh centuries CE. The frontier was adjusted later under the Ming, who built the Great Wall and its western terminus, the magnificent fort at Jiayuguan ("Barrier of the Pleasant Valley"). This seems to show that when the Chinese, Romans, or anyone else had a reasonably good idea as to where a road went, generally because they built it themselves, they could refer to it by a specific name. But the idea that a merchant beginning a journey in Chang'an or Samarkand thought he was traveling on the great Silk Roads was an idea whose time had not come. For merchants travelling from South Asia to Samarkand, the notion would simply not make sense at all.

When it was fully functioning, there is no question that the Silk Roads comprised the longest overland commercial network in history.[43] It is often put at roughly five thousand miles long, but this comes with many *ifs*, *ands*, and *buts*. First, where did it begin, and where did it end? On the eastern side, the beginning or end of the Silk Roads was China and more specifically the great city of Chang'an. The western side was less firmly set. At times it was certain cities, most often ports that connected into maritime systems on the eastern rim of the Mediterranean or the Black seas. At other times it did not make it that far, and the terminus would have been somewhere in the Persian Empire or its successor, the Islamic Caliphate. Early in the system's history, Silk Roads traffic didn't even make it to Persia but rather turned left in Central Asia and ended up in northwestern India, where it could connect into the Arabian Sea-Indian Ocean maritime system.[44] Hedin used Xian and the ancient Phoenician port of Tyre as his termini, from which he concluded that the length was six thousand miles "as the crow flies and including bends".[45] In any case, to get from one side to the other, traffic had to flow through one great corridor, Central Asia. In ancient times, Central Asia was on the periphery, a buffer zone separating the urbanized and settled lands of civilization lying to the east, west, and south from the grazing lands of roaming nomads. As long-distance commerce developed and the various settled lands began shooting feelers toward each other, they did so via Central Asia, which went from being a frontier to a heartland.

Rather than a single route or road, then, it can be more useful to understand premodern trade, both local and regional, but also at larger scales that might be understood as global trade, as webs of intersecting networks. What mattered more was that goods could be carried across boundaries, rather than necessarily that they traveled down the same road or route. Merchants traded along paths that were made up of connections of marked and unmarked paths, trails, and occasionally actual roads. At the least, as in some of the Trans-Saharan routes, they made up little more than a general line of travel. Old trade routes often followed the annual movements originally set down by nomadic pastoralists. Routes were partially determined by geographical factors such as topography, the location of watering spots, and the availability of pasture. Routes often did not run in straight lines, and longer, even circuitous routes were preferred if they were more secure or avoided difficult mountains, deserts, or the payment of prohibitive protection costs.

River valleys provided natural corridors. Traversing mountainous regions such as the great Pamir Knot that crossed Eurasia depended on passes often grouped together in their own complex of systems. The presence of facilities, in particular caravansaries and storage depots as well as places to buy supplies and seek shelter, when necessary, was a critical factor. At sea, of course, the path becomes more nebulous still, with sites along the way denoting the direction of travel rather than being points that a traveler would pass over. The route was defined by the starting point, stopping points along the way, and of course the final destination. When considering the longest-distance trade in the premodern world, it was not likely that a commodity would travel the whole distance with a single merchant or on a single ship: it certainly would travel beyond the limit of any single road.

Major trading systems were organized to take advantage of roads, ports and other facilities through which chains of relays could pass and where exchanges were made. The backbones of such systems were trunk lines into which smaller systems fed. Connectors and occasionally even trunk lines could materialize, disappear, or shift due to climatic, hydrological, geopolitical, and other considerations. Routes connected specific points, usually cities where merchants clustered, that served as trade nexuses. Upon arriving at a city, a merchant could catch another caravan to travel farther on to where there was a particular demand for a commodity he was carrying, but eventually he would sell his goods, buy other goods, and return to his home base. Stretches of river were often integrated into cross country systems, and land systems often connected into maritime systems at ports.

Up until the time of the Mongol Empire, virtually everyone who ventured on what is now considered to be the Silk Roads traveled on only some particular part of it that went to where they intended to do business. When that was accomplished, they turned around and went back. This was also the case for all the other so-called "Roads" that have been used describe wider systems that shaped the premodern trading world. Small traders using parts of long-distance networks to engage in what would be thought of as regional or even short-term commercial ventures represented the huge majority of cargoes being moved. The weight-to-distance ratio ensured that only the most valuable commodities made it very far. One source of confusion is in using the word "Road", another great convenience but one, if taken literally, that can be very misleading. Over time modern scholars studying long distance trade would discern or invent other Roads, among the most reputed being the Incense and Spice Roads, several versions of the Fur Road, the Bamboo and Steppe Roads, and earlier more shrouded constructs like the Lapis Lazuli (sometimes called a "Route") and the Amber (sometimes labelled a "Trail"). But the Silk Roads and its like were not roads. They were complex networks of routes, in a sense supersystems directed across specific landscapes integrating a multitude of many smaller systems that were mostly used by locals. Trade moved through their channels, joining settlements large and small in the commercial transport of cargo. They served as the connection between production and distribution. They were the means by which trade negotiated distance; networks were composed of links used as commercial circuits. A typical large network would handle an enormous variety of commodities ranging from the bulkiest of cheap goods like grains, common textiles, wood, and base metal products to the most luxurious of textiles, exotic spices and aromatics, gems, and precious metal objects. But networks also had their own inventory that included a few products considered to be their specialties, the most special of which often accounts for their modern names.

The routes taken by traders were not uniform, and, for the most part, they were not linear; they meandered, zigzagged, and even crisscrossed. A system could be made up of a series of parallel roads. There were instances of two roads leaving from the same place and headed for the same destination but going different ways and having no lateral contact with each other. Sometimes they were little more than patchworks of pathways, some more beaten than others, mountain passes that often became series of passes, and at worst in some desert places, little more than directions signaled by landmarks. They tied together cities, oases, wells, mines, camps, and anything else that for commercial purposes was worth going to. Networks were intended to reach from one central place to another, the ends determined by population clusters and the presence of markets. They also plugged into the hinterlands they crossed, loading and offloading cargo as they went. In favored places that were more settled and commercially developed, parts of networks could be composed of actual roads intentionally constructed by current or long forgotten governments. Merchants who traveled over them were always taxed and sometimes otherwise harassed in various ways by the authorities, but even when countries were at war with each other, some arrangement, formal or informal, was usually worked out for those who were engaged in legitimate commerce. Nevertheless, on long distance trade routes in general, human boundaries were as much of a challenge as geographical and climatic factors, and systems that flowed across multiple cultural and ethnic borders could be very fragile. Fortunately, while conditions in one place or another may have appeared troublesome or even chaotic, most of the time they represented transient political and economic situations. Commerce was adaptable; merchants could always move.

Long distance networks came in shapes reflecting the merging and patching processes that brought them together. Larger systems absorbed smaller systems that usually kept some elements of their own special nature or function. The shape that a large network took centered on the role its backbone or spine played. The simplest model has a distant backbone often referred to as the trunk line, for which other roads served as auxiliaries in the form of feeders, branches, and connectors. A system that had many feeders is sometimes referred to as a capillary system. All but the most local stretches between minor villages served some feeder, branch, or connector function giving access to the outside. As one insightful Chinese observer noted: "There are also roads running from each country which intersect in turn in the south and in the north. By following [these roads] it is possible to reach any point."[46] Often branch and connector routes were older than the trunk lines they came to serve. As early as 1935, Herrmann's atlas made an attempt at examining the numerous branches of the Silk Roads, where supplemental roads intersected trunk roads, commercial nodes or hubs often materialized in the form of trade centers that became cities.[47]

Backbones often split into sections that in themselves qualified as backbones, making the model somewhat more complicated. For example, from the great commercial hub of Merv, an entryway into Central Asia from the west, the main Silk Roads split, one part going north into the land of the Türks, the other toward Tukharistan and the city of Balkh (Afghanistan) on the way to India.[48] Nor were such splits always dramatic. Along the great routes, portions of caravans would veer off to head toward another city or a place where they knew water or pasturage was available or even to a relatively minor market town if it was noted for producing some special product ranging from knives to melons. The main arteries of a system like the Silk Roads flowed into and out of such cities as Samarkand, Bukhara, Balkh, Merv, Herat, Nishapur, and Kashgar, where travelers could change directions and pick up a different section of the network or take a connector route into a different system.

Out of the cities, roads separated to go in several directions, then split again; side roads could split off main roads, then rejoined the main road later. Great rivers often intersected transcontinental latitudinal routes, creating short cuts as, for example, in the western section of the Steppe Road, which ran from the Black Sea across the Dnieper, Donets, Don, and Volga rivers to above the Caspian Sea and into Central Asia. Major trading systems often crossed parallel bands of ecotones, transition areas between adjacent ecological zones or even whole ecozones as between desert and steppe, steppe and river valley, river valley and forest, or any of the above and mountain regions. Different environments offered different products. Entrepots tended to be established at ecotones, where often transportation modes changed, as in camels for donkeys and oxen or, in some places, donkeys for human porterage. Although it was at one of the far ends of the great Afro-Eurasian land mass, sub-Saharan West Africa, for example, was a great place to trade since parallel bands of ecozones and ecotones were compressed within the fairly short distance that lay from the edge of the Sahara to the Guinea coast, allowing for the exchange of a wide variety of raw materials and products.

Case Study: The Trans-Saharan Route

The Trans-Saharan route in West Africa is a useful case study for assessing how multiple economic systems could be linked through a long-distance trading exchange that was brought about through multiple intersecting networks and points of exchange. Rather than a single road, the route consisted of parallel roads with shapes more like candelabra or webs than shafts. One or another of the passages could play the role of principal artery, but this fluctuated according to conditions and was not likely to have the resilience, stability, or amount of traffic to become a permanent trunk road. By one count, for example, the Trans-Saharan had a half dozen main roads but with only two or three being active at any one time. Long-distance commercial systems almost always had designated beginnings and ends. The ends often connected with the beginnings of other systems since it would be rare that all the goods arriving at the end of a particular system would be consumed there. They might fade into capillary systems, which eventually trickled down to a point of consumption. But to keep some structure to the whole concept of a commercial system and how such systems worked, there should be locations, however broadly or narrowly defined, that could be declared as anchoring one side and the other. For the Trans-Saharan system trade in the north started in cities of the Maghrib (literally "the West", the term used in central and eastern Arab lands to refer to the habitable portions of North Africa beyond Egypt), collectively referred to as the "northern termini". The capital that fueled Trans-Saharan trade tended to be concentrated more at the northern than the southern end, and many large-scale merchants along with those who bankrolled them lived in places like Fez, Marrakesh, Temen, Tunis, and Tripoli.

Fez was located about one hundred fifty miles from both the Mediterranean and the Atlantic. Well situated on the east-west trade route that connected Egypt and al-Andalus (Muslim Spain) in the heart of a productive agricultural region, Fez alternated with its great rival to the south, Marrakesh, as the capital of Morocco, and often each was the capital of its own independent state. Marrakesh had been founded to take the surplus population of an older trade center at Aghmat with the intention of serving as a fortress. Two local tribes ended up squabbling over the location, each insisting the town be built on its territory and given its name. Finally, the shaykhs of a larger, more powerful tribe imposed a compromise. They found, according to the city's historian Ibn Idhari (*c.*1312): "a desert place with no living thing except gazelles and ostriches and nothing growing except lotus trees and colocynths".[49] Marrakesh turned out to be not as unattractive as Ibn Idhari's description may imply, and it was located in a strategic spot close to the point where the High Atlas Mountains, the Sahara, and the Maghrib all came together.

They became the capital of two succeeding empires, but neither Fez nor Marrakesh was a port. On the Mediterranean, the city of Tangier was, and it was much older than either, its origins going back to Punic times. But Tangier was always more Mediterranean than Moroccan, its access to the hinterland interrupted by rough topography. It proved to be a better gateway to Spain than to Morocco, leave aside the Sahara. Moving eastward across what today comprises the state of Algeria, only occasionally did this land constitute a separate political entity before the sixteenth century. Its greatest city, Tlemcen, went back to Roman times when it was a military settlement, but Tlemcen was also not a port. By the tenth century it was a bustling center for merchants not just as a northern terminus for the Trans-Saharan but also for east-west trade.

Unlike the great northern termini on the western side of the Maghrib, Tripoli and Tunis were major ports. Tripoli was another ancient Punic city, but unlike Tangier it had been trading with the Sahara since Carthaginian times, at first in a trickle trade and later more directional, reaching into the major oases of the desert, particularly the Fezzan, and involving among other items a mysterious gem called the "carbuncle".[50] Over the centuries the desert slowly gobbled up Tripoli's hinterland, leaving little productive area from which to draw locally made goods, unlike Fez and Marrakesh. Tripoli served as a door into and out of Africa, bringing in imports from Egypt, the Mediterranean, and Europe, and sending out exports from Central and West Africa. Tunis was a much younger place. Invading Arabs founded Tunis across the bay from Carthage, the latter being too Roman and too Christian to suit them. The Romans had referred to the territory around Carthage as "Africa", so to the Arabs this became Ifriqiya. Tunis inherited the Mediterranean connections of Carthage and important inland contacts once Islam began to penetrate the Sahara. In the centuries following the Arab conquest, Ifriqiya was the center of Arab maritime power in the Mediterranean, and Tunis flourished.

From Marrakesh to Tripoli cities did not depend on Trans-Saharan trade in the manner of their counterparts farther south on the desert edge. In northern termini cities the Trans-Saharan system was an important pillar of the economy, but it was not the whole foundation. Their commercial contacts extended in all directions not just south into the desert; to them the Trans-Saharan was different only in its high risk, high return character. Trans-Saharan trade was so risky merchants tended to cooperate rather than compete: if they were successful, plenty of profit could be made all around. As a result, no monopoly ever developed. Ibn Khaldun (1332–1406), the North African polymath and sometimes statesman, offers a lesson in economics, which he sums up by advising his readers to buy cheap and sell dear. He uses Trans-Saharan trade as his example:

> Therefore the merchants who dare to enter the Sudan country are the most prosperous and wealthy of all people. The distance and the difficulty of the road they travel are great. They have to cross a difficult desert which is made almost inaccessible by fear and beset by thirst. Therefore the goods of the Sudan country are found only in small quantities among us, and they are particularly expensive. The same applies to our goods among them.[51]

Some of the big dealers had their home offices in the northern termini cities, and the most successful became very rich. In the mid-thirteenth century five brothers of a merchant family from Tlemcen named Maqqari established a

Trans-Saharan network with two staying in Tlemcen, two moving to Walata, (a city on the other side of the Sahara northwest of Timbuktu), and one setting up in the city of Sijilmasa. All the brothers married local women and had sons and grandsons who branched out. They became sinews in the trade between Egypt, the Maghrib, and the Western Sudan, establishing routes, digging wells, collecting commercial information, organizing caravans, and providing security for other merchants. The family dabbled in politics, ingratiating itself with local rulers: "When they had gained the confidence of the kings, the earth became submissive to their travelling upon it. Their wealth knew no bounds and became more than could be counted."[52] Nevertheless, despite the great profits that were made in the early years of the Trans-Saharan, commerce remained a matter of family firms that did not evolve into large-scale enterprises. As for the Maqqari family, after several generations through misfortune and mismanagement their business frittered away.

Goods and people from the northern termini cities made their way south to gather at what has come to be known variously as the "staging posts", "break-of-bulk points", or "rendezvous points", usually the major city of an oasis on the northern rim of the desert. Most of these had been founded between the mid-eighth and the mid-eleventh centuries although a few, like Ghadames (border of Tunisia, Algeria, and Libya) and Ghat (Libya) went back into the classical period. Sijilmasa, in the oasis of Tafilelt, was for a time the most important and best known because it was associated with the gold trade of Ghana and Mali. The Syrian-Egyptian geographer Ibn Fadl Allāh al-Umari (1301–49) called it "one of the biggest cities of the West and most celebrated in the world. It stands on a big river and is possessed of imposing palaces, high buildings, and tall gates".[53] Sijilmasa's size was surpassed only by its wealth. The peripatetic geographer Ibn Hawqal (wr. 988), who visited the town between 947 and 951 CE, reported that merchants from Iraq had settled there, bringing their business acumen:

> They, their children, and their trade flourish, their light caravans are constantly on the move and their heavy caravans are incessant to obtain enormous profits, fat gains, and abundant benefits. Merchants in the countries of Islam seldom approach them in affluence. I have seen a promissory note written concerning a debt owned by Muhammad b. Abī Sa'dūn in Awdaghust, and witnessed by assessors, for 42,000 dinars ... I have never seen or heard anything comparable to this story in the East [meaning the Islamic heartland].[54]

On the eastern side of the Maghrib, towns in two large oases, the Fezzan and Ouargla, served as staging posts for Tripoli and Tunis. Both were inhabited by merchants belonging to a dissident sect of Islam, the Ibadiyya, who had become rich from the gold and slave trades. Ouargla was heavily irrigated and capable of producing tons of excellent quality dates, the mainstay of man and beast headed into the desert.[55]

Staging posts were huge entrepots in and out of which enormous amounts of goods poured. Caravans assembled there: provisions were obtained, water bags filled, food loaded, camels rented or purchased, and drivers, guards, and guides secured. Partnerships and other legal arrangements were made based on Islamic law, and credit was available when needed. Both large and small traders were welcomed, the petty merchants attaching themselves to caravans organized by the big dealers. Staging posts were also important as listening stations, places for merchants to gather intelligence as to which products were selling high or low, which routes were safe, and which strategies seemed to be working to ensure maximum profits. This was the border between the inhabited and the uninhabited portions of the journey. The Trans-Saharan was a long trip, depending on the point of crossing between 1,200 and 2,000 miles, but it spanned only one ecozone. It was essentially a bridge. Places along the trip were supplied preferentially, skipping large stretches of intervening space.

After leaving the staging posts, caravans would stop at two types of places, mines, generally salt but also copper, alum, and gem mines, and "refreshment stations". If they weren't in a hurry, they stopped at both since neither served very well as a substitute for the other. Refreshment stations, also referred to as "halting places" and "way stations", were built around wells and ponds, the lifegiving source of a settlement. They were often organized as *ksars* (qusūrs), fortified mudbrick-constructed villages. A large caravan could overwhelm a small *ksar*; since camels drank so much at a sitting, large caravans could stop only at holes that held enormous amounts of water. Some of the big oases had an abundance lying about in stagnant pools that made them very unhealthy places. This did not deter the caravans: stagnant water was better than no water. Some trading took place at refreshment stations, particularly among small traders who limited their activity to making circuits between staging posts and refreshment stations. Such merchants specialized in knowing the market conditions in their own sector; beyond it, they could be easy prey for local shysters. The largest firms operated long distance networks in which goods were handled by agents, partners, brokers, and proxies.

The greatest of the refreshment stations was Tuwat (Tuat). Lying between Morocco to the northwest, Tripoli and Ifriqiya to the northeast, and Timbuktu and Gao to the south, Tuwat was a series of oases rather than a single large well. Nature had favored Tuwat with a lot of water, part of the large reserves that lie close to the surface in the northern Sahara. This water was exploited by use of subterranean aqueducts, the foggaras, a system of connecting tunnels and vertical shafts designed to tap into the water table where it was higher than the land, often at a spring in a cliff or plateau. Foggaras were used to irrigate date palms, which require a lot of water until their root systems developed. They proved to be the most important crop in the oases because they could take as much direct sunlight as the Sahara could give without wilting. The most bountiful oases like Tuwat and Ouargla contained over a million trees, beneath whose shade vegetable crops were also grown. Nevertheless, oases were crowded places, and despite their abundance, they were rarely self-sufficient; grain usually had to be brought in by passing caravans. Most of the income in oases was generated through the same caravan-supporting service industries that could be found at staging posts. As havens for rest and relaxation, some refreshment stations developed substantial prostitution businesses.

In 1447 Antonio Malfante, representing the Centurione banking house of Genoa, left the port of Honein on the Maghribian coast and headed inland. Italian merchants had enjoyed commercial relations with the states of the Maghrib for centuries. In 1272 and 1433, for example, Genoa signed commercial treaties with the Hafsid kings of Tunis stipulating, among other things, that Genoese merchants were not to import counterfeit silver coins into Hafsid lands. They did anyway. This silver helped to pay for gold since most West African gold that came into Europe did so through Genoa via Spain or the Maghrib. A great bullion shortage in fifteenth-century Europe provided added impetus for seeking a direct link with the gold-producing areas of West Africa, bypassing Maghribian and Spanish intermediaries, and outflanking the Portuguese, who had started creeping down the western Atlantic coast. Most importantly, Genoese agents gained the rights to trade in the African interior. They and their rivals from other Italian cities began appearing in places like Marrakech, Tlemcen, and Sijilmasa. Malfante traveled by horseback as part of a caravan, stopping after seven days at the oasis of Tabalbalet. He was not impressed, noting that it was "a ksour where dwelt very poor people who supported themselves on water and a little sandy ground. They sow little, living upon the numerous date palms."[56]

From Tabalbalet, with five more days of travel, Malfante reached Tuwat, where he engaged in business for a while. He wrote a letter to an associate back in Genoa about the people of Tuwat, providing the earliest description of that oasis from a European. Tuwat, Malfante observed, was an oligarchy divided into eighteen quarters, each ruled by a chief who "protects his followers, whether they be in the right or no".[57] A foreign merchant was expected to make a deal with one of these chiefs, who became his protector. The system worked well, though, providing merchants with much better security than they had in Tlemcen or Tunis. Malfante's patron was a rich fellow worth 100,000 doubles (estimated at more than 16,000 gold ounces). Malfante's protector's brother was the most important merchant in Timbuktu, so Malfante was told.

The main town in Tuwat was Tamentit (which Malfante calls De Amamento), where the populace was polarized between the very rich and the very poor. The rich got their money from trade, particularly gold, while the poor subsisted on low-grade dates and occasionally the meat of castrated camels. Wheat and barley from Maghribian caravans and millet and dried fish from the other direction were also available. Malfante's interest in Tuwat was the gold trade, so when not directly engaged in business himself, he gathered information on the lands south of the Sahara. His patron had spent thirty years in Timbuktu and another fourteen farther south in the land of the Sudan, which extended "endlessly". Malfante wanted to know about trade, and the news was excellent. He was told that a great river traversed the land of the Sudan, flowing by Timbuktu and eventually coming out in Egypt as the Nile. The great river was the Niger, and, of course, it does not eventually flow into the Nile. But it was convenient for people to tie together one river for which the upper part of its course was known but not its outlet and another river for which its outlet and lower course were known but not its source of upper part. In any case, the patron reported that the river was full of boats, and traders came from the north with copper and salt. Egyptian merchants brought a half million head of cattle and camels, "a figure which is not fantastic in this region".[58]

All of the merchants came for gold. The trade was so lucrative that even as far away as Tuwat traders would not bother with a business venture unless they could make one hundred percent profit. Malfante may have been shocked by what seemed an exorbitant markup in prices without apparently realizing the extraordinarily high-risk conditions under which such trade operated. He was out of his league and ended up losing two thousand doubles in a year of trading. Many times he asked his patron where the gold came from, and each time the response was the same: "I was fourteen years in the Land of the Blacks, and I have never heard nor seen anyone who could reply from definite knowledge."[59] If Malfante's patron had spent that much time trading in the south and his brother was that important, he was being more then circumspect with his Genoese guest. But why spoil a good thing by inviting Italians into the market? The only other information Malfante got was that the gold came from "a distant land, and ... from a definite zone" and that his patron had been in places "where silver was as valuable as gold".[60]

Other Italian travelers probably wrote letters back from Africa both of a business and personal nature, but only one of note has survived, and it is very brief. Benedetto Dei (1418–92), a widely traveled representative of the Florentine commercial house of Portinari, wrote in late 1469 that he was in Timbuktu, "a very dry country. There is much business there in selling broad cloth, serges, and woolen fabric like that which is made in Lombardy."[61] If Dei was the first European to reach Timbuktu, a feat for which a number of eighteenth- and nineteenth-century British and other European explorers would later sacrifice their lives, the unassuming four lines he sent back may rate as one of the most understated announcements in the history of European geographical discovery.

The Trans-Saharan *per se* ended at the southern reaches of the Sahara where the desert gave way first to a transition zone known as the Sahel ("shore") and farther southward, the savanna and forest regions. In the Sahel urban life began again in the form of great trade centers that served as a combination of southern terminus and staging posts. These had originated as nomadic camps; those in favorable locations became trading towns, and the most successful emerged as cities. Merchants from North Africa usually stopped at cities in the Sahel. They regarded these as ports of the great sand sea and referred to their camels by the Arabic word for ship. In the late first millennium CE when the Trans-Saharan system was coming together, the most important were Awdaghust in the west and Tadmekka in the east, both located some distance north of the great bend in the Niger River. According to al-Bakri:

> The people of Awdaghust enjoy extensive benefits and huge wealth. The market there is at all times full of people, so that owing to the great crowd and the noise of the voices it is almost impossible for a man to hear the words of one sitting beside him. Their transactions are in gold.[62]

Tadmekka, also called al-Suk ("the market"), was located in the Adrar des Iforas about 150 miles from the northeasternmost point of the Niger Bend. The date of Tadmekka's founding does not so much as warrant a guess. The first mention of it comes in Ibn Hawqal, but the reason for Tadmekka's location is more apparent than the date. The straightest path between the Maghrib and the Niger Bend crosses through some of the worst parts of the Sahara including the Tanezrouft ("Region of Thirst"). So, trade routes were developed around the desert's center. While Awdaghust's great wealth was based on the gold trade with the ancient kingdom of Ghana directly to its south, Tadmekka's trade was more diversified with strong markets in slaves, salt, and copper as well as some gold.

In the centuries after 1100 CE, Trans-Saharan routes gradually shifted toward the south and east in the direction of the Niger Bend as the climate became drier and new, more productive gold mines were opened up. This benefited two cities in particular, a new one centering on a popular well that became known as Timbuktu ("the well of Buktu") and an old fishing village that reinvented itself known as Gao, referred to in Arabic sources oddly as "KawKaw." Some of the commodities that arrived by caravan in Timbuktu, Gao, and other Sahelian ports were consumed there, but these cities mostly served as transit stations where arriving goods were sold, repacked, and sent farther south into a web of regional systems that had been woven across West Africa.

Although he was a Tuwati, a man of the desert and Sahel, Malfante's patron was unusual if indeed he spent fourteen years trading somewhere south of Timbuktu. Rarely did a merchant from the north continue beyond Timbuktu or other Sahelian cities although a colony of Maghribians did live up the Niger in the city of Jenne, and the mid-fourteenth-century traveler Ibn Battuta stayed with other Moroccans while visiting the Malian capital, the exact location of which is still uncertain. Some very brave or very greedy North African merchants traded in their camels for donkeys in Timbuktu, on which they ventured as far south as they dared or until their donkeys died from disease. But only those with gold fever. For most, the Niger River was a convenient boundary. Beyond, so they were warned by the Sudanese who were their trading partners in the Sahel, lived the Lamlam and the Damdam, a land of cannibals, naked women, and fetish worshippers, altogether a threatening, disgusting, and nasty place of real and imagined dangers. Plenty of money could be made just going to a place like Timbuktu without risking body and soul.

Commodities from the north were more varied than those that came up from the south since the Trans-Saharan could carry not only North African and Mediterranean products but goods from across Eurasia. However, the Trans-Saharan became storied for two items in particular, one from the south representing the most valuable of commodities, the other from the north representing the most mundane: gold and salt respectively. At times they were reportedly traded directly one for the other.[63] Gold was special because there was not very much of it in the world at the time, and along with its more pedestrian cousin, silver, it could be negotiated or used as a means of value for every other commodity. In West Africa gold came from three major fields that were discovered and played out in succession and various minor ones stretching from the Upper Senegal and Upper Niger river basins to the Akan forest region of modern Ghana. This gold started out mostly in the form of gold dust. Once safely hidden in a bag tucked away somewhere on a camel or, more likely, on the merchant himself, it would be transported to North Africa. There some of it would be transformed into dinars and some sent farther on to the north and east.

In 1252 Europe began to shift from silver-based to gold-based currencies. Two centuries of sustained commercial and demographic growth had created the need for a new monetary system to provide extended means of payment. Local production could hardly keep up with demand, and the value of gold skyrocketed. Even after the gold bubble burst in the mid-fourteenth century and the value of gold fell to a more realistic level, Europe was left with a gold-based currency and the need for a steady supply of the metal, further increasing the demand for it in West Africa. Much of the West African gold that flowed from North Africa to Europe, however, did not stay there. In the early second millennium CE, Europeans were increasingly developing a taste for luxuries, many of which came from India and China, still the great engines driving large scale international trade. Some European gold went across ancient networks operated by Jews and Eastern Christians (Nestorians) and later by Italians and Armenians into the Silk Roads system. Far more went to Egypt, joining other stocks of gold that had come directly from North Africa or West Africa itself. Much of this was shipped down the Red Sea and into the maritime system of the Indian Ocean. The money trail left by Sudanese gold can become very tangled.

The amount of gold exported across the Trans-Saharan remains an unsolved question. Verifiable statistics are non-existent, leaving only scattered bits of anecdotal information. For those who have ventured to make estimates, the trend has been to revise downward from optimistic guesses at up to nine tons per year to a range from around a ton to perhaps two in exceptional years.[64] This does not sound like very much, and compared to modern operations it is virtually a drop in the bucket. One widely quoted statement maintains that for the fourteenth century about two-thirds of the Old World's gold production came from West Africa, but this is not an estimate based on hard evidence; it barely qualifies as someone's guess.[65] Nevertheless, Sudanese gold had an enormous impact on the monetization of Islamic and European economies, and was vital for the expansion of international trade and commercial revitalization.

If the impact of Sudanese gold on the international scene is accepted as canon – even a ton a year can result in a lot of gold over the course of seven or more centuries – this does not address the impact of the gold trade on the Trans-Saharan system. When the importance of Sudanese gold to the outside world was combined with anecdotes from Arab authors, fanciful stories soon followed of hidden cities paved with gold and caravans with strings of camels laden with gold winding through the Sahara. Al-Umari, who is fairly reliable on most matters, got completely carried away: "For they [trans-Saharan merchants] set out with valueless articles and return with bullion as their camels' burden."[66] The Andalusian scholar Abd al-Mu'min al-Sharishi, who lived more than a century before al-Umari, talked to various Trans-Saharan merchants from whom he was able to get a more realistic picture: "Anyone who journeys there [Ghana] with thirty camels comes back with three camels, or two: one for him to ride on, and a second for water ... The price in gold realized from the loads of the thirty camels may be got into one travelling-bag."[67] Al-Umari, however, became one of the most commonly used sources for medieval West African history while al-Sharishi remains largely neglected.

A dromedary's burden could be up to three hundred pounds, which means that if more recent figures are accepted, the total quantity of gold exported on the Trans-Saharan for a year could have been carried by one caravan of seven or so laden camels. Getting Sudanese gold across the desert may have been crucial for economies north of the Sahara, but seven camels a year (or even seventy) hardly a system makes. Trans-Saharan gold is sometimes compared with silk on the Silk Roads or spices in Indian Ocean commerce, but in terms of quantity this is misleading. Substantially sized camel caravans crossing the Taklamakan Desert between China and the Pamirs really could be laden with silk, or ships riding the monsoon from southern Indian ports bound for the Red Sea could have their holds full of pepper or cinnamon.

The most important mines in the Sahara produced salt. Sodium chloride is necessary for the human body to carry on certain physiological functions, and people who consume a fair amount of meat and fish get enough salt from these foods since flesh, blood, milk, and urine all contain salt. But plants have a lower salt content, so people who exist primarily on grains and other vegetable matter need a supplement. Rock deposits of salt in sub-Saharan West Africa were so meager people often had to extract their daily dosage from burning saline-rich grasses, millet straw, or cattle dung. The ashes were dissolved in water, then repeatedly boiled and filtered until only the salt residue was left. Rock salt from the mines of the Sahara, however, enjoyed a consistent reputation for quality. It had been formed when ancient inland seas dried up and were buried, producing a salt that was so dense it was like rock. It was considered tastier, purer, and in every other way superior to salt from any other source, including seawater. And usually it was more expensive. In the Western Sudan the type of salt consumed often reflected a person's social class and economic standing. The Sudanese craved rock salt. They licked it rather than ground and sprinkled it so as not to lose any flakes. Children savored it as a snack; adults sipped it dissolved in water.

The Trans-Saharan gold trade was in a league by itself because it transcended the weight-to-value issue. Going north, gold was carried in a purse or at most a sack or two on a camel whose principal load was something else, often food or another commodity likely to be consumed in a desert oasis even if the gold itself would move on and eventually exit the system. What has been touted as the salt-for-gold trade was mostly a salt-for-food trade. Gold was along for the ride. The Trans-Saharan thus combined directional trade in which goods like gold and a few other valuables like civet (for perfume) from the south and manufactured goods from the north were taken from one side of the system to the other together with inter-regional trade in commodities like salt and foodstuffs. Although gold, which had a value-to-weight ratio that was off the chart, was the most valuable item exported across the entire desert, grain, which had the lowest value-to-weight ratio, was the most important sent into the desert, and salt picked up along the way, another low value-to-weight commodity, was the most important to come out.

Notes

1 Hamdallah Mustawfi, *Nuzhat al-Qulub*, trans. G. Le Strange, *The Geographical Part of the Nuzhat-Al-Qulūb* (Leiden, 1919). This text formed part of a Persianate tradition that dated to the eleventh-century, see Gerald R. Tibbetts, "The Balkhī School of Geographers" in J. B. Harey and David Woodward (eds.), *The History of Cartography, vol. 2, book 1: Cartography in the Traditional Islamic and South Asian Societies* (Chicago, 1992), pp. 108–36.

2 The Wāqwāq Islands were described as more than a hundred islands to the east of China and have been identified as Japan, Indonesia or even Madagascar, see: Ibn Khurradādhbih, *Kitāb al Masālik w'al Mamālik*, p. 50; and Gabriel Ferrand, *Le Wakway est-il Japan?* (Paris, 1932).

3 The Island of Barṭāyil has never been conclusively identified and has been presumed to refer to clove producing or trading parts of the Maluku Islands or Indonesia.

4 Herodotus, *The Histories*, book 4, part 196. For a range of examples and analysis of silent trade see: William A. Haviland et al., *Anthropology: The Human Challenge* (Boston, 2004), p. 461; Francesca Trivellato, Leor Halevi, and Catia Antunes (eds.), *Religion and Trade: Cross-Cultural Exchanges in World History* (Oxford, 2014), pp. 73–85; James Woodburn, "Silent Trade with Outsiders: Hunter Gatherers' Perspectives" in *HAU: Journal of Ethnographic Theory* 6:2 (2016), pp. 473–96.

5 Ibrāhīm Ibn Wasīf Shāh, *Akbār al-Zamān* [The History of Time], trans. Carra de Vaux, *L'abrégé des Merveilles* (Paris, 1898), chap. 4.
6 Al-Biruni, *Taḥqīq mā li-al-Hind*, trans. Edward Sachau, *Beruni's India: Account of the religion, philosophy, literature, geography, chronology, astronomy, customs, laws, and astrology of India, about AD 1030* (London, 1888), p. 309.
7 Zhao Rukuo, *Zhu Fan Zhi* [Records of Foreign People], trans. Friedrick Hirth and W. W. Rockhill, *Chau Ju-Kua: His Work on the Chinese and Arab Trade in the Twelfth and Thirteenth Centuries, entitled Chu-fan-chï* (St Petersburg, 1911), p. 104.
8 Ibn Battuta, *The Rihla*, trans. H. A. R. Gibb and C. F. Beckingham (eds.), *The Travels of Ibn Battuta, AD 1325–54*, 4 vols. (London, 1994), p. 151.
9 Alvise da Cadamosto, *The Voyages of Alvise Cadamosto and Pero de Sintra*, trans. G. R. Crone, *The Voyages of Cadamosto and other Documents on Western Africa in the Second Half of the Fifteenth Century* (London, 1937), pp. 22–3. Accounts of silent trade in West Africa have attracted particular attention from historians – often focusing on the accuracy of particular accounts. See, P. F. de Moraes Farias, "Silent Trade: Myth and Historical Evidence", *History in Africa* 1 (1974), pp. 9–24.
10 Samuel Bowles questions whether this trade should have been considered "really so odd" and highlights its potential as an exchange mechanism, see *Microeconomics: Behaviour, Institutions, and Evolution* (Princeton, NJ, 2004), pp. 233–49.
11 Susan Whitfield, "Was there a Silk Road?", *Asian Medicine* 3:2 (2008), p. 206, pp. 201–13.
12 Anver Greif, *Institutions and the Path to the Modern Economic: Lessons from Medieval trade* (Cambridge, 2006), pp. 70–1.
13 Douglas North, "Institutions", *Journal of Economic Perspectives* 5:1 (1991), pp. 97–9; Paul R. Milgrom, Douglas C. North, and Barry R. Weingast, "The Role of Institutions in the Revival of Trade: The law merchant, private judges, and the Champagne fairs", *Economics and Politics* 2:1 (1990), pp. 1–23.
14 See Andre Gunder Frank, *ReOrient: Global economy in the Asian Age* (Berkeley, CA, 1998).
15 Francesca Trivellato, *The Familiarity of Strangers: The Sephardic diaspora, Livorno, and cross-cultural trade in the early modern period* (New Haven, CT, 2009), pp. 157–61.
16 Ann Stahl, *Making History in Banda: Anthropological visions of Africa's past* (Cambridge, 2001); Edmond Smith and Mariana Boscariol, "Akan Relations, Commercial Networks, and the Portuguese Empire in West Africa, 1482–1637", *Journal of World History* 33:4 (2022), pp. 609–38.
17 Curtin, *Cross-Cultural Trade*, pp. 38–59.
18 Francesca Trivellato, *The Familiarity of Strangers: The Sephardic diaspora, Livorno, and cross-cultural trade in the early modern period* (New Haven, CT, 2009), p. 1.
19 Francesca Trivellato, *The Familiarity of Strangers: The Sephardic diaspora, Livorno, and cross-cultural trade in the early modern period* (New Haven, CT, 2009), 7.
20 Natalie Rothman, "Between Venice and Istanbul: Trans-Imperial Subjects and Cultural Mediation in the Early Modern Mediterranean", PhD Dissertation, University of Michigan (2006), pp. xiv, 40–81.
21 Christopher Edens, "Dynamics of Trade in the Ancient Mesopotamian 'World System'", *American Anthropologist* 94:1 (1992), pp. 118–39.
22 John W. Chaffee, *The Muslim Merchants of Premodern China: The history of a maritime Asian trade diaspora, 750–1400* (Cambridge, 2018).
23 See, for instance, Sebouh Aslanian, *From the Indian Ocean to the Mediterranean: The global trade networks of the Armenian merchants of New Julfa* (California,

2010); Jawaid Akhtar, "Gujarati Merchants in the Indonesian Archipelago in the 17th Century", *Proceedings of the Indian History Congress* 54 (1993), pp. 273–7; Ivor Wilks, "Wangara, Akan and Portuguese in the Fifteenth and Sixteenth Centuriers, 1: The Matter of Bitu", *The Journal of African History* 23:3 (1982), pp. 333–49.

24 Kenneth Pomeranz and Steven Topik, *The World that Created Society, Culture, and the World Economy, 1400-the Present* (Armonk, NY, 1999), p. 7.

25 Christopher Bayly used the concept of "communities of mercantile trust" in "'Archaic' and 'Modern' Globalisation in the Eurasian and African Arena, c. 1750–1850" in A. G. Hopkins (ed.), *Globalisation in World History* (London, 2002), p. 59. Aslanian draws on concept of "social capital" to interpret these relationships: Sebouh Aslanian, *From the Indian Ocean to the Mediterranean: The global trade networks of the Armenian merchants of New Julfa* (California, 2010), pp. 166–74. Edmond Smith uses "communal governance": "Governance" in William Pettigrew and David Veevers (eds.), *The Corporation as a Protagonist in Global History, c. 1550–1750* (Leiden, 2018), pp. 163–86.

26 Competition within commercial communities was of course common, and conflicts of interest between competing merchants could have significant repercussions for the stability of these groups. See, Bhaswati Bhattacharya, "The 'Book of Will' of Petrus Woskan (1680–1751): Some insights into the global commercial network of the Armenians in the Indian Ocean", *Journal of Economic and Social History of the Orient* 51:1 (2008), pp. 67–98.

27 Francesca Trivellato, "Sephardic Merchants in the Early Modern Atlantic and Beyond: Towards a Comparative Historical Approach to Business Cooperation" in Richard L. Kagan and Philip Morgan (eds.), *Atlantic Diasporas: Jews and Crypto-Jews in the Age of Mercantilism, 1500–1800* (Baltimore, 2005), pp. 101–3.

28 Francesca Trivellato, *The Familiarity of Strangers: The Sephardic diaspora, Livorno, and cross-cultural trade in the early modern period* (New Haven, CT, 2009), p. 157.

29 Sebouh Aslanian, *From the Indian Ocean to the Mediterranean: The global trade networks of the Armenian merchants of New Julfa* (California, 2010), p. 166.

30 Philippe Beaujard, *The Worlds of the Indian Ocean: A global history, vol. 2: From the seventh century to the fifteenth century CE* (Cambridge, 2019), p. 299.

31 Subhi Y. Labib, "Capitalism in Medieval Islam", *The Journal of Economic History* 29:1 (1969), pp. 92–3.

32 Philippe Beaujard, *The Worlds of the Indian Ocean: A global history, vol. 2: From the seventh century to the fifteenth century CE* (Cambridge, 2019), pp. 300–2.

33 Philippe Beaujard, *The Worlds of the Indian Ocean: A global history, vol. 2: From the seventh century to the fifteenth century CE* (Cambridge, 2019), pp. 300–2.

34 Philippe Beaujard, *The Worlds of the Indian Ocean: A global history, vol. 2: From the seventh century to the fifteenth century CE* (Cambridge, 2019), pp. 300–2.

35 Philippe Beaujard, *The Worlds of the Indian Ocean: A global history, vol. 2: From the seventh century to the fifteenth century CE* (Cambridge, 2019), 302–5.

36 A safe conduct of Sultan Qalāwūn, quoted in Philippe Beaujard, *The Worlds of the Indian Ocean: A global history, vol. 2: From the seventh century to the fifteenth century CE* (Cambridge, 2019), p. 299.

37 Francesca Trivellato, *The Familiarity of Strangers: The Sephardic diaspora, Livorno, and cross-cultural trade in the early modern period* (New Haven, CT, 2009), pp. 1–2.

38 Ida Nursoo, "Indiginous Law, Colonial Injustice and the Jurisprudence of Hybridity", *The Journal of Legal Pluralism and Unofficial Law*, 50, 1 (2018), pp. 56–70.

39 Aslanian has suggested that these spaces began to disappear in the eighteenth and nineteenth centuries "for the most part after the erection of cultural, linguistic and national boundaries". See Sebouh Aslanian, *From the Indian Ocean to the Mediterranean: The global trade networks of the Armenian merchants of New Julfa* (California, 2010), p. 66.
40 Much like "global", "premodern" and "Eurasia" are used in this book to show connections and commonalities between otherwise disparate experiences of trading in the past.
41 John Hill, *Through the Jade Gate to Rome: A study of the Silk Roads during the later Han Dynasty 1st to 2nd centuries*, vol. 1 and 2 (2009), p. ix.
42 Sven Hedin, *Silk Road* (London, 1938), p. 226.
43 David Christian, "Silk Roads or Steppe Roads? The Silk Roads in World History", *Journal of World History* 11:1 (2000), p. 10, pp. 1–26.
44 Sally Hovey Wriggins, *The Silk Road Journey with Xuanzang* (Colorado, 2004).
45 Sven Hedin, *Silk Road* (London, 1938), p. 228.
46 Zhang Guand-da, B. A. Litvinsky, "Historical Introduction" in Zhang Guand-da, B. A. Litvinsky, and R. Shabani Samghabadi (eds.), *History of Civilizations of Central Asia, vol 3: The crossroads of civilization: A.D. 250 to 750* (Paris, 1996), p. 31, pp. 19–35.
47 Albert Herrmann, *Historical and Commercial Atlas of China* (Boston, MA, 1935).
48 Ibn Khurradādhbih, *Kitāb al Masālik w'al Mamālik*, p. 50; and Gabriel Ferrand, *Le Wakway est-il Japan?* (Paris, 1932), p. 18.
49 Ibn Idhari, *Al-Bayan al-Mughrib*, trans. Nehemiah Levtzion and J. F. P. Hopkins (eds.), *Corpus of Early Arabic Sources for West African History* (Cambridge, 1981), pp. 226–7.
50 Strabo, *Geographica*, vol. 17, book 3, part 19.
51 Ibn Khaldun, *Muqaddimah*, trans. Franz Rosenthal in N. J. Dawood (ed.), *The Muqaddimah: An Introduction to History* (Princeton, NJ, 2005), p. 464.
52 Ibn al-Khatib quoted in Nehemiah Levtzion and J. F. P. Hopkins (eds.), *Corpus of Early Arabic Sources for West African History* (Cambridge, 1981), pp. 307–8.
53 Ibn Fadl Allāh al-Umari quoted in Nehemiah Levtzion and J. F. P. Hopkins (eds.), *Corpus of Early Arabic Sources for West African History* (Cambridge, 1981), p. 275.
54 Ibn Hawqal quoted in Nehemiah Levtzion and J. F. P. Hopkins (eds.), *Corpus of Early Arabic Sources for West African History* (Cambridge, 1981), pp. 45.
55 Madeleine Rouvillois-Brigol, *Le Pays de Ouargla (Sahara Algérien)* (Paris, 1975).
56 Antoine Malfante, "Letter from Tuat, 1447", trans. Gerald Roe Crone (ed.), *The Voyages of Cadamosto and other Documents on Western Africa in the Second Half of the Fifteenth Century* (London, 1937), p. 85.
57 Antoine Malfante, "Letter from Tuat, 1447", trans. Gerald Roe Crone (ed.), *The Voyages of Cadamosto and other Documents on Western Africa in the Second Half of the Fifteenth Century* (London, 1937), p. 85.
58 Antoine Malfante, "Letter from Tuat, 1447", trans. Gerald Roe Crone (ed.), *The Voyages of Cadamosto and other Documents on Western Africa in the Second Half of the Fifteenth Century* (London, 1937), p. 90.
59 Antoine Malfante, "Letter from Tuat, 1447", trans. Gerald Roe Crone (ed.), *The Voyages of Cadamosto and other Documents on Western Africa in the Second Half of the Fifteenth Century* (London, 1937), p. 90.
60 Antoine Malfante, "Letter from Tuat, 1447", trans. Gerald Roe Crone (ed.), *The Voyages of Cadamosto and other Documents on Western Africa in the Second Half of the Fifteenth Century* (London, 1937), p. 90.
61 Benedetto Dei, "Letter from Timbuktu, 1469", quoted in Richard Smith, "The Image of Timbuktu in Europe before Caillié", *Proceedings of the Meeting of the French Colonial Historical Society* 8 (1985), p. 14, pp. 12–22.

62 Al-Bakrī, *Kitāb al-Masālik wa-al-Mamālik*, trans. Nehemiah Levtzion and J. F. P. Hopkins (eds.), *Corpus of Early Arabic Sources for West African History* (Cambridge, 1981), p. 68.

63 Abu Hamid al-Gharnati and Al-Umari, both quoted in Nehemiah Levtzion and J. F. P. Hopkins (eds.), *Corpus of Early Arabic Sources for West African History* (Cambridge, 1981), pp. 132, 273.

64 One of the few estimates from someone in the know comes from the sixteenth-century Portuguese explorer and administrator Pacheco Pereira. He put the annual Portuguese coastal trade in gold, about which he had good information, at somewhat over 2,200 pounds. On the Trans-Saharan gold trade, his estimate, which was no more than a guess, was between 9,000 and 10,000 pounds. See Duarte Pacheco Pereira, *Esmeraldo de Situ Orbis*, trans. George Kimble (ed.), *Esmeraldo de Siter Orbis* (London, 1937). The eminent French scholar Raymond Mauny, *Tableau Géographique de L'Ouest Africain au Moyen Age: D'Après les Sources Écrites, la Tradition et l'Archéologie* (Dakar, 1961), p. 298, led the way for modern historians with an estimate of 9,000 kgs per year from the sixteenth through the nineteenth centuries, a period in which West African gold exports were declining. It was first questioned in Vitorino Magalhaes-Godinho, *L'Économie de l'Empire Portugais aux XVe et XVIe Siècles* (Paris, 1969), p. 119, and thereafter estimates have moved downward as in Philip Curtin, "Africa and the Wider Monetary World, 1250–1850" in J. F. Richards (ed.), *Precious Metals in the Later Medieval and Early Modern Worlds* (Durham, NC, 1983), p. 240, who sees 1,500 kgs as "a more probably figure." Ralph Austen, *African Economic History: Internal development and external dependency* (Portsmouth, NH, 1987), p. 36, sees a high point at something over a ton a year.

65 Andrew Watson, "Back to Gold – and Silver", *The Economic History Review* 20 (1967), pp. 30–1.

66 Al-Umari quoted in Nehemiah Levtzion and J. F. P. Hopkins (eds.), *Corpus of Early Arabic Sources for West African History* (Cambridge, 1981), p. 274.

67 Nehemiah Levtzion and J. F. P. Hopkins (eds.), *Corpus of Early Arabic Sources for West African History* (Cambridge, 1981), p. 152.

6 Commodities of the Premodern World

The Premodern Market Stall

In the detailed mercantile account of markets along the Silk Roads by Francesco Balducci Pegolotti (1290–1347), it is possible to get some sense of the scope and complexity of global exchanges that were taking place across Eurasia, and how a premodern market stall might come to be stocked simultaneously with goods carried from sites as distant as China, Indonesia, Russia, and England. Pegolotti was an Italian merchant and politician from Florence, who wrote the *Libro di Divisamenti di Paesi* (The Book of the Descriptions of Countries) sometime around 1340, in which he sought to set out his mercantile knowledge of trade across Europe and into Asia. He was well traveled and had traded across Europe during his time as factor for the Bardi Company, and he had spent time in Antwerp, London, and Cyprus. Perhaps his most ambitious venture came in 1335, when he sought and obtained privileges from the King of Lesser Armenia to boost the Bardi Company's position in the Gulf of İskenderun at the port of Aiazzo. This was the Mediterranean terminus of a route that carried goods from India, via Baghdad and Tabriz, and connected Pegolotti directly to the long-distance trading routes that feature prominently in his book.[1]

Of particular interest are his comments on the route to "Cathay", and his descriptions of major ports and market towns along the way. For merchants from Italy planning to travel the whole way to Khanbaliq, a capital of the Mongol-led Yuan Dynasty in China, he recommended they carry goods valued at approximately 25,000 gold florins, as well as silver to cover the costs of travel. The main commodity needed when reaching their eastern destination would be silver, but some Italian linens as well as "some bales of the very finest stuffs which go in small bulk" would be suitable for the journey too. For their return journey they would be carrying silk.[2] As this suggests, the for a merchant traversing the length of the Silk Roads, the trade would include an extremely limited number of commodities that would travel the whole distance with them. However, this focus on the seemingly simple exchange of precious metals for silk only reveals one small part of the webs of exchange that made up the wider pathways and flows of goods

DOI: 10.4324/9781003052890-7

across the system, and the mundane goods of everyday travel like supplies of food or the provision of animals, were just as important. Global trade in the premodern world simply could not function without the intersection of local, regional, and continental trading routes.

Major markets represented key meeting points where these different levels of commercial activity came together. Pegolotti's description of the markets in Constantinople show the wide array of commodities that were available for merchants at this key crossing point between Europe and Asia, where the Mediterranean meets the Black Sea. Starting with consumable goods, Constantinople was well stocked with varieties from across the wider Mediterranean trading world. These included simple products like suet, honey, rice, cheese, dates, almonds, pistachios, chestnuts, and walnuts. Others were less common and came from specific origins such as raisins from Syria, dried figs from Majorca and Spain, olive oil of Apulia, and wine from Greece, Italy, Crete, and Romania. Soaps from Venice, Ancona and Apulia in Italy, as well as from Cyprus and Rhodes, also fall into this category. Consumables also included some of the most luxurious and expensive commodities, with some that had traveled the furthest distances of anything available in Constantinople. Cumin, saffron, round pepper, long pepper, ginger, brazilwood, incense, sugar, cinnamon, cinnabar, cassia, mace and cloves were all available – some of which had come from as far as the Maluku Islands even though knowledge of these distant spice islands was still uncertain. Metals, too, were available, but do not seem to have been too notable, with Pegolotti simple noting that iron, tin and lead "of every kind" was available, although the availability of copper, coral, and amber all allude to prestige objects like jewelry that was certainly available during this period. Likewise, an array of animal products could be found like horse, ox, and buffalo hides, as well as Slavonian squirrel, martin, goat and skins, but there was no mention of particularly rare and luxurious furs on Constantinople's market stalls. Finally, the array of textiles available reveal the presence of goods produced from the very westernmost parts of Eurasia, in the form of British woolen broadcloths, and from the very easternmost parts, with an array of silk on offer like silk gauze, dressed silk, silk velvets, and damasks. Other textile commodities included materials for cloth production, such as raw silk, gold thread, cotton wool, cotton yarn, flax from Alexandria and Romania, camlet wool, washed wool from Romania, and wool from Turkey. There were also goods needed for dyeing and staining such as madder, alum, henna, safflower, sulfur, and orpiment – an orange-yellow arsenic sulfide mineral that was used for making pigments. Among these was another link to long distance trade, with indigo available that was likely transported from South Asia either via the Red Sea or the longer overland route via Tabriz noted above.[3] In the markets of Constantinople, then, goods from across the world were available, and whether they were seeking a block of cheese or cloth of gold, premodern merchants who traveled to the city were sustaining highly connected webs of exchange that tied together these far-flung geographies.

Discussions of commodities often begin with the premise that in the premodern world they can be divided into two groupings. The first is often referred to as "luxury goods". These can be defined in a negative sense in that they were items that were not necessary for common everyday living. They had high value, brought prestige to their owners, and were intended for elite consumption. The initial cost of production may have been high (although not necessarily). They were often exotic, meaning not produced locally, and the distance they had traveled was often factored into their perceived value. In some cases, staple goods in domestic markets could become luxury goods in far off markets. But where they were being sold, they had to be scarce in quantity. They were often used for display and conspicuous consumption. Merchants who engaged in selling luxury goods were assumed to enjoy higher profits per unit than was generated by the sale of other goods. The other grouping of commodities is referred to by a variety of terms, each having a slightly different nuance including staples, utilitarian, practical use, functionally based, bulk, local, and subsistence. Again, these can be defined negatively. They were not high value, generally did not travel long distances, did not bring prestige to their owners, and were not scarce in quantity. The exchange of such products was far more common and, although far less studied, far more important in the everyday lives of people than that of luxury goods carried by long-distance trade.

Indeed, there was a difference between the grain market and the gem market. However, a slightly deeper look shows an increasingly complicated picture. Commodities did not always fall into two discrete groupings, the boundaries between them could be quite fluid, and the perceived value of a particular product could change over time. Dividing commodities by category becomes more complicated, for example, when considering among the most commonly traded of all goods in the premodern world, textiles. These ranged from the most luxurious silk to the most commonplace woolen and hemp products. Such a range was also evident for ceramics, comestibles, metal products, and virtually all categories of commodities. Luxury products could be exchanged for staples, one example being that of Javanese merchants trading boatloads of rice and cheap cotton textiles for the most expensive of spices in the Maluku and Banda islands. And while overland caravan traffic was limited in most cases by the weight to value ratio, even a modest size ship like an Indian Ocean dhow had far too much space to carry only small luxury goods. One of the most important trade networks to develop in this period, the Trans-Saharan, was based on three products carried over long distance by camels: salt coming from the north to be exchanged for food and gold coming from the south.

Once the networks were in place to help carry merchants and people from one place to another, they still had to go through the actual process of exchanging goods. The practice of pure barter, that is, not bartering at a specific rate or using some standard of value, was relatively rare in the premodern world. Bartering by using some explicit measures of value such as a certain length of cloth of a particular grade or a certain measure of grain was common in societies not monetized and under-monetized including some that were very advanced in other ways. As noted earlier, multiple reports exist from places ranging from the African interior to the Artic tundra to the borderlands of Tibet of "Dumb Barter" or the "Silent Trade", but such reports were noted because they were so unusual. Exchanging primitive valuables and gift exchange between people of power were important practices at earlier times, and it appears that they survived in various forms including, for example, Chinese tribute trade. In most places at most times during the period under discussion, the use of money was more common than barter.

Money is usually thought of as coins, but other items could serve a true money function in the form of money such as cowrie shells in West Africa and Bengal or commodity money such as bolts of silk in China or rice in the Khmer Empire. There was also the use of gold and silver not minted into coins in the form of gold dust, marked bags, ingots, bars, plates, jewelry, and bullion traded by weight. Copper and tin were also used but more spottily. Coins could be minted from precious or base metals, the latter including copper, tin, lead, and iron. The most effective use of coins in commerce came when they were standardized for fineness and weight. Debasement, depreciation, inflation, and counterfeiting were all too common and tended to undermine marketplace confidence. When matters got too out-of-hand, as in the tenth century in parts of the crumbling Abbasid state, merchants resorted to weighing rather than counting coins. Coins known for their fineness and weight often served as international currencies as did the Islamic dirham-dinar and later the gold coinage issued by the most prominent Italian states, especially the ducat, florin, and genovino. At different times the Chinese government forbade the export of their copper cash coins and actively promoted the export in shiploads to Southeast Asia. The most daring monetary policy of this period came with the issuing of paper money by the Song dynasty in China. This was continued under the Yuan dynasty but dropped under the Ming due to severe inflation. Outside of China this experiment with fiduciary money was tried in the Ilkhanate, a close ally of the Yuan dynasty, and Korea. In Europe banknotes served a similar purpose.

In trying to understand who traded what and why, it should not be forgotten that in the premodern world the demand for goods, both of the luxury and general use varieties, typically outran supply. The luxury market boomed during the heyday of the Caliphate in the West and the Tang and Song dynasties in the East. But the long durée trend through the millennium was the expansion of trade, and with it the increased importance of the bulk market and the sale of low-value items.

Global Commodities in Primary Sources

Whereas Pegolotti account reveals the array of global commodities available in a single well-connected marketplace, other commentators offered more information about the origins and value of different goods that were produced across the premodern world. In this section, evidence from four authors who were writing towards the end of the period covered in this book, (from Africa, western Asia, eastern Asia, and Europe) is used to show how a range of different commodities were understood and represented by interested commentators. This begins with an assessment of agricultural and animal products, then metals and mineral products, before finally considering textiles and other manufactured goods. The focus, of course, is on products that could be traded at least within wider regional commercial systems, which means that almost all commodities discussed included some processing by workers before they were dispatched on their journeys to distant markets. This included the preservation of agricultural and animal products, the smelting of metal into ingots, or the complex manufacture of textiles and other products that passed through many hands before reaching the market.

First, the famous Berber traveler Ibn Battuta (1304–68/9) spent thirty years traversing North Africa and Eurasia between 1325 and 1354. Towards the end of his life, he dictated an account of these journeys that is known as *The Rihla* or *A Gift to Those Who Contemplate the Wonders of Cities and the Marvels of Travelling*.[4] Second, the Persian historian Hamdallah Mustawfi (1281–1340s), who served in the Ilkhanate, completed the *Nuzhat al-Qulub* towards the end of his life and included a detailed geography of Iran and its surroundings, as well as commentary about the most famous features of other parts of the world.[5] Third, Ma Huan (*c.*1380–*c.*1460) was a Chinese translator and traveler who accompanied Admiral Zheng He on three of his famous expeditions across maritime Asia and the Indian Ocean World. Ma Huan took notes on the geography, politics, climate, economy, and local customs of places he visited across these voyages, and produced from these his *Yingya Shenglan,* which was completed in 1451.[6] Fourth, and finally, Tomé Pires (*c.*1468–*c.*1524/40) was a Portuguese diplomat and colonial administrator, as well as an apothecary, who served in India, Melaka, and China. While in Melaka he wrote the *Suma Oriental* which described the geography, people, and commerce of the Asian coastline the whole way from the Red Sea to Japan.[7]

Natural Products

Many agricultural commodities were not intended for long-distance trade and were consumed locally. This is not to say that they were not traded across greater distances, however, and in regions where producing food was particularly difficult, like some parts of maritime Southeast Asia, the import of rice and other agricultural products was essential. Their very ubiquity meant that many basic commodities received limited attention from commentators. Corn, cereal, rice and fruits were the most common agricultural commodities mentioned by Mustawfi and appeared regularly across his book.

However, he became more specific when it came to more unusual outputs, such as sugarcane in the marshy area of Hawizeh which "grows here abundantly", and in nearby Tarazak where "sugarcane grows better and more abundantly here than anywhere else in Khuzestan, being larger in size and finer".[8]

Battuta also included some basic details of agricultural goods available in different regions, and these crops also appear when he reported events like famine, when describing the provisions needed for a journey or provided by a generous host, and when they were part of a particular dish unique to a region he was visiting.[9] He also took care to describe the practices of agricultural communities that he visited. For example, he provided a detailed account of "the cereals which the people of India sow and use for food" that covered topics such as how they sowed their fields twice a year and rice three times a year, how they made bread, the cereals they fed to draught animals, and the variety of grains and legumes that were harvested.[10] Some towns were also noted for the particular quality of their agricultural produce, whether "rice of an excellent sort" from Sarasati or the "fine flavored sugarcanes, which are unexcelled in the rest of that country" found in Malabar.[11]

Ma Huan, too, noted the most important agricultural crops and practices on places that he visited. In Java, where "the climate is continuously hot, like summer", he thought it worth noting that "rice in the fields ripens twice in one year", but that "barley and wheat are entirely non-existent".[12] Nearby Palembang was more richly furnished in agricultural produce. Here, "the people are very rich and prosperous" and the "soil of the land is very fertile", allowing for rice to be sown once and harvested three times each year.[13] Conversely, in Champa, he described how "men take up fishing for a livelihood; they seldom go in for agriculture, and therefore rice and cereals are not abundant. In the local varieties of rice the kernel is small, long, and reddish. Barley and wheat are both wanting."[14] For the most part, Ma Huan was not impressed by the agricultural outputs of lands he visited, perhaps because China was so productive in this respect.[15] That said, he did take care to describe the sweeter things when he found them, and when visiting Bengal, Ma Huan took note that "they have such things as granulated sugar, white sugar, crystallized sugar, crystallized fruits, honey-preserves, and crystallized ginger".[16]

Pires, despite focusing more on goods carried between different markets that often combined produce from a variety of areas, did share information about the richness of particular regions. He explained that "the land of Shiraz is the choicest of Persia, a land abounding in wheat, wine, meat, fruits and – like our own country – not lacking in nuts, chestnuts and dried figs".[17] Cambay likewise was "abundant in all kinds of wheat, barley, millet, vegetables, fruits" and consequently "the land is thickly populated and has beautiful cities both on the coast and inland, as well as large villages" – its agricultural surplus meant that merchants from Arabia who who came took wheat and rice home with them, as well as more luxurious goods obtained in Cambay's marketplaces.[18] Bengal, too, was "very productive of many foodstuffs: meat, fish, wheat", and these were all notably cheap.[19]

Agricultural products were not only simply for consumption but were often a resource needed to produce manufactured commodities, notably textiles. When Mustawfi described the goods of Kufa in Iràq included "fine crops of cotton, corn, and other cereals are raised in the vicinity", the inclusion of cotton alongside cereals is no surprise and is a combination of commodities that appear together across the *Nuzhat al-Qulub*.[20] Ma Huan makes a similar observation about the cultivation of cotton and silk taking place together on the northern coast of Sumatra, but he insisted that despite having mulberry trees and rearing silk worms, "they do not understand how to reel off silk" and only cotton was used when producing cloth.[21]

As well as agricultural goods and vital supplies themselves, the infrastructure required to produce them also drew attention. In some places, Mustawfi reported fairly simple agricultural production, but sophisticated infrastructure was also in use. In Konya, "a large town, of the province of Cappadocia", where "the climate is temperate", he described how "the water is from the hills round; and to keep the water pure, at each city gate there is a great dome built (over a tank), and outside each dome there are some 300 spouts by which the water flows out. The crops here are plentiful and excellent, consisting of cotton, corn and other cereals".[22] Similarly large-scale planning was needed to support the silk-producing town of Junabad, a location where "the desert sands are in sight" and "waters got from underground channels, which same are often four leagues in length, with pits going down to them that average 700 cubits in depth".[23] Of just as much importance but somewhat less sophistication, Pires noted that "it is a think worth seeing" how in a city as "famous and rich as Aden" their "drinking water has to be brought in a cart".[24]

Agricultural commodities were more commonly referenced in relation to long-distance trade where practices of preservation enabled their transportation over vast distances. Dried fruits, remarkably, were traded from one end of Eurasia to the other, and places where these were produced were connected with export markets far and wide. Mustawfi was able to identify at least one trans-continental fruit exporting provide in Iran, noting that "the fruits from here [Isfahan] are exported to India and to Greece".[25] Likewise, in the town of Wabkana on the edge of the desert near Bukhara, Battuta described how its inhabitants preserved grapes and yellow plums, after which "people carry the dried fruit to India and China".[26] In Cannanore, Pires reported that there was a busy export trade in dried coconuts: "all the ships take them when they depart". He explained that "oil is made from them, and they are also eaten".[27] A charming account of long-distance fruit trade is glimpsed in Battuta's account of his time in Delhi. After acknowledging that the "melons of Khwarazm have no equal in any country in the world, east or west", he noted "a remarkable thing is that they are cut into strips, dried in the sun, and packed in reed baskets". Once prepared, the melon strips were "exported from Khwarazm to the remotest parts of India and China, and of all the dried fruits there are none which excel them in sweetness". This was a familiar process for Battuta, and he shared that the same process was used in Morocco and Malaga with figs. While in Delhi, he was kept in good stock of the sweet melon by the Sultan Muhammad bin Tughlaq, who made sure "to give pleasure to the foreigners [at his court] by sending to them the fruit of their own countries".[28]

As well as goods that would be transported long-distances, these authors also highlighted the importance of consumable goods for major trading centers. These often depended on imported agricultural goods, especially those that served as emporium at the connecting point of multiple trading networks, rather than being a major producer of particular goods themselves. In Ormuz, that Battuta recognized was a "fine large city, with magnificent bazaars" that served as the "port of India and Sind", he noted that "their food is fish and dried dates exported to them from Basra and Oman".[29] On his own visit to Ormuz, Ma Huan likewise noted the variety of foodstuffs available on the island, including "roast mutton, roast chicken, roast meat, wafer cakes, *ha-la-sa* [probably harissa], and all kinds of cereal foods". Rice (and wheat too) was "bought in different places and comes here to be sold; the price is extremely cheap". Notably, as well as these perishable goods, he noted that "foreign ships from every place and foreign merchants travelling by land all come to this country to attend the market and trade; hence the people of the country are all rich".[30] Pires made similar observations about Jeddah on the Arabian Red Sea coastline. With "no natural products or fruits except dates", the city depended on supplied carried from Zeila and Berbera in the Horn of Africa. This was made possible because of Jeddah's role as an entrepot connecting the Indian Ocean and the Mediterranean, where "all the merchandise of India is unloaded", that helped make it a "great trading city".[31] Despite travelling a shorter distance than the spices and other Indian goods that flowed through the city, the perishable goods that came to Ormuz or Jeddah were still vitally important for the functioning of the city's role a long-distance trading hub.

While consumable goods were essential, probably the most significant agricultural products in the world of premodern global trade were spices of various sorts. The rarity of such, and consequently the massive profits that could be found in transporting them great distances, was a major incentive for traders to reach destinations across the world. Such was their prominence, regions that produced them were sometimes defined by their presence. When Battuta "reached the land of Malabar" he was able to describe it quite simply: "the pepper country".[32] This reputation was not only held by travelers from western Eurasia, and Battuta reported that upon telling a South Asian Princess called Urdujā that he had traveled from India she confirmed "the pepper country?" before, by this account, suggesting that "I must invade it and take possession of it. Its wealth and its soldiers please me".[33] Likewise, the Maluku Islands, the only place in the world that grew nutmegs and cloves were known as the Spice Islands for hundreds of years. When describing this region, Pires carefully clarified which islands and goods were available and had clearly sought out information from more knowledgeable traders from nearby regions. These confirmed that "this merchandise is not known anywhere else in the world except in these places; and I asked and enquired very diligently whether they had this merchandise anywhere else and everyone said not". Indeed, according to Pires: "Malay merchants say that God made Timor for sandalwood and Banda for mace and the Maluku for cloves".[34]

Unlike many other commodities, the importance and sometimes mystery of these goods meant that they received considerable attention from travelers. For instance, such was pepper's value, Battuta took considerable time to describe pepper in detail while he was in Malabar:

> The pepper trees resemble grape vines; they are planted alongside coco-palms and climb up them in the same way that vines climb, except that they have no shoots, that is to say tendrils, like those of vines. The leaves of the trees resemble those of stocks, and some of them resemble the leaves of briar. It produces its fruit in small clusters, the grains of which resemble the grains of *abu qinninah* [the date palm] when they are green. In the autumn, they gather the grains and spread them on mats in the sun, just as is done with grapes in order to obtain raisins; they keep on turning them until they are thoroughly dried and become black, and then sell them to the merchants. Most people in our country suppose that they roast them with fire and that it is because of that they become crinkled, but it is not so since this results only from the action of the sun upon them. I have seen pepper grains in the city of Calicut being poured out for measuring by the bushel, like millet in our country.[35]

As this suggests, despite its familiarity to consumers across Eurasia, both the plants themselves and the methods of preparing pepper were unfamiliar. Considering the value of pepper in the premodern world, the notion of pouring grains by the bushel must have seemed like a remarkable display of wealth.

Nutmeg, cloves, and mace, as noted above, were products unique to the Maluku Islands and their origins were uncertain and sometimes mythologized in literature from Europe, the Islamic World, and China. This is clear in Battuta's efforts to describe them, and his efforts to persuade his readers that his portrayal was accurate. Much like his account of pepper in Malabar, he was similarly fascinated by the growing and collection of spices from the Maluku Islands. Despite not visiting the source of nutmegs and cloves, Battuta took some care to learn about them during his stay in Sumatra and assured his readers that he would "relate about them what we have seen ourselves, have examined with care and verified":[36]

> The clove trees are of a great age and huge. There are more of them in infidel than in Muslim country. They are not privately owned as they are so common. What is brought to our country is the wood. What people in our country call "the flower of the clove" is what falls from the flowers and is like orange flowers. The fruit of the clove is the nutmeg, known among us as the perfume nut. The flower that is formed within it is mace. I have seen all this and been witness to it.[37]

Yet, despite his bold assertion of accuracy, his understanding remained minimal, and he was unable to identify either that these spices came from different plants or their precise origin. Battuta, though, was certainly not alone in this respect.

Rather than being from the same tree, cloves were actually from the dried buds of the tree *Syzygium caryophyllata*, while nutmegs were seeds from the tree *Myristica fragrans*, and mace was made from the reddish seed covering of the nutmeg seed. By the time Pires was writing, the Maluku Islands were becoming more easily visited and understood, but knowledge about them was still keenly sought after. Thus, after rattling through quick descriptions of other islands in the region, Pires turned his attention the Banda islands "as we are so fond of the fruits of its soil". Banda, he explained, had six islands, of which "five produce mace and one has a volcano", and described the process of harvesting mace and nutmeg on the islands: "the mace is a fruit like peaches or apricots, and when it is ripe it opens and the outer pulp falls, and that in the inside turns red, and this is the mace on the nutmeg, and they gather them and put them to dry. This fruit is ripe all through the year; it is gathered every month".[38] In the Maluku Islands, too, Pires noted that there were five islands that produced the precious cloves and described how they were harvested:

> After flowering it [the fruit of the clove tree] turns green and then it turns red; then they gather it, some by hand and some beaten down with a pole, and red as it is they spread it out on mats to dry, and it turns black. They are small trees. Cloves grow like myrtle berries, a great many heads grow together. All this fruit is in the hands of the natives, and it all comes through their hands to the seacoast.[39]

Once reaching the coast, these products were sold for goods carried from across Asia, notably cotton cloth from India, by merchants that had traveled just as far. Having left these islands, these commodities would reach consumers across Asia, Europe, and Africa, often following routes that had been in existence for centuries as enduring testaments to the longevity and scale of long-distance trade in the premodern world.

As well as spices, the trading world of maritime Asia was host to an array of prized aromatics, medicines, and prestige display items that were exported long-distances. Despite not being quite so scarce as cloves or nutmeg were lent luxurious status by their rarity as well as their practical use for consumers. In Siam, for instance, Ma Huan reported that "the country produces yellow *su* incense, *Lo-ho su* incense, laka-wood, sinking incense, rose-wood, cardamoms, chaulmoogra seeds, dragon's blood, liana nodes, sapan-wood, flower tin, elephants' teeth, kingfishers' feathers, and other such things".[40] In Sumatra, Battuta described a range of aromatics that were available, including incense and Indian aloes, while goods including "musk in powder and pods", "apothecary's camphor in large quantities", and rhubarb were highlighted in Pires's account of China.[41] Like his fellow authors' descriptions of spice trees, Ma Huan too sought to describe the natural sources of more unusual commodities that he came across. In Dhufar, he explained that "the land produces frankincense; this incense is in truth the gum from a tree; this tree resembles an elm-tree, but its leaves are pointed and long; [and] the people there continually cut the tree, get the incense, and sell it".[42] In Java, another aromatic that he called "*Chin-yin* incense", which was probably benzoin and obtained as a resin from tree in the *Styrax* genus, was similarly described, but only in its gum state: "this incense resembles the black glue used by silversmiths for inlaying silver articles; inside there is a lump like a kind of white wax in the middle". Unlike its Arabian namesake, Ma Huan thought benzoin was "very pungent and irritates the nose", no matter how popular it was among "western foreigners".[43]

Agricultural commodities, then, whether everyday consumables like rice or rare spices like nutmeg and cloves, were a common source of commodities that played important roles in long-distance trade. They were not, of course, the only commodities available. Animals that were reared or hunted were also valuable. These, similarly, accounted for commodities that might be consumed within a local community, traded across a regional economy, or, in some special circumstances, be traded at a trans-continental scale. As such, these authors similarly took care to describe the animal products that were available. Mustawfi drew attention to the relationship between environment, animal rearing and agriculture, describing how in the "rugged mountain region" of Daylaman on the borders of Gilan near the Caspian Sea, Mustawfi noted that "sheep are plentifully reared" and "cattle pasture is common and nutritious", even though cotton and fruits were harder to grow in the harsh climate.[44] Elsewhere, it was the richness of the land and consequent rearing of particularly noteworthy livestock that drew his attention. In Qazvin, "the game-preserves and pastures are rich, more especially in fodder for camels, which here is superior to elsewhere: whereby the camels of Qazvin are of higher price than camels from other lands".[45] Isfahan, likewise, was blessed in this regard with "rich pasture lands, and every four-footed beast that is fattened here becomes twice as strong as it would if fattened elsewhere".[46] Mogadishu, "a town of enormous size" on the East African coast, was notably rich in livestock, and Battuta described how "its inhabitants are merchants possessed of vast resources; they own large numbers of camels, of which they slaughter hundreds every day" for food and "also have quantities of sheep".[47]

Some animals were prized enough to be involved in long-distance exchanges. Battuta described that "sheep brought from the land of the Turks" were given as presents in India alongside horses and camels.[48] Likewise, Arabian "thoroughbred horses" were exported from Yemen to India.[49] Pires, too, noted this trade, and described how horses sold via Ormuz were prized commodities in ports across India, with cities like Goa acting as intermediary markets for their sale deep into the interior of the subcontinent.[50] At a larger scale still, Battuta also recorded that mass transport of horses from Azov, at the mouth of the Don River, which served as an entry point into commercial networks into the Eurasian steppes, as well as an important base for Genoese traders to trade with the region. From here, "horses are exported to India in droves, each one numbering six thousand horses or more or less". These were herded by a drover "who looks after them and their pasturage, like sheep", across the long overland route to Multan in Sind. Here, they were sold for "a handsome profit ... for they sell the cheapest of them in the land of India for a hundred silver dinars, and often sell them for twice or three times as much". In India, they were prized not for speed, but because "what they prize in these horses is strength and length of pace".[51]

Sometimes, animal products were notable precisely because they had traveled great distances for trade. Unfortunately, one consequence of this is that knowledge of their origins was often limited. Therefore, when Mustawfi sought to describe Saqsin and Bolghar, cities on the Volga River, he was able to say little more than their having "many districts and plains" despite recognizing that "most of the furs in trade are brought from here".[52] Other animals were transported as living gifts over vast distances not because of their practical value but because of their value as prestige items for monarchs. Ma Huan described numerous animals that were sent to China. These included an ostrich "with black markings", a patterned zebra, and a spotted leopard. Less familiar still was a giraffe that was dispatched to the Chinese court and would go on to be painted by Shen Du. The giraffe, Ma Huan explained, was distinguished by a head "carried on a long neck" and "on its head it has two fleshy horns, beside the ears; it has the tail of an ox and the body of a deer". He was also particularly descriptive of a lion "which resembles a tiger's [body] in shape; it is a dark-yellow color, without stripes", and remarked that "the noise of its roar is like thunder. All the beasts, when they see it, fall down and dare not rise; it is indeed the king among the beasts".[53]

Mineral Products

Natural products provided a significant array of commodities for premodern traders, even as their perishability meant that the distances that many could be transported were limited. For mineral products, this was no concern, and instead the restrictions on the scale of long-distance trade was due to either the lack of demand for a product (iron, for instance, was for the most part too common to justify very long-distance trade) or the costs of transporting it (carrying a heavy commodity like stone was very expensive, and only undertaken over large distances if it was remarkably profitable to do so). Many mineral products that had everyday uses, such as stone for buildings or iron where it was abundant in the form of tools, were rarely observed by authors – it was simply too similar for readers wherever they were to find interesting. However, for certain mineral products our authors did take care to outline their origins and key markets, especially for material that was rare or particularly useful.

In this vein, while Mustawfi took little time expanding on sources of iron, copper or lead, which were commonly found nearby, other metals that had important practical uses but were less readily available did receive his attention. Tin was most easily sourced, he believed, "at Qal'ah, on the Indian frontier of China". This was most likely a reference to Kalah, the famous port of Kedah in the Malay Peninsula, and the term Qal'ah derived from the Malay word for tin, kalang. Additional sources that were similarly distant and only minimally understood, included "the tin mines of the Islands of Kalah [likely the same Kalah in Kedah] and Sarbuzah in the Indian Sea, and there are mines in the Frank Country".[54] More extreme still, in terms of the very limited information available to Mustawfi, was the metal zinc. He knew that zinc was not found anywhere in Iran and that "philosophers have said regarding it, that it might be taken as a comparison for non-existence". However, "in certain books ... it [is] stated that mines of it exist in China, where they make of this metal arms for war, and it gives an edge that is harder than iron".[55]

Battuta's and Pires's accounts reveal only limited interest in mines of any sort, while Ma Huan pays them even less attention. Where Battuta did take an interest, it was often to indicate the importance of certain metals within the economies of places he visited. In Kumish, in al-Iraq, he described a "a populous city which is visited by merchants from al-Traq and Syria, and in which there are silver mines", while the nearby town of Arzanjan had "well-organized bazaars, and there are manufactured in it fine fabrics which are called by its name" and was home to "mines of copper, from which they make utensils" and lampstands.[56] In Beirut he simply noted that "fruit and iron are exported from there to Egypt".[57] His description was richer when providing details about the workings of a copper mine outside Takadda in West Africa where "they dig it from the ground and bring it to the town where they smelt it in their houses. This is done by male and female slaves". The copper was then smelted into rods that were transported to destinations across the wider African region, including to Gobir, Bornu, and Kanem – the last of which was connected with trade routes running further east to the Indian Ocean coast.[58]

Pires takes a different approach, instead describing the abundance of certain products in different parts of maritime Asia. For example, he alluded to the local availability of copper in Sri Lanka by describing the "large houses of prayer, with copper pillars, and with roofs covered with lead and copper".[59] Likewise, when listing commodities available in China, Pires noted that "copper", "vases of copper", and "countless copper bracelets" were all available (while noting that he "did not see much" silver or gold), which again recognizes the relative available of different metals locally without taking interest in their production or origin specifically.[60] Similarly, there were some mentions of iron (from Sumatra, India, and China) and lead (from Siam), as traded commodities, but little further detail was recorded.[61]

Commodities that would only come to have greater value in later centuries also crop up in these accounts, notably coal, but of course our authors paid them no particular attention. Mustawfi, for instance, described how in the mountains of Ferghana, through which passed a key trading route between central and south Asia, there were mines that produced numerous valuable commodities including "turquoise, quicksilver, copper, lead, gold, naphtha, bitumen, asphalt, sal ammoniac and copperas". Notably, too, was "found here a stone [coal] used for fuel", although there is nothing to suggest that this was exported.[62] Indeed, Battuta makes no mention of coal being used in the region, and expressed disbelief that the use of "charcoal is unknown" in India, Persia or Khorasan, let alone the use of coal. Instead, Battuta described coal only in reference to China, where "they kindle stones in which the fire blazes up as it does in charcoal".[63] These descriptions were interesting asides about an unusual mineral rather than accounts of a potentially valuable trading good.

While minerals of all sorts were a valuable commodity for many economies, some metals like silver and gold were valued less for their practical applications and more for their prestige and beauty, as well as their utility as bullion. In Mustawfi's geographic study, sites where precious metals were mined are not numerous in his description of the Ilkhanate. The closest deposits were probably in the Ilaq and Ranik mountains, in Turkistan, there were "mines of silver and gold", as well as in Damghan in Iran where "ingots of gold are found here in the soil", but most were much further afield.[64] In a detailed section describing where gold could be found across the world, he described sources of the rare metal that included both well known deposits within the Islamic world as well as those that were likely only carried as rumors. Most gold, he believed, came from "the hot regions" that included "many mines of metal". However, for the best quality and output, the north African Maghrib region was without equal. Such was its reputation that "many say that from all times in Maghrib people who were acquainted with the art of Alchemy have made gold, for which cause it is that gold there is very abundant". More practically, Mustawfi understood that "the mines of Andalusia too are excellent, and very profitable", as was the "mine at

Al-Bajjah in Abyssinia" and "those in the desert lying between Egypt, Nubia, Abyssinia and the Red Sea". As well as the location of gold mines, he also took care to explain which were particularly challenging: the mine at Sijilmasa in the Maghrib "gives a great output, but the road thither is difficult, and the mine is troublesome to work".[65]

Other sources of gold were known only by rumor. Far to the east in "the Waqwaq Isles", likely to mean Japan, Mustawfi understood that there was a mine that reportedly "gives immense returns, so much so that most of the government edicts of that people are inscribed in gold". Less distant but more unsettling were accounts of mines in the Rāng Mountains in Turkistan, and he warned that while gold was easily found on the surface "it is a notable fact that if the large ingots are carried off then a death occurs among the people here". Some rumors received more critical treatment, and he questioned whether "much celebrated" stories regarding a mine in Sistan were to be believed. Here, during the Ghaznavid Empire, "a golden tree in the earth" had purportedly been discovered, but Mustawfi considered that this was "hardly credible, for how should a metal be a growing thing like a plant, seeing that metal is more of the nature of an inorganic fossil than of a vegetable?". He warned his readers that the "truth seems to be that the mine really never existed, and that the account of it is but a fable told to amuse and entertain ignorant folk".[66]

Mustawfi gave silver mines a similar treatment to gold mines, but, being "mostly in cold countries, and the best, by reason of the purity of the ore, and the abundant output, are those in the Frank countries [Europe]", less details were provided regarding their precise locations or other information.[67] Battuta offered more information related to silver, but often this too was shaped by his interest in the distant people who produced it as much as the commodity itself. In "the mountains of the Rus" were "silver mines, and from it are imported the *sawm*, that is, the ingots of silver with which selling and buying are done in this land". These mines were overseen by the Rus, "who are Christians; they have red hair, blue eyes, and ugly faces, and are treacherous folk".[68]

A similar difficulty in discerning the origins of precious metals is apparent in Ma Huan's text. While gold and silver appear regularly throughout his account, usually when describing coins or decorative displays of wealth, he does not mention any mines or offer detail in where gold and silver were sourced: at least beyond sharing a "traditional story" from Calicut about an ox that excreted gold for the people.[69] He did, though, make note of where gold was available as a traded good, describing how Java was an emporium for all manner of precious metals and gemstones: "foreigners from every place come here in great numbers to trade. Gold, all kinds of precious stones, and all varieties of foreign goods are sold in great quantities. The people are very wealthy".[70]

Pires, on the other hand, was much more dedicated in trying to identity the sources of gold, even when the precise details were fairly minimal. When describing Abyssinians, he is able to provide no more than simple noting that "they have foodstuffs in their land and gold".[71] This, alongside gold sourced from Egypt, entered the Indian Ocean through Aden and Ormuz, which would, of course, then be exchanged for goods from across Asia in emporium like Cambay, or carried further still.[72] Gold was also available from Menangkabau in Champa where "gold in big pieces" was available thanks to a nearby mine.[73] Although it was beyond his own experience, Pires understood that Japan was also a source of gold and copper, and supplied much of the precious metal that was available in maritime eastern Asia.[74] Other sources of gold in Asia, he suggests, included Siam, Cambodia and Dai Viet, where gold was among the commodities he believed were available for visiting merchants. Otherwise, Pires discussed gold mainly in reference to its usage as currency and on occasion decorative items: in Siam "the lords wear as many as nine gold ones, with beautiful treble, contralto and tenor tones".[75]

As well as metals, mineral products that were sought after by long-distance traders also included stones of various sorts, with precious gems representing some of the rarest and most sought-after goods in the global marketplace. Certain gemstones, like spices, were found only in specific locations, leading to speculative ideas about their origins and ongoing uncertainty about where they could be found. Mustawfi shared a number of stories about these locations, but often with only scarce information, such as his note that "sapphire mines lie near the equator, for there the power of the heat is greatest, and the sapphire is only able to get to its maturity after the lapse of time under a powerful heat".[76] This would not, of course, be much use for an enterprising merchant seeking to purchase them. Emeralds, likewise, were incredibly rare, but Mustawfi was able to offer a more precise location for what he believed what their source, in this case at Mount Mokattam in Egypt: "in the whole world there is no other emerald mine but this".[77] In relation to other gems, the location might be precise, but the knowledge about it was wrapped in mythology. Mustawfi told a tale how, on a mountain in Sarandib on the island of Sri Lanka, "one of the most famous of mountains", there were "mines of corundum [likely rubies or sapphires], emery and rock crystal" and that "on these grounds great pieces of diamond are strewn about". Yet, despite the great wealth this would suggest, its fame instead came from it being "where Adam fell (to earth, when ejected from Paradise)" and that "a footprint of Adam may be seen on a rock here". This fantastical history of the mountain perhaps goes some way to explain the other commodities available nearby, including "odorous woods", "musk and civet", numerous medicinal herbs, and a nearby pearl fishery.[78] Elsewhere on Sri Lanka, Mustawfi believed, were valleys where diamonds could be found – the only source of the precious gems in the world. Unfortunately, "fear of the vipers that live in these valleys" meant that "none dare go there". Instead, "only by tricks and artifices, using birds to carry forth the same, is it possible to get the stones out from these valleys, and it is because of this that all the pieces of diamond are so small".[79]

Manufactured Products

Manufactured products appeared less in these accounts than we might expect, at least in terms of information about their sources and production. That being said, descriptions of rulers and other figures were often replete with details of the richness of the possessions, and these often included rich silks, cottons and other fabrics, as well as jewelry, weaponry bearing precious stones, and other signs of prestige. In Champa, Ma Huan described how the king "on his body he wears a long robe of foreign cloth with small designs worked in threads of the five colors", while the king in Dhufar "uses a white, fine foreign cloth to bind round his head; on his body he wears [a robe] which has fine silk embroidery in a blue floral design" and "on his feet he wears foreign boots".[80] In both cases, it was the foreignness of the cloth that drew Ma Huan's attention. In a more extreme display of wealth, Battuta note that on his visit to Sultan Muhammad bin Tughluq of Delhi, even "the elephants are adorned with silk, gold, and precious stones"![81]

Mustawfi's account of the Ilkhanate spends less time on finished products than he does agricultural commodities, but he does take care to note where the raw materials for textile production could be found. Predominantly his focus was on cotton, which was grown across Iran, but there were occasional references to other products, especially when of particularly high quality.[82] In Sivas, in Rüm, he noted that "the climate here is cold. Crops of corn, fruits and cotton are raised, and the wool of Sivas, which is so renowned, comes from the district".[83] Elsewhere, he described sites where silk was harvested, such as in Qabalah near Darband which "produces excellent silk, also corn and other cereals" or in Junabad where "excellent silk is obtained here in abundance".[84]

Battuta, too, took note of some locations where raw materials for textiles production were particularly plentiful. Torbat-e Jam was notable because "most of its trees are mulberries, and silk is to be had there in quantities".[85] In Bush, Battuta reported that "this town is the chief centre of the Egyptian linen industry, and it is exported thence to all parts of Egypt and to Africa", while the silk fabrics of Nishapur in northern Iran were taken by merchants to India and beyond.[86] When travelling on the East African coast, Battuta noted that the "woven fabrics" made in Mogadishu were "unequalled" in quality and were "exported from it to Egypt and elsewhere".[87] In Aksaray, it was "rugs of sheep's wool ... which have no equal in any country" that drew Battuta's attention, and such were their quality that merchants carried them as far as Egypt, India and even China.[88]

Ma Yuan gives a clearer insight into the range of textile products available, especially, as well as other manufactured goods. In Bengal, he noted that the "land produces five or six kinds of fine cloths" that he named and described in detail. These comprised of: *pi* which was white and "as fine as starched paper; *man-che-t'i* which was orange and "closely-woven and strong"; a cotton crepe called *sha-na-pa-fu*; *hsin-pai-ch'in-ta-li* which was a fine cotton gauze; a "good, triple-thread cotton cloth" known as *sha-t'a-erh*; and a cotton cloth with a "raised flossy surface" called *mo-hei-mo-li*. As well as these cotton textiles, Bengal was also well supplied with raw silk from its mulberry trees, although Ma Yuan believed that they "do not understand how to make silk-floss". Additionally, lacquered objects of various types were available, as was a "glossy and smooth" type of paper. All of these, it seems likely, were among the "local products" that were obtained in Bengal for the return voyage to China.[89]

In a similar vein, much of the information about textiles in Pires's text comes in sections where he is describing their sale rather than their production. For example, he described that in the past merchants had sold poor quality cloth, but now high quality Indian cottons were the most sought after commodity: "the chief merchandise for Banda is the Gujarat cloth, to wit, red and black *bretangis*, *cafutos*, white and black *maindis*, *corafones* cloth, *patolas*, and after these cloth from Bengal and after Bengal from Coromandel".[90] However, some sites of production are mentioned. In Shiraz he reported that there was "a great deal of silk from which rich cloths are made, and many kinds of camlet in fine colors and very good".[91] This was produced at a greater scale still in China, where he considered silk the "chief merchandise" from the country, including "raw white silk in large quantities" but also finished cloths including "loose colored silks, many in quantity, satins of that all colors, damask checkered *enrolados* in all colors, taffetas and other thin silk cloths called *xaas*".[92]

As well as textiles, other manufactured goods were also sought after, and those that were carried the greatest distances often combined utility with beauty, with their particular value often coming from the rarity of their component products or the quality of their decoration. Ma Huan was particularly appreciative of the knives made in Java "which are all made of steel" and decorated "with most intricate patterns drawn in very delicate lines". As well as the blades, the handles were notable in their use of gold, rhinoceros horn or ivory that were "engraved with representations of human forms or devils' faces, the craftsmanship being very fine and skilful".[93] Pires drew attention to manufacturing quality in Liuqiu, which was renowned for its metalwork. Here, the people were "great draftsmen and armourers. They make gilt coffers, very rich and well-made fans, swords, many arms of all kinds after their fashion". When it came to armaments, Pires suggested "just as we in our kingdoms speak of Milan [for its reputation in this regard], so do the Chinese and all the other races speak of the *Lequios*". Consequently, the islands exports were dominated by "gold, copper, and arms of all kinds, coffers [and] boxes (*caxonjas*) with gold leaf veneer".[94]

Chinese porcelain was renowned despite pottery of other sorts being produced all over Eurasia, was also a commodity that was transported vast distanced. Battuta described how "Chinese pottery is made only in the city of Zaitun [Quanzhou] and Sin Kalan [Guangzhou]" and was "made from an earth from mountains there which burns like charcoal". Not only was it "the most superb kind of pottery" but in China "the price is that of pottery in our country, or less". Consequently, it was "exported to India and other parts of the world" and even "reaches our country in the Maghrib".[95] In the other direction, he described briefly that in Malaga "is made the wonderful gilded pottery that is exported to the remotest countries".[96] The value of Chinese porcelain was also reflected in Ma Huan's account which described how Chinese commodities were sought after in markets. In Champa "they very much like the dishes, bowls, and other kinds of blue porcelain articles" that were carried from China, as well as silk. In return, they "bring their pale gold and give it in exchange" as well as rhinoceros horns, elephant ivory and incense.[97] Likewise, in Java "the people of the country are very fond of the blue patterned porcelainware", and also silk, musk, and beads. These were purchased with copper coins and exchanged for "foreign products".[98] In Sri Lanka, similar goods, including colored silk-taffeta and porcelain, were traded for "precious stones and pearls", while in Dhufar the Chinese visitors received frankincense, myrrh and other aromatics.[99] In Aden Chinese goods were sold for rubies, large pearls, the "stems of coral trees" and even lions, zebra, leopards, and ostriches![100]

Across their descriptions, these authors revealed the array of commodities that were being traded in premodern markets. They gave some indication of the way in which different commodities were valued, and the ways in which contemporaries might have understood their connection to wider exchanges of goods across Eurasia. However, as much as the commodities themselves, it is often how and where these authors place them that reveal details about the practice and structure of premodern trade. Whether in emporium that attracted merchants from across vast regions or in gift exchanges between rulers, the collection of global commodities into the same spaces and contexts do much to attest to the intensity of connection across Eurasia during this period, even as the particular value of commodities sometimes depended on a rarity that stemmed from their production far from the major centers of population or wealth.

Global connections and the gathering of commodities together is clear in Pires's observation of the global exchanges that were taking place in Aden, a city to which merchants from across maritime Asia traveled to trade, and whose own merchants "go everywhere". Here, he described a market that functioned primarily as a meeting point for various different trades and traffics. It was not the source of any particular commodity but an emporium:

> This town has a great trade with the people of Cairo as well as with those of all India, and the people of India trade with it. There are many important merchants in the city with great riches, and many from other

> countries live there also. This city is a meeting place for merchants. It is one of the four great trading cities in the world, and it has dealings inside the straits with Jeddah, to which it trades most of the spices and drugs in exchange for the said [merchandise]. It trades cloth to Dahlak and receives seed pearls in exchange; it trades coarse cloths and various trifling things to Zeila and Berbera in exchange for gold, horses, slaves and ivory; it trades with Socotra, sending cloth, straw of Mecca, Socotrine aloes, and dragon's-blood; it trades with Ormuz, whence it brings horses; and out of the goods from Cairo it trades gold, foodstuffs, wheat, and rice if there is any, spices, seed pearls, musk, silk and any other drugs; it trades with Cambay, taking there the merchandise from Cairo and opium, and returning large quantities of cloth, with which it trades in Arabia and the Islands, and seeds, glass beads, beads from Cambay, many carnelians of all colours, and chiefly spices and drugs from Melaka, cloves, nutmeg, mace, sandalwood, cubeb, seed pearls and things of that sort.
>
> It takes a great quantity of madder and raisins to Cambay, and also to Ormuz; it trades with the kingdom of Goa, and takes there all sorts of merchandise and horses both from [Aden] itself and from Cairo, and receives in return rice, iron, sugar, fine muslin, and quantities of gold; it trades with Malabar in India, where the main market was Calicut, whence it took pepper and ginger; and it traded merchandise from Melaka with Bengal in return for many kinds of white cloths, and it traded the merchandise from Melaka also with Pegu in exchange for lac, benzoin, musk and precious stones, rice also from Bengal, rice from Siam, and merchandise from China which comes through Ayutthaya. And in this way it has become great, prosperous and rich, and the king receives all his revenues from Aden alone, for all the rest is nothing.[101]

Pires makes it abundantly clear how the city's wealth and the goods that flowed through it were dependent on linkages that brought together many different commodities in a complex web of exchanges rather than down a single route. The commercial links that made this possible were long-distance and multi-direction, and Aden benefited from direct links across maritime Asia from Egypt to Siam: gateways to Mediterranean and Chinese markets respectively.

An exchange of gifts between the Yuan Emperor of China and the Sultan of Delhi, described by Battuta, shows how different types of commodities could be transported together during long-distance exchanges. In this case, "five hundred pieces of velvet cloth, including a hundred of those which are manufactured in the city of Zaitun [Quanzhou], and a hundred of those which are manufactured in Khansa [Hangzhou], five maunds of musk, five robes adorned with jewels, five embroidered quivers, and five swords, as well as one-hundred enslaved people", had been sent to India.[102] In return came a similarly diverse array of gifts, which are worth recounting in full:

> A hundred thoroughbred horses saddled and bridled, a hundred male slaves, a hundred Hindu singing- and dancing-girls, a hundred pieces of *bairami* cloth, which are made of cotton and are unequalled in beauty each piece being worth a hundred dinars, a hundred lengths of the silk fabrics called *khazz*, in which the silk material of each is dyed with four or five different colours, four hundred pieces of the fabrics known as *salahi*, a hundred pieces of *shirin-baf,* a hundred pieces of *shan-baf*, five hundred pieces of *mir'izz* woollens, one hundred of them black and a hundred each in white, red, green, and blue, a hundred lengths of Greek linen, a hundred pieces of blanket cloth, a *seracha* [large tent], six pavilions, four candelabra in gold and six in silver enamelled, four golden basins with ewers to match, and six silver basins, ten embroidered robes of honor from the Sultan's own wardrobe and ten caps worn by him, one of them encrusted with pearls, ten embroidered quivers one of them encrusted with pearls, ten swords one of them with a scabbard encrusted with pearls, *dastban,* that is gloves, embroidered with pearls, and fifteen eunuchs.[103]

In this single exchange between China and India goods of many of the types described throughout this chapter were present, especially after the supplies for the journeys were taken into account. Long-distance trade in the premodern world could connect producers and consumers from across the widest expanse of Eurasia, and in doing so helped create and was dependent on the formation of webs of exchange that crossed and connected the world.

Notes

1 Francis Balducci Pegolotti, *Libro di Divisamenti di Paesi* [The Book of the Descriptions of Countries], trans. in Henry Yule (ed.), *Cathay and the Way Thither, vol. 2* (London, 1866), pp. 279–82.
2 Francis Balducci Pegolotti, *Libro di Divisamenti di Paesi* [The Book of the Descriptions of Countries], trans. in Henry Yule (ed.), *Cathay and the Way Thither, vol. 2* (London, 1866), pp. 293–5.
3 Francis Balducci Pegolotti, *Libro di Divisamenti di Paesi* [The Book of the Descriptions of Countries], trans. in Henry Yule (ed.), *Cathay and the Way Thither, vol. 2* (London, 1866), pp. 302–6.
4 Ibn Battuta, *The Rihla*, trans. H. A. R. Gibb and C. F. Beckingham (eds.), *The Travels of Ibn Battuta, AD 1325–54*, 4 vols. (London, 1994).
5 Hamdallah Mustawfi, *Nuzhat al-Qulub*, trans. G. Le Strange, *The Geographical Part of the Nuzhat-Al-Qulūb* (Leiden, 1919).
6 Ma Huan, *Yingya Shenglan* [The Overall Survey of the Ocean's Shores], trans. J. V. G. Mills, *Ma Huan, Ying-Yai Sheng-Lan: "The overall survey of the ocean's shores, 1433"* (Cambridge, 1970).

7 Tomé Pires, *Suma Oriental que trata do Mar Roxo até aos Chins* [An Account of the East, from the Red Sea to China], trans. Armando Cortesão (ed.), *The Suma Oriental of Tome Pires* (London, 1944).
8 Hamdallah Mustawfi, *Nuzhat al-Qulub*, trans. G. Le Strange, *The Geographical Part of the Nuzhat-Al-Qulūb* (Leiden, 1919), pp. 109–10.
9 Ibn Battuta, *The Rihla*, trans. H. A. R. Gibb and C. F. Beckingham (eds.), *The Travels of Ibn Battuta, AD 1325–54*, 4 vols. (London, 1994), pp. 545, 608, 734.
10 Ibn Battuta, *The Rihla*, trans. H. A. R. Gibb and C. F. Beckingham (eds.), *The Travels of Ibn Battuta, AD 1325–54*, 4 vols. (London, 1994), pp. 611–12.
11 Ibn Battuta, *The Rihla*, trans. H. A. R. Gibb and C. F. Beckingham (eds.), *The Travels of Ibn Battuta, AD 1325–54*, 4 vols. (London, 1994), pp. 617, 808.
12 Ma Huan, *Yingya Shenglan* [The Overall Survey of the Ocean's Shores], trans. J. V. G. Mills, *Ma Huan, Ying-Yai Sheng-Lan: "The overall survey of the ocean's shores, 1433"* (Cambridge, 1970), p. 91.
13 Ma Huan, *Yingya Shenglan* [The Overall Survey of the Ocean's Shores], trans. J. V. G. Mills, *Ma Huan, Ying-Yai Sheng-Lan: "The overall survey of the ocean's shores, 1433"* (Cambridge, 1970), p. 99.
14 Ma Huan, *Yingya Shenglan* [The Overall Survey of the Ocean's Shores], trans. J. V. G. Mills, *Ma Huan, Ying-Yai Sheng-Lan: "The overall survey of the ocean's shores, 1433"* (Cambridge, 1970), p. 79.
15 Ma Huan, *Yingya Shenglan* [The Overall Survey of the Ocean's Shores], trans. J. V. G. Mills, *Ma Huan, Ying-Yai Sheng-Lan: "The overall survey of the ocean's shores, 1433"* (Cambridge, 1970), p. 103.
16 Ma Huan, *Yingya Shenglan* [The Overall Survey of the Ocean's Shores], trans. J. V. G. Mills, *Ma Huan, Ying-Yai Sheng-Lan: "The overall survey of the ocean's shores, 1433"* (Cambridge, 1970), p. 162.
17 Tomé Pires, *Suma Oriental que trata do Mar Roxo até aos Chins* [An Account of the East, from the Red Sea to China], trans. Armando Cortesão (ed.), *The Suma Oriental of Tome Pires* (London, 1944), p. 24.
18 Tomé Pires, *Suma Oriental que trata do Mar Roxo até aos Chins* [An Account of the East, from the Red Sea to China], trans. Armando Cortesão (ed.), *The Suma Oriental of Tome Pires* (London, 1944), pp. 33, 43.
19 Tomé Pires, *Suma Oriental que trata do Mar Roxo até aos Chins* [An Account of the East, from the Red Sea to China], trans. Armando Cortesão (ed.), *The Suma Oriental of Tome Pires* (London, 1944), p. 88.
20 Hamdallah Mustawfi, *Nuzhat al-Qulub*, trans. G. Le Strange, *The Geographical Part of the Nuzhat-Al-Qulūb* (Leiden, 1919), pp. 37, 42, 59–62, 67–71, 74, 76–7, 86–90, 98–103, 105, 108, 114–15, 118, 120, 124, 137, 140–1, 143, 149, 152–3, 156–7, 159, 242, 244.
21 Ma Huan, *Yingya Shenglan* [The Overall Survey of the Ocean's Shores], trans. J. V. G. Mills, *Ma Huan, Ying-Yai Sheng-Lan: "The overall survey of the ocean's shores, 1433"* (Cambridge, 1970), p. 119.
22 Hamdallah Mustawfi, *Nuzhat al-Qulub*, trans. G. Le Strange, *The Geographical Part of the Nuzhat-Al-Qulūb* (Leiden, 1919), pp. 97–8.
23 Hamdallah Mustawfi, *Nuzhat al-Qulub*, trans. G. Le Strange, *The Geographical Part of the Nuzhat-Al-Qulūb* (Leiden, 1919), p. 142.
24 Tomé Pires, *Suma Oriental que trata do Mar Roxo até aos Chins* [An Account of the East, from the Red Sea to China], trans. Armando Cortesão (ed.), *The Suma Oriental of Tome Pires* (London, 1944), p. 17.
25 Hamdallah Mustawfi, *Nuzhat al-Qulub*, trans. G. Le Strange, *The Geographical Part of the Nuzhat-Al-Qulūb* (Leiden, 1919), p. 56.
26 Ibn Battuta, *The Rihla*, trans. H. A. R. Gibb and C. F. Beckingham (eds.), *The Travels of Ibn Battuta, AD 1325–54*, 4 vols. (London, 1994), p. 550.

27 Tomé Pires, *Suma Oriental que trata do Mar Roxo até aos Chins* [An Account of the East, from the Red Sea to China], trans. Armando Cortesão (ed.), *The Suma Oriental of Tome Pires* (London, 1944), p. 83.
28 Ibn Battuta, *The Rihla*, trans. H. A. R. Gibb and C. F. Beckingham (eds.), *The Travels of Ibn Battuta, AD 1325–54*, 4 vols. (London, 1994), p. 547.
29 Ibn Battuta, *The Rihla*, trans. H. A. R. Gibb and C. F. Beckingham (eds.), *The Travels of Ibn Battuta, AD 1325–54*, 4 vols. (London, 1994), p. 400.
30 Ma Huan, *Yingya Shenglan* [The Overall Survey of the Ocean's Shores], trans. J. V. G. Mills, *Ma Huan, Ying-Yai Sheng-Lan: "The overall survey of the ocean's shores, 1433"* (Cambridge, 1970), pp. 165–9.
31 Tomé Pires, *Suma Oriental que trata do Mar Roxo até aos Chins* [An Account of the East, from the Red Sea to China], trans. Armando Cortesão (ed.), *The Suma Oriental of Tome Pires* (London, 1944), p. 11.
32 Ibn Battuta, *The Rihla*, trans. H. A. R. Gibb and C. F. Beckingham (eds.), *The Travels of Ibn Battuta, AD 1325–54*, 4 vols. (London, 1994), p. 805.
33 Ibn Battuta, *The Rihla*, trans. H. A. R. Gibb and C. F. Beckingham (eds.), *The Travels of Ibn Battuta, AD 1325–54*, 4 vols. (London, 1994), p. 886.
34 Tomé Pires, *Suma Oriental que trata do Mar Roxo até aos Chins* [An Account of the East, from the Red Sea to China], trans. Armando Cortesão (ed.), *The Suma Oriental of Tome Pires* (London, 1944), p. 204.
35 Ibn Battuta, *The Rihla*, trans. H. A. R. Gibb and C. F. Beckingham (eds.), *The Travels of Ibn Battuta, AD 1325–54*, 4 vols. (London, 1994), p. 807.
36 Ibn Battuta, *The Rihla*, trans. H. A. R. Gibb and C. F. Beckingham (eds.), *The Travels of Ibn Battuta, AD 1325–54*, 4 vols. (London, 1994), p. 882.
37 Ibn Battuta, *The Rihla*, trans. H. A. R. Gibb and C. F. Beckingham (eds.), *The Travels of Ibn Battuta, AD 1325–54*, 4 vols. (London, 1994), p. 882.
38 Tomé Pires, *Suma Oriental que trata do Mar Roxo até aos Chins* [An Account of the East, from the Red Sea to China], trans. Armando Cortesão (ed.), *The Suma Oriental of Tome Pires* (London, 1944), pp. 205–6.
39 Tomé Pires, *Suma Oriental que trata do Mar Roxo até aos Chins* [An Account of the East, from the Red Sea to China], trans. Armando Cortesão (ed.), *The Suma Oriental of Tome Pires* (London, 1944), pp. 213–16.
40 Ma Huan, *Yingya Shenglan* [The Overall Survey of the Ocean's Shores], trans. J. V. G. Mills, *Ma Huan, Ying-Yai Sheng-Lan: "The overall survey of the ocean's shores, 1433"* (Cambridge, 1970), p. 106.
41 Ibn Battuta, *The Rihla*, trans. H. A. R. Gibb and C. F. Beckingham (eds.), *The Travels of Ibn Battuta, AD 1325–54*, 4 vols. (London, 1994), p. 881; Tomé Pires, *Suma Oriental que trata do Mar Roxo até aos Chins* [An Account of the East, from the Red Sea to China], trans. Armando Cortesão (ed.), *The Suma Oriental of Tome Pires* (London, 1944), p. 125.
42 Ma Huan, *Yingya Shenglan* [The Overall Survey of the Ocean's Shores], trans. J. V. G. Mills, *Ma Huan, Ying-Yai Sheng-Lan: "The overall survey of the ocean's shores, 1433"* (Cambridge, 1970), p. 152.
43 Ma Huan, *Yingya Shenglan* [The Overall Survey of the Ocean's Shores], trans. J. V. G. Mills, *Ma Huan, Ying-Yai Sheng-Lan: "The overall survey of the ocean's shores, 1433"* (Cambridge, 1970), p. 101.
44 Hamdallah Mustawfi, *Nuzhat al-Qulub*, trans. G. Le Strange, *The Geographical Part of the Nuzhat-Al-Qulūb* (Leiden, 1919), pp. 65–6.
45 Hamdallah Mustawfi, *Nuzhat al-Qulub*, trans. G. Le Strange, *The Geographical Part of the Nuzhat-Al-Qulūb* (Leiden, 1919), p. 64.
46 Hamdallah Mustawfi, *Nuzhat al-Qulub*, trans. G. Le Strange, *The Geographical Part of the Nuzhat-Al-Qulūb* (Leiden, 1919), p. 56.
47 Ibn Battuta, *The Rihla*, trans. H. A. R. Gibb and C. F. Beckingham (eds.), *The Travels of Ibn Battuta, AD 1325–54*, 4 vols. (London, 1994), p. 374.

48 Ibn Battuta, *The Rihla*, trans. H. A. R. Gibb and C. F. Beckingham (eds.), *The Travels of Ibn Battuta, AD 1325–54*, 4 vols. (London, 1994), p. 742.
49 Ibn Battuta, *The Rihla*, trans. H. A. R. Gibb and C. F. Beckingham (eds.), *The Travels of Ibn Battuta, AD 1325–54*, 4 vols. (London, 1994), p. 382.
50 Tomé Pires, *Suma Oriental que trata do Mar Roxo até aos Chins* [An Account of the East, from the Red Sea to China], trans. Armando Cortesão (ed.), *The Suma Oriental of Tome Pires* (London, 1944), pp. 20–1, 58, 62.
51 Ibn Battuta, *The Rihla*, trans. H. A. R. Gibb and C. F. Beckingham (eds.), *The Travels of Ibn Battuta, AD 1325–54*, 4 vols. (London, 1994), pp. 478–9.
52 Hamdallah Mustawfi, *Nuzhat al-Qulub*, trans. G. Le Strange, *The Geographical Part of the Nuzhat-Al-Qulūb* (Leiden, 1919), p. 252.
53 Ma Huan, *Yingya Shenglan* [The Overall Survey of the Ocean's Shores], trans. J. V. G. Mills, *Ma Huan, Ying-Yai Sheng-Lan: "The overall survey of the ocean's shores, 1433"* (Cambridge, 1970), pp. 158–9.
54 Hamdallah Mustawfi, *Nuzhat al-Qulub*, trans. G. Le Strange, *The Geographical Part of the Nuzhat-Al-Qulūb* (Leiden, 1919), p. 194.
55 Hamdallah Mustawfi, *Nuzhat al-Qulub*, trans. G. Le Strange, *The Geographical Part of the Nuzhat-Al-Qulūb* (Leiden, 1919), p. 194.
56 Ibn Battuta, *The Rihla*, trans. H. A. R. Gibb and C. F. Beckingham (eds.), *The Travels of Ibn Battuta, AD 1325–54*, 4 vols. (London, 1994), pp. 436–7.
57 Ibn Battuta, *The Rihla*, trans. H. A. R. Gibb and C. F. Beckingham (eds.), *The Travels of Ibn Battuta, AD 1325–54*, 4 vols. (London, 1994), p. 85.
58 Ibn Battuta, *The Rihla*, trans. H. A. R. Gibb and C. F. Beckingham (eds.), *The Travels of Ibn Battuta, AD 1325–54*, 4 vols. (London, 1994), p. 974.
59 Tomé Pires, *Suma Oriental que trata do Mar Roxo até aos Chins* [An Account of the East, from the Red Sea to China], trans. Armando Cortesão (ed.), *The Suma Oriental of Tome Pires* (London, 1944), p. 84.
60 Tomé Pires, *Suma Oriental que trata do Mar Roxo até aos Chins* [An Account of the East, from the Red Sea to China], trans. Armando Cortesão (ed.), *The Suma Oriental of Tome Pires* (London, 1944), 125.
61 Tomé Pires, *Suma Oriental que trata do Mar Roxo até aos Chins* [An Account of the East, from the Red Sea to China], trans. Armando Cortesão (ed.), *The Suma Oriental of Tome Pires* (London, 1944), pp. 17, 62, 108, 125, 156–7.
62 Hamdallah Mustawfi, *Nuzhat al-Qulub*, trans. G. Le Strange, *The Geographical Part of the Nuzhat-Al-Qulūb* (Leiden, 1919), p. 188.
63 Ibn Battuta, *The Rihla*, trans. H. A. R. Gibb and C. F. Beckingham (eds.), *The Travels of Ibn Battuta, AD 1325–54*, 4 vols. (London, 1994), pp. 545–6.
64 Hamdallah Mustawfi, *Nuzhat al-Qulub*, trans. G. Le Strange, *The Geographical Part of the Nuzhat-Al-Qulūb* (Leiden, 1919), pp. 183, 185.
65 Hamdallah Mustawfi, *Nuzhat al-Qulub*, trans. G. Le Strange, *The Geographical Part of the Nuzhat-Al-Qulūb* (Leiden, 1919), pp. 192–3.
66 Hamdallah Mustawfi, *Nuzhat al-Qulub*, trans. G. Le Strange, *The Geographical Part of the Nuzhat-Al-Qulūb* (Leiden, 1919), pp. 192–3.
67 Hamdallah Mustawfi, *Nuzhat al-Qulub*, trans. G. Le Strange, *The Geographical Part of the Nuzhat-Al-Qulūb* (Leiden, 1919), p. 193.
68 Ibn Battuta, *The Rihla*, trans. H. A. R. Gibb and C. F. Beckingham (eds.), *The Travels of Ibn Battuta, AD 1325–54*, 4 vols. (London, 1994), pp. 498–9.
69 Ma Huan, *Yingya Shenglan* [The Overall Survey of the Ocean's Shores], trans. J. V. G. Mills, *Ma Huan, Ying-Yai Sheng-Lan: "The overall survey of the ocean's shores, 1433"* (Cambridge, 1970), p. 139.
70 Ma Huan, *Yingya Shenglan* [The Overall Survey of the Ocean's Shores], trans. J. V. G. Mills, *Ma Huan, Ying-Yai Sheng-Lan: "The overall survey of the ocean's shores, 1433"* (Cambridge, 1970), p. 90.

71 Tomé Pires, *Suma Oriental que trata do Mar Roxo até aos Chins* [An Account of the East, from the Red Sea to China], trans. Armando Cortesão (ed.), *The Suma Oriental of Tome Pires* (London, 1944), p. 8.
72 Tomé Pires, *Suma Oriental que trata do Mar Roxo até aos Chins* [An Account of the East, from the Red Sea to China], trans. Armando Cortesão (ed.), *The Suma Oriental of Tome Pires* (London, 1944), pp. 17, 47.
73 Tomé Pires, *Suma Oriental que trata do Mar Roxo até aos Chins* [An Account of the East, from the Red Sea to China], trans. Armando Cortesão (ed.), *The Suma Oriental of Tome Pires* (London, 1944), p. 113.
74 Tomé Pires, *Suma Oriental que trata do Mar Roxo até aos Chins* [An Account of the East, from the Red Sea to China], trans. Armando Cortesão (ed.), *The Suma Oriental of Tome Pires* (London, 1944), p. 131.
75 Tomé Pires, *Suma Oriental que trata do Mar Roxo até aos Chins* [An Account of the East, from the Red Sea to China], trans. Armando Cortesão (ed.), *The Suma Oriental of Tome Pires* (London, 1944), p. 102.
76 Hamdallah Mustawfi, *Nuzhat al-Qulub*, trans. G. Le Strange, *The Geographical Part of the Nuzhat-Al-Qulūb* (Leiden, 1919), p. 196.
77 Hamdallah Mustawfi, *Nuzhat al-Qulub*, trans. G. Le Strange, *The Geographical Part of the Nuzhat-Al-Qulūb* (Leiden, 1919), p. 195.
78 Hamdallah Mustawfi, *Nuzhat al-Qulub*, trans. G. Le Strange, *The Geographical Part of the Nuzhat-Al-Qulūb* (Leiden, 1919), pp. 186–7.
79 Hamdallah Mustawfi, *Nuzhat al-Qulub*, trans. G. Le Strange, *The Geographical Part of the Nuzhat-Al-Qulūb* (Leiden, 1919), p. 195.
80 Ma Huan, *Yingya Shenglan* [The Overall Survey of the Ocean's Shores], trans. J. V. G. Mills, *Ma Huan, Ying-Yai Sheng-Lan: "The overall survey of the ocean's shores, 1433"* (Cambridge, 1970), pp. 79, 151.
81 Ibn Battuta, *The Rihla*, trans. H. A. R. Gibb and C. F. Beckingham (eds.), *The Travels of Ibn Battuta, AD 1325–54*, 4 vols. (London, 1994), p. 663.
82 Hamdallah Mustawfi, *Nuzhat al-Qulub*, trans. G. Le Strange, *The Geographical Part of the Nuzhat-Al-Qulūb* (Leiden, 1919), pp. 37, 42, 59–62, 67–71, 74, 76–7, 86–90, 98–103, 105, 108, 114–15, 118, 120, 124, 137, 140–1, 143, 149, 152–3, 156–7, 159, 242, 244.
83 Hamdallah Mustawfi, *Nuzhat al-Qulub*, trans. G. Le Strange, *The Geographical Part of the Nuzhat-Al-Qulūb* (Leiden, 1919), p. 95.
84 Hamdallah Mustawfi, *Nuzhat al-Qulub*, trans. G. Le Strange, *The Geographical Part of the Nuzhat-Al-Qulūb* (Leiden, 1919), pp. 93, 143.
85 Ibn Battuta, *The Rihla*, trans. H. A. R. Gibb and C. F. Beckingham (eds.), *The Travels of Ibn Battuta, AD 1325–54*, 4 vols. (London, 1994), p. 580.
86 Ibn Battuta, *The Rihla*, trans. H. A. R. Gibb and C. F. Beckingham (eds.), *The Travels of Ibn Battuta, AD 1325–54*, 4 vols. (London, 1994), p. 60.
87 Ibn Battuta, *The Rihla*, trans. H. A. R. Gibb and C. F. Beckingham (eds.), *The Travels of Ibn Battuta, AD 1325–54*, 4 vols. (London, 1994), p. 374.
88 Ibn Battuta, *The Rihla*, trans. H. A. R. Gibb and C. F. Beckingham (eds.), *The Travels of Ibn Battuta, AD 1325–54*, 4 vols. (London, 1994), p. 432.
89 Ma Huan, *Yingya Shenglan* [The Overall Survey of the Ocean's Shores], trans. J. V. G. Mills, *Ma Huan, Ying-Yai Sheng-Lan: "The overall survey of the ocean's shores, 1433"* (Cambridge, 1970), pp. 164–5.
90 Tomé Pires, *Suma Oriental que trata do Mar Roxo até aos Chins* [An Account of the East, from the Red Sea to China], trans. Armando Cortesão (ed.), *The Suma Oriental of Tome Pires* (London, 1944), p. 207.
91 Tomé Pires, *Suma Oriental que trata do Mar Roxo até aos Chins* [An Account of the East, from the Red Sea to China], trans. Armando Cortesão (ed.), *The Suma Oriental of Tome Pires* (London, 1944), p. 29.

92 Tomé Pires, *Suma Oriental que trata do Mar Roxo até aos Chins* [An Account of the East, from the Red Sea to China], trans. Armando Cortesão (ed.), *The Suma Oriental of Tome Pires* (London, 1944), p. 125.
93 Ma Huan, *Yingya Shenglan* [The Overall Survey of the Ocean's Shores], trans. J. V. G. Mills, *Ma Huan, Ying-Yai Sheng-Lan: "The overall survey of the ocean's shores, 1433"* (Cambridge, 1970), p. 88.
94 Tomé Pires, *Suma Oriental que trata do Mar Roxo até aos Chins* [An Account of the East, from the Red Sea to China], trans. Armando Cortesão (ed.), *The Suma Oriental of Tome Pires* (London, 1944), p. 130.
95 Ibn Battuta, *The Rihla*, trans. H. A. R. Gibb and C. F. Beckingham (eds.), *The Travels of Ibn Battuta, AD 1325–54*, 4 vols. (London, 1994), p. 889.
96 Ibn Battuta, *The Rihla*, trans. H. A. R. Gibb and C. F. Beckingham (eds.), *The Travels of Ibn Battuta, AD 1325–54*, 4 vols. (London, 1994), p. 940.
97 Ma Huan, *Yingya Shenglan* [The Overall Survey of the Ocean's Shores], trans. J. V. G. Mills, *Ma Huan, Ying-Yai Sheng-Lan: "The overall survey of the ocean's shores, 1433"* (Cambridge, 1970), p. 85.
98 Ma Huan, *Yingya Shenglan* [The Overall Survey of the Ocean's Shores], trans. J. V. G. Mills, *Ma Huan, Ying-Yai Sheng-Lan: "The overall survey of the ocean's shores, 1433"* (Cambridge, 1970), p. 97.
99 Ma Huan, *Yingya Shenglan* [The Overall Survey of the Ocean's Shores], trans. J. V. G. Mills, *Ma Huan, Ying-Yai Sheng-Lan: "The overall survey of the ocean's shores, 1433"* (Cambridge, 1970), pp. 129, 153.
100 Ma Huan, *Yingya Shenglan* [The Overall Survey of the Ocean's Shores], trans. J. V. G. Mills, *Ma Huan, Ying-Yai Sheng-Lan: "The overall survey of the ocean's shores, 1433"* (Cambridge, 1970), p. 155.
101 Tomé Pires, *Suma Oriental que trata do Mar Roxo até aos Chins* [An Account of the East, from the Red Sea to China], trans. Armando Cortesão (ed.), *The Suma Oriental of Tome Pires* (London, 1944), pp. 16–17.
102 Ibn Battuta, *The Rihla*, trans. H. A. R. Gibb and C. F. Beckingham (eds.), *The Travels of Ibn Battuta, AD 1325–54*, 4 vols. (London, 1994), p. 773.
103 Ibn Battuta, *The Rihla*, trans. H. A. R. Gibb and C. F. Beckingham (eds.), *The Travels of Ibn Battuta, AD 1325–54*, 4 vols. (London, 1994), pp. 773–4.

Bibliography

Primary Sources

Anon., *Hudūd al-Ālam*, trans. Vladimir Minorsky, *A Persian Geography, 372 AD–982 AD* (London, 1970)

Anon., *Periplus Maris Erythraei*, trans. Lionel Casson (ed.), *The Periplus Maris Erythraei: Text with introduction, translation, and commentary* (Princeton, NJ, 1989)

Al-Bakrī, *Kitāb al-Masālik wa-al-Mamālik*, trans. Nehemiah Levtzion and J. F. P. Hopkins (eds.), *Corpus of Early Arabic Sources for West African History* (Cambridge, 1981)

Ibn Battuta, *The Rihla*, trans. H. A. R. Gibb and C. F. Beckingham (eds.), *The Travels of Ibn Battuta, AD 1325–54*, 4 vols. (London, 1994)

Al-Biruni, *Taḥqīq mā li-al-Hind*, trans. Edward Sachau, *Beruni's India: Account of the religion, philosophy, literature, geography, chronology, astronomy, customs, laws, and astrology of India, about AD 1030* (London, 1888)

Alvise da Cadamosto, *The Voyages of Alvise Cadamosto and Pero de Sintra*, trans. G. R. Crone, *The Voyages of Cadamosto and other Documents on Western Africa in the Second Half of the Fifteenth Century* (London, 1937)

Ibn Faḍlān, *Risāla*, trans. Richard Frye, *Ibd Fadlan's Journey to Russia: A tenth-century traveler from Bagdad to the Volga* (Princeton, NJ, 2005)

Fan Ye, *Hou Hanshou*, trans. John Hill, *Through the Jade Gate to Rome: A study of the Silk Roads during the later Han Dynasty 1st to 2nd centuries* (2009)

Bento de Gois, *De Christiana expeditione apud Sinas*, trans. Henry Yule, *Cathay and the Way Thither: Being a collection of medieval notices of China, vol. 4* (1916)

Ban Gu, *Han Shu*, trans. Anthony François Paulus Hulsewé and M. A. N. Loewe (eds.), *China in Central Asia: The Early Stage: 125 BC–AD 23; an Annotated Translation of Chapters 61 and 96 of the History of the Former Han Dynasty* (Leiden, 1979)

Herodotus, *The Histories*, trans. Robin Waterfield (Oxford, 2008)

Ma Huan, *Yingya Shenglan*, trans. J. V. G. Mills, *Ma Huan, Ying-Yai Sheng-Lan: "The overall survey of the ocean's shores, 1433"* (Cambridge, 1970)

Ibn Idhari, *Al-Bayan al-Mughrib*, trans. Nehemiah Levtzion and J. F. P. Hopkins (eds.), *Corpus of Early Arabic Sources for West African History* (Cambridge, 1981)

Cosmas Indicopleustes, *Topographia Christiana*, trans. J. W. M. Crindle, *The Christian Topography* (London, 1897)

Flavius Josephus, *De Bello Judaico*, trans. H. Thackery, *The Jewish War* (Cambridge, MA, 1927–8)

Ibn Jubayr, *Rihla*, trans. Ronald Broadhurst (ed.), *The Travels of Ibn Jubayr: Being the chronicle of a medieval Spanish Moor concerning his journey to the Egypt of Saladin, the holy cities of Arabia, Baghdad the city of the Caliphs, the Latin kingdom of Jerusalem, and the Norman kingdom of Sicily* (London, 1952)

Ibn Khaldun, *Muqaddimah*, trans. Franz Rosenthal in N. J. Dawood (ed.), *The Muqaddimah: An Introduction to History* (Princeton, NJ, 2005)
Ibn Khurradādhbih, *Kitāb al Masālik w'al Mamālik*, trans. Michael Jan de Goeje, *Ibn Khurradādhbih's Kitāb Al-Masālik Wa L-Mamālik and Part of the Kitāb Al-Kharāj by Qudāma Ibn Ja'far* (Leiden, 1889)
Antoine Malfante, "Letter from Tuat, 1447", trans. Gerald Roe Crone (ed.), *The Voyages of Cadamosto and other Documents on Western Africa in the Second Half of the Fifteenth Century* (London, 1937)
Hamdallah Mustawfi, *Nuzhat al-Qulub*, trans. G. Le Strange, *The Geographical Part of the Nuzhat-Al-Qulūb* (Leiden, 1919)
Francesco Balducci Pegolotti, *Libro di Divisamenti di Paesi*, trans. Henry Yule, *Cathay and the Way Thither: Being a collection of medieval notices of China, vol. 3* (London, 1914)
Duarte Pacheco Pereira, *Esmeraldo de Situ Orbis*, trans. George Kimble (ed.), *Esmeraldo de Siter Orbis* (London, 1937)
Tomé Pires, *Suma Oriental que trata do Mar Roxo até aos Chins*, trans. Armando Cortesão (ed.), *The Suma Oriental of Tome Pires* (London, 1944)
Pliny, *Naturalis Historia*, trans. John Bostock, *The Natural History* (Perseus Digital Library: http://data.perseus.org/citations/urn:cts:latinLit:phi0978.phi001.perseus-eng1:12.32)
Marco Polo, *Il Libro di Marco Polo detto il Milione*, trans. Hugh Murray, *Travels of Marco Polo* (Edinburgh, 1845)
Procopius, *Hypèr tōn Polémon Lógoi*, trans. Henry Bronson Dewing, *History of the Wars* (Cambridge, MA, 1914–40)
Claudius Ptolemy, *The Geography*, trans. Edward Stevenson (New York, 1932)
Sima Qian, *Records of the Grand Historian*, trans. Burton Watson, *Records of the Grand Historian* (Hong Kong, 1993)
Zhao Rukuo, *Zhu Fan Zhi*, trans. Friedrick Hirth and W. W. Rockhill, *Chau Ju-Kua: His Work on the Chinese and Arab Trade in the Twelfth and Thirteenth Centuries, entitled Chu-fan-chï* (St Petersburg, 1911)
Al-Sa'di, *Tarikh al-Sudan*, trans. John Hunwick, *Timbuktu and the Songhay Empire: Al-Sadi's Tarikh al-Sudan down to 1613 and other contemporary documents* (Leiden, 1999)
Diodorus Siculus, *Bibliotheca Historica*, trans. Charles Henry Oldfather, *Library of History: Loeb classic library, vol. 3* (Cambridge, MA, 1935)
Strabo, *Geographica*, trans. Horace Jones, *The Geography of Strabo* (Cambridge, 1924)
Ibrāhīm Ibn Wasīf Shāh, *Akbār al-Zamān*, trans. Carra de Vaux, *L'abrégé des Merveilles* (Paris, 1898)
Sharaf Al-Zamān Ṭāhir Marvazī, trans. V. Minorsky, *Sharaf al-Zamān Ṭāhir Marvazī on China, the Turks, and India* (London, 1942)

Secondary Literature

Saidov Abdukakhor, "The Ferghana Valley: The pre-colonial legacy" in S. Frederick Starr (ed.), *Ferghana Valley: The heart of central Asia* (Armonk, NY, 2011), pp. 3–28
Jeremy Adelman and Stephen Aron, "From Borderlands to Borders: Empires, nation-states, and the peoples in between in North American history", *The American Historical Review* 104:3 (1999), pp. 814–41
S. A. M. Adshead, *Central Asia in World History* (London, 1993)
S. Maqbul Ahmad, "Cartography of al-Sharīf al-Idrīsī" in J. B. Harley and D. Woodward (eds.), *The History of Cartography, vol. 2, book 1: Cartography in the traditional Islamic and South Asian societies* (Chicago, 1992), pp. 156–74

Jawaid Akhtar, "Gujarati Merchants in the Indonesian Archipelago in the 17th Century", *Proceedings of the Indian History Congress* 54 (1993), pp. 273–7

Albert Ammerman and Christopher Polglase, "The Exchange of Obsidian at Neolithic Sites in Italy" in Christopher Scarre and Frances Healey (eds.), *Trade and Exchange in Prehistoric Europe: Proceedings of a conference held at the University of Bristol* (Oxford, 1992), pp. 101–8

Runni Andrew Anderson, *Alexander's Gate, Gog and Magog, and the Inclosed Nations* (Cambridge, MA, 1932)

David Anthony, *The Horse, the Wheel, and Language: How Bronze-Age riders from the Eurasian steppes shaped the modern world* (2007)

Benjamin S. Arbuckle and Emily L. Hammer, "The Rise of Pastoralism in the Ancient Near East", *Journal of Archaeological Research* 27 (2019), pp. 391–449

Sebouh Aslanian, *From the Indian Ocean to the Mediterranean: The global trade networks of the Armenian merchants of New Julfa* (California, 2010)

Ralph Austen, *African Economic History: Internal development and external dependency* (Portsmouth, NH, 1987)

Jan Albert Bakker et al., "The Earliest Evidence of Wheeled Vehicles in Europe and the Near East", *Antiquity* 73:282 (1999), pp. 778–90

Warwick Ball, "Following the Mythical Road", *Geographical* 70:3 (1998)

Thomas Barfield, *The Perilous Frontier: Nomadic empires and China* (Oxford, 1989)

Christopher Bayly, "'Archaic' and 'Modern' Globalisation in the Eurasian and African Arena, c. 1750–1850" in A. G. Hopkins (ed.), *Globalisation in World History* (London, 2002)

Philippe Beaujard, *The Worlds of the Indian Ocean: A global history, vol. 2: From the seventh century to the fifteenth century CE* (Cambridge, 2019)

James Belich, John Darwin, and Chris Wickham (eds.), *The Prospect of Global History* (Oxford, 2016)

Peter Bellwood, *Prehistory of the Indo-Malaysian Archipelago (revised edition)* (Sydney, 2007)

Norbert Benecke and Angela von den Dreisch, "Horse Exploitation in the Kazakh Steppes during the Neolithic and Bronze Ages" in Marsha Levine, Colin Renfrew and Katie Boyle (eds.), *Prehistoric Steppe Adaptation and the Horse* (Cambridge, 2003), pp. 69–82

Craig Benjamin, *Empires of Ancient Eurasia: The first Silk Roads Era, 100 BCE–250 CE* (Cambridge, 2018)

Rafi Benvenisti, *Economic Life at the Dawn of History in Mesopotamia and Ancient Egypt: The birth of market economy in the third and second millennia BCE* (Berlin, 2024)

Bhaswati Bhattacharya, "The 'Book of Will' of Petrus Woskan (1680–1751): Some insights into the global commercial network of the Armenians in the Indian Ocean", *Journal of Economic and Social History of the Orient* 51:1 (2008), pp. 67–98

Peter Bietenholz, *Historia and Fabula: Myths and legends in historical thought from Antiquity to the Modern Age* (Leiden, 1994)

Brian Boeck, *Imperial Boundaries: Cossack communities and empire-building in the age of Peter the Great* (Cambridge, 2010)

Nicole Boivin and Michael Frachetti (eds.), *Globalization in Prehistory: Contact, exchange and the "people without history"* (Cambridge, 2018)

Samuel Bowles, *Microeconomics: Behaviour, Institutions, and Evolution* (Princeton, NJ, 2004)

John Andrew Boyle, "Alexander and the Mongols" in *The Journal of the Royal Asiatic Society* 2 (1979), pp. 123–36

Alison Brooks et al., "Long-distance Stone Transport and Pigment Use in the Earliest Middle Stone Age", *Science* 360 (2018), pp. 90–94

Ursula Brosseder and Bryan K. Miller, "Global Networks and Local Agents in the Iron Age Eurasian Steppe" in Nicole Boivin and Michael Frachetti (eds.), *Globalization in Prehistory: Contact, exchange and the 'People Without History* (Cambridge, 2018), pp. 162–83

Elizabeth Brumfiel and Timothy Earle, *Specialization, Exchange and Complex Societies* (Cambridge, 1997)

Marius Canard, "La relation du voyage d'Ibn Fadlân chez les Bulgares de la Volga", *Annales* 16 (1958), pp. 41–145

M. Cary and E. H. Warmington, *The Ancient Explorers* (London, 1929)

John W. Chaffee, *The Muslim Merchants of Premodern China: The history of a maritime Asian trade diaspora, 750–1400* (Cambridge, 2018)

Gerard Chaliand, trans. A. M. Berrett, *Nomadic Empires: From Mongolia to the Danube* (London, 2003)

Claudia Chang, *Rethinking Prehistoric Central Asia: Shepherds, farmers and nomads* (London, 2019)

J. Chapman and B. Gaydarska, "The Provision of Salt to Tripolye Mega-Sites" in A. Korvin-Piotrovsky, V. Kruts and S. Rizhov (eds.), *Tripolye Settlement-Giants* (Kiev, 2003), pp. 203–11

John Chapman, "The Standard Model, the Maximalists and the Minimalists: New interpretations of Trypillia mega-sites", *Journal of World Prehistory* 30:3 (2017), pp. 221–37

K. N. Chaudhuri, *Asia before Europe: Economy and civilization of the Indian Ocean from the rise of Islam to 1750* (Cambridge, 1990)

Tamara Chin, "The Invention of the Silk Road, 1877", *Critical Inquiry* 40:1 (2013), pp. 194–219

Georg Christ, *Trading Conflicts: Venetian merchants and Mamluk officials in late medieval Alexandria* (Leiden, 2012)

David Christian, "State Formation in the Inner Eurasian Steppes" in David Christian and Craig Benjamin (eds.), *Silk Road Studies II: World of the Silk Roads: Ancient and modern* (Turnhout, 1998), pp. 51–76

David Christian, "Silk Roads or Steppe Roads? The Silk Roads in World History", *Journal of World History* 11:1 (2000), pp. 1–26

David Christian and Craig Benjamin (eds.), *Silk Road Studies II: World of the Silk Roads: Ancient and modern* (Turnhout, 1998)

David Cook, *Contemporary Muslim Apocalyptic Literature* (Syracuse, 2005)

Frederick Cooper, "What Is the Concept of Globalization Good for? An African Historian's Perspective", *African Affairs* 100:399 (2001), pp. 189–213

Roger Cribb, *Nomads in Archaeology* (Cambridge, 1990)

Philip Curtin, "Africa and the Wider Monetary World, 1250–1850" in J. F. Richards *(ed.), Precious Metals in the Later Medieval and Early Modern Worlds* (Durham, NC, 1983)

Philip Curtin, *Cross-Cultural Trade in World History* (Cambridge, 1984)

Federico De Romanis, *The Indo-Roman Pepper Trade and the Muziris Papyrus* (Oxford, 2020)

Aleksandr Diachenko and Francesco Menotti, "The Gravity Model: Monitoring the formation and development of the Tripolye culture giant-settlements in Ukraine", *Journal of Archaeological Science* 39:8 (2012), pp. 2810–7

Robert Drews, *Early Riders: The beginnings of mounted warfare in Asia and Europe* (Abingdon, 2004)

Paula Doumani Dupuy, "Bronze Age Central Asia" in Oxford Handbooks Editorial Board (eds.), *The Oxford Handbook of Topics in Archaeology* (Oxford, 2014)

Timothy Earle, Jens-Henrik Bech, and Chiara Villa, "New Early Neolithic and Late Bronze Age Amber Finds from Thy", *Antiquity* 97:391 (2022), pp. 70–85

Sauer Eberhard, *Dariali: The 'Caspian Gates' in the Caucasus from antiquity to the Age of the Huns and Middle Ages* (Oxford, 2020)
Patricia Ebrey, *Chinese Civilisation and Society: A sourcebook* (London, 1981)
Christopher Edens, "Dynamics of Trade in the Ancient Mesopotamian 'World System'", *American Anthropologist* 94:1 (1992), pp. 118–39
Tali Erickson-Gini and Yigal Israel, "Excavating the Nabataean Incense Road", *Journal of Eastern Mediterranean Archaeology & Heritage Studies* 1:1 (2013), pp. 24–53
Kasper Grønlund Evers, *Worlds Apart Trading Together: The organisation of long-distance trade between Rome and India in Antiquity* (Bicester, 2017)
Gabriel Ferrand, *Le Wakway est-il Japan?* (Paris, 1932)
Adam Fong, "Together They Might Make Trouble': Cross-Cultural Interactions in Tang Dynasty Guangzhou, 618–907 CE", *Journal of World History* 25:4 (2014), pp. 475–92
Michael Frachetti, "Multiregional Emergence of Mobile Pastoralism and Non-uniform Institutional Complexity across Eurasia", *Current Anthropology* 53:1 (2012), pp. 2–38
Irene Franck and David Brownstone, *The Silk Road: A history* (New York, 1986)
Andre Gunder Frank, *ReOrient: Global economy in the Asian Age* (Berkeley, CA, 1998)
Peter Frankopan, *The New Silk Roads: The present and future of the world* (London, 2018)
Bisserka Gaydarska (ed.), *Early Urbanism in Europe: The Trypillia megasites of the Ukrainian forest-steppe* (Berlin, 2020)
Dragoş Gheorghiu, "A Fire Cult in South European Chalcolithic Traditions? On the relationship between ritual contexts and the instrumentality of fire" in Dragoş Gheorghiu, D. Barrowclough and C. Malone (eds.), *Cult in Context: Reconsidering ritual in archaeology* (Oxford, 2007), pp. 269–84
John-Paul Ghobrial, "The Secret Life of Elias of Bablylon and the Uses of Global Microhistory", *Past & Present* 222 (2014), pp. 51–93
Marija Gimbutas, *The Goddesses and Gods of Old Europe: 6500–3500 BC: Myths and cult images* (London, 1982)
Peter Golden, "The Qipcac of Medieval Eurasia: An example of stateless adaption in the steppe" in Gary Seaman and Daniel Marks (eds.), *Rulers from the Steppe: State formation on the Eurasian periphery* (Los Angeles, CA, 1991)
Anver Greif, *Institutions and the Path to the Modern Economic: Lessons from Medieval trade* (Cambridge, 2006)
Zhang Guand-da, B. A. Litvinsky, "Historical Introduction" in Zhang Guand-da, B. A. Litvinsky, and R. Shabani Samghabadi (eds.), *History of Civilizations of Central Asia, vol 3: The crossroads of civilization: AD 250 to 750* (Paris, 1996), pp. 19–35
Jan Gyllenbok, *Encyclopaedia of Historical Metrology, Weights and Measures, vol. 1* (Switzerland, 2018)
Karl Reinhold Haellquist (ed.), *Asian Trade Routes: Continental and maritime* (London, 1991)
Valerie Hansen, *The Silk Road: A new history* (Oxford, 2012)
William A. Haviland et al., *Anthropology: The human challenge* (Boston, 2004)
Thomas N. Headland and Lawrence A. Reid, "Hunter-Gatherers and their Neighbors from Prehistory to the Present", *Current Anthropology* 30:1 (1989), pp. 43–66
Sven Hedin, *Silk Road* (London, 1938)
Albert Herrmann, *Die Alten Seidenstrassen Zwischen China und Syria* (Berlin, 1910)
Albert Herrmann, *Historical and Commercial Atlas of China* (Boston, MA, 1935)
John Hill, *Through the Jade Gate to Rome: A study of the Silk Roads during the later Han Dynasty 1st to 2nd centuries, vol. 1 and 2* (2009)

Geoffrey Hindley, *A History of Roads* (London, 1972)
Colleen Ho, "Overland Trade in the Mongol World" in Michael Hope and Timothy May (eds.), *The Mongol World* (New York, 2022), pp. 484–504
William Honeychurch, *Inner Asia and the Spatial Politics of Empire: Archaeology, mobility, and culture contact* (New York, 2015)
B. Horejs et al., "The Aegean in the Early 7th Millennium BC: Maritime networks and colonisation", *Journal of World Prehistory* 28 (2015), pp. 289–330
George Hourani, *Arab Seafaring in the Indian Ocean in the Ancient and Early Medieval Times* (Princeton, NJ, 1995 [1963])
James Howard-Johnston, "The Fur Trade in the Early Middle Ages" in Jacek Gruszczyński, Marek Jankowiak, and Jonathan Shepard (eds.), *Viking-Age Trade: Silver, slaves and Gotland* (London, 2020), pp. 57–74
Mei-Ling Hsu, "Chinese Maritime Cartography: Sea charts of pre-modern China", *Imago Mundi* 40 (1988), pp. 96–112
Geoffrey Hudson, *Europe and China: A survey of their relations from the earliest times to 1800* (London, 1961)
Hsiao-Chun Hung et al., "Ancient Jades Map 3000 Years of Prehistoric Exchange in Southeast Asia", *Proceedings of the National Academy of Sciences of the United States of America* 104:50 (2007), pp. 19,745–50
Tim Ingold, *The Perception of the Environment: Essays of livelihood, dwelling and skill* (London, 2000)
Sechin Jagchid and Van Jay Symons, *Peace, War, and Trade along the Great Wall: Nomadic-Chinese interaction through two millennia* (Bloomington, IN, 1989)
Cat Jarman, *River Kings: A new history of Vikings from Scandinavia to the Silk Roads* (London, 2021)
A. M. Khazanov, "Characteristic Features of Nomadic Communities in the Eurasian Steppes" in W. Weissleder (ed.), *The Nomadic Alternative: Modes and models of interaction in the African-Asian Deserts and Steppes* (The Hague, 1978), pp. 119–26
A. M. Khazanov, trans. Julia Crookenden, *Nomads and the Outside World* (Cambridge, 1984)
Michael Khodarkovsky, *Russia's Steppe Frontier: The making of a colonial empire, 1500–1800* (Bloomington, 2002)
Philip Kohl, "The Ancient Economy, Transferable Technologies and the Bronze Age World System: A view from the northeastern frontier of the ancient Near East" in Michael John Rowlands, Larsen Mogens, and Kristian Kristiansen (eds.), *Centre and Periphery in the Ancient World* (Cambridge, 1987), pp. 143–64
Philip Kohl, *The Making of Bronze Age Eurasia* (Cambridge, 2007)
Kristian Kristiansen and Johan Ling, "A Triangular Middle Bronze Age Trade System of Amber, Copper and Tin, 1500–1300 BC" in C. C. Bakels, Q. P. J. Bourgeois, D. R. Fontijn, and R. Jansen (eds.), *Local Communities in the Big World of Prehistoric Northwest Europe* (Leiden, 2018), pp. 41–5
Luc Kwanten, *Imperial Nomads: A history of central Asia, 500–1500* (Leicester, 1979)
Hermann Kulke, "The Naval Expeditions of the Cholas in the Context of Asian History" in Hermann Kulke, K. Kesavapany, and Vijay Sekhuja (eds.), *Nagapattinam to Suvarnadwipa: Reflections on the Chola naval expeditions to Southeast Asia* (Singapore, 2009), pp. 1–19
E. E. Kuzmina and Victor Mair, *The Prehistory of the Silk Road* (Philadelphia, PA, 2015)
Subhi Y. Labib, "Capitalism in Medieval Islam", *The Journal of Economic History* 29:1 (1969), pp. 92–3
C. C. Lamberg-Karlovsky, "The Bronze Age *khanates* of Central Asia", *Antiquity* 68:259 (1994), pp. 401–2
Justin Leidwanger and Carl Knappett, "Maritime Networks, Connectivity, and Mobility in the Ancient Mediterranean" in Justin Leidwanger and Carl Knappett (eds.), *Maritime Networks in the Ancient Mediterranean World* (Cambridge, 2018)

Katheryn Linduff, "A Walk on the Wild Side: Late Shang appropriation of horses in China" in Marsha Levine, Colin Renfrew and Katie Boyle (eds.), *Prehistoric Steppe Adaptation and the Horse* (Cambridge, 2003), pp. 139–62

Katherine Linduff and Jianun Mei, "Metallurgy in Ancient Eastern Asia: Retrospect and Prospects", *Journal of World Prehistory* 22:3 (2009), p. 274, pp. 265–81

Johan Ling, Richard Chacon and Kristian Kristiansen (eds.), *Trade Before Civilisation: Long distance exchange and the rise of social complexity* (Cambridge, 2022)

M. A. Littauer and J. H. Crouwel, *Wheeled Vehicles and Ridden Animals in the Ancient Near East* (1979)

Jiun-Yu Liu, "Intertwined Maritime Silk Road and Austronesian Routes: A Taiwanese archaeological perspective", *Journal of Global History* 18:3 (2023), pp. 384–400

Xinru Liu, *The Silk Road in World History* (New York, 2010)

Xinru Liu, "Silk Road Trade and Foreign Economic Influences" in Debin Ma and Richard von Glahn (eds.), *The Cambridge Economic History of China, vol. 1, to 1800* (Cambridge, 2022), pp. 203–40

Xinru Liu and Lynda Norene Shaffer, *Connections Across Eurasia: Transportation, communication, and cultural exchange on the Silk Roads* (New York, 2007)

Janet Abu Lughod, *Before European Hegemony: The world system AD 1250–1350* (1989)

Michael MacDonald, *Literacy and Identity in Pre-Islamic Arabia* (Surrey, 2009)

Vitorino Magalhaes-Godinho, *L'Économie de l'Empire Portugais aux XVe et XVIe Siècles* (Paris, 1969)

Cornelia Magda-Mantu, Gheorghe Niculescu, and Ana-Maria Vlad, "Painting pigments for ceramic decoration in the Cucuteni-Tripolye cultural complex" in F. Draşovean (ed.), *Festschrift für Gheorghe Lazarovici zum 60. Geburstag* (Timişoara, 2001), pp. 191–210

James Mallory, *In Search of the Indo-Europeans: Language, archaeology and myth* (London, 1989)

Raymond Mauny, *Tableau Géographique de L'Ouest Africain au Moyen Age: D'Après les Sources Écrites, la Tradition et l'Archéologie* (Dakar, 1961)

Marcel Mauss, *The Gift: Forms and functions of exchange in archaic societies* (London, 2002 [1925])

Timothy May, *The Mongol Empire* (Edinburgh, 2022)

Michael McCormick, *Origins of the European Economy: Communications and commerce, AD 300–900* (Cambridge, 2001)

Susan Keech McIntosh (ed.), *Beyond Chiefdoms: Pathways to complexity in Africa* (Cambridge, 1999)

Melanie Michailidis, "Samanid Silver and Trade along the Fur Route", *Medieval Encounters* 18:4–5 (2012), pp. 315–38

Olivia Milburn, "Aromas, Scents, and Spices: Olfactory culture in China before the arrival of Buddhism", *Journal of the American Oriental Society* 136:3 (2016), pp. 441–64

Paul R. Milgrom, Douglas C. North, and Barry R. Weingast, "The Role of Institutions in the Revival of Trade: The law merchant, private judges, and the Champagne fairs", *Economics and Politics* 2:1 (1990), pp. 1–23

James Millward, *Eurasian Crossroads: A history of Xingiang* (London, 2007)

P. F. de Moraes Farias, "Silent Trade: Myth and Historical Evidence", *History in Africa* 1 (1974), pp. 9–24

Frederick Mote, *Imperial China, 900–1800* (Cambridge, MA, 2003)

Stuart Munro-Hay, *Aksum: An African civilisation of late Antiquity* (Edinburgh, 1991)

M. Murillo-Barroso, A. Martín Cólliga, and M. Martinón-Torres, "The Earliest Baltic Amber in Western Europe", *Scientific Reports* 13 (2023), article 14250

Douglas North, "Institutions", *Journal of Economic Perspectives* 5:1 (1991), pp. 97–9
Ida Nursoo, "Indiginous Law, Colonial Injustice and the Jurisprudence of Hybridity", *The Journal of Legal Pluralism and Unofficial Law* 50:1 (2018), pp. 56–70
Rahul Oka and Chapurukha M. Kusimba, "The Archaeology of Trading Systems, Part 1: Towards a new trade synthesis", *Journal of Archaeological Research* 16:4 (2008), pp. 339–95
Sandra Olsen, "The Exploitation of Horses at Botai, Kazakhstan" in Marsha Levine, Colin Renfrew and Katie Boyle (eds.), *Prehistoric Steppe Adaptation and the Horse* (Cambridge, 2003), pp. 83–104
Ludovic Orlando, "Back to the Roots and Routes of Dromedary Domestication", *Proceedings of the National Academy of Sciences of the United States of America*, 113, 24 (2016), pp. 6588–90
P. Petrequin, F. Jeudy, and C. Jeunesse, "Neolithic Quarries, the Exchange of Axes and Social Control in the Southern Vosger" in Christopher Scarre and Frances Healey (eds.), *Trade and Exchange in Prehistoric Europe: Proceedings of a conference held at the University of Bristol* (Oxford, 1992), pp. 45–60
K. Polanyi, "Traders and Trade" in J. A. Sabloff (ed.), *Ancient Civilizations and Trade* (Alburquerque, 1975), pp. 133–54
Kenneth Pomeranz and Steven Topik, *The World that Created Society, Culture, and the World Economy, 1400-the Present* (Armonk, NY, 1999)
Sebastian Prange, *Monsoon Islam: Trade and faith on the medieval Malabar coast* (Cambridge, 2018)
C. Refrew, "Trade and Culture Process in European Prehistory", *Current Anthropology* 15 (1969), pp. 151–69
Jan Retsö, "The Domestication of the Camel and the Establishment of the Frankincense Road from South Arabia", *Orientalia Suecana*, 40 (1991), pp. 187–219
Janet Rizvi, *Trans-Himalayan Caravans: Merchant princes and peasant traders in Ladakh* (Oxford, 1999)
Morris Rossabi, *China and Inner Asia: From 1368 to the present day* (London, 1975)
Morris Rossabi, "The 'Decline' of the Central Asian Caravan Trade" in James Tracy (ed.), *The Rice of Merchant Empires: Long distance trade in the early modern world, 1350–1750* (Cambridge, 1990)
Natalie Rothman, "*Between Venice and Istanbul: Trans-Imperial Subjects and Cultural Mediation in the Early Modern Mediterranean*", PhD Dissertation, University of Michigan (2006), pp. xiv, 40–81
Madeleine Rouvillois-Brigol, *Le Pays de Ouargla (Sahara Algérien)* (Paris, 1975)
C. Runnels and T. H. Van Andel, "Trade and the Origins of Agriculture in the Eastern Mediterranean", *Journal of Mediterranean Archaeology* 1:1 (1988), pp. 83–109
Jeremy Sabloff and C. C. Lamberg-Karlovsky (eds.), *Ancient Civilization and Trade* (Albuquerque, 1975)
M. D. Sahlins, "On the Sociology of Primitive Exchange" in S. Gudeman (ed.), *Economic Anthropology* (Cheltenham, 1998), pp. 82–140
Gary Seaman and Daniel Marks, *Rulers from the Steppe: State formation on the Eurasian periphery* (Los Angeles, CA, 1991)
Sarah Semple, "Materializing Inequalities in Past, Present and Future", *World Archaeology* 54:4 (2022), pp. 493–501
T. Sen, "The Formation of Chinese Maritime Networks to Southern Asia, 1200–1450", *Journal of the Economic and Social History of the Orient* 49:4 (2006), pp. 421–53
Stephen Shennan, "Exchange and Ranking: The role of amber in the earlier Bronze Age of Europe" in Colin Renfrew and Stephen Shennan (eds.), *Ranking, Resources and Exchange: Aspects of the archaeology of early European society* (Cambridge, 1982), pp. 33–45

Andrew Sherratt, "Mobile Resources: Settlement and exchange in early agricultural Europe" in Colin Renfrew and Stephen Shennan (eds.), *Ranking, Resource and Exchange: Aspects of the archaeology of early European society* (Cambridge, 1982), pp. 13–26

Kurakichi Shiratori, "On the Ts'ung-ling Traffic Route Described by C. Ptolemaeus", *The Memoirs of the Research Department of the Toyo Bunko* (1957), pp. 1–34

Søren Michael Sindbæk, "Local and Long-Distance Exchange" in Stefan Brink, *The Viking World* (London, 2008), pp. 150–8

Denis Sinor, "The Establishment and Dissolution of the Türk Empire" in Denis Sinor (ed.), *The Cambridge History of Early Inner Asia* (Cambridge, 1990)

Jonathan Karam Skaff, "Survival in the Frontier Zone: Comparative perspectives on identity and political allegiance in China's inner Asian borderlands during the Sui-Tang Dynastic transition (617–630)", *Journal of World History* 15:2 (2004), pp. 117–53

Robin Skeates, "Neolithic Exchange in Central and Southern Italy" in Christopher Scarre and Frances Healey (eds.), *Trade and Exchange in Prehistoric Europe: Proceedings of a conference held at the University of Bristol* (Oxford, 1992), pp. 109–14

Edmond Smith, "Governance" in William Pettigrew and David Veevers (eds.), *The Corporation as a Protagonist in Global History, c. 1550–1750* (Leiden, 2018)

Edmond Smith, "Commercial Culture in Contested Spaces" in Cátia A. P. Antunes and Francisco Bethencourt (eds.), *Merchant Cultures: A global approach to spaces, representations and worlds of trade, 1500–1800* (Brill, 2022)

Edmond Smith and Mariana Boscariol, "Akan Relations, Commercial Networks, and the Portuguese Empire in West Africa, 1482–1637", *Journal of World History* 33:4 (2022), pp. 609–38

Richard Smith, "The Image of Timbuktu in Europe before Caillié", *Proceedings of the Meeting of the French Colonial Historical Society* 8 (1985), pp. 12–22

Arnold Spekke, *The Ancient Amber Routes and the Geographical Discovery of the Eastern Baltic* (Stockholm, 1957)

Ann Stahl, *Making History in Banda: Anthropological visions of Africa's past* (Cambridge, 2001)

Aurel Stein, *Innermost Asia: Detailed report of explorations in Central Asia, Kan-su and eastern Iran* (Oxford, 1928)

Robert R. Stieglitz, "Long-Distance Seafaring in the Ancient Near East", *The Biblical Archaeologist*, 47:3 (1984), pp. 134–42

Richard Stoneman (ed.), *The Greek Alexander Romance* (London, 1991)

Sanjay Subrahmanyam, *Three Ways to Be Alien: Travails and encounters in the early modern world* (Waltham, MA, 2011)

Eric Tagliacozzo, Helen F. Siu, and Peter C. Perdue, "Introduction: Spatial assemblages" in Eric Tagliacozzo, Helen F. Siu, and Peter C. Perdue (eds.), *Asia Inside Out: Connected places* (Cambridge, MA, 2015)

W. W. Tarn and G. T. Griffith, *Hellenistic Civilisation* (London, 1952)

Filip Taterka, "Hatshepsut's expedition to the land of Punt – novelty or tradition?", *Current Research in Egyptology 2015: Proceedings of the Sixteenth Annual Symposium* (2016), pp. 114–23

Gerald R. Tibbetts, "The Balkhī School of Geographers" in J. B. Harey and David Woodward (eds.), *The History of Cartography, vol. 2, book 1: Cartography in the Traditional Islamic and South Asian Societies* (Chicago, 1992), pp. 108–36

Joan Todd, "A Reappraisal of the Prehistoric and Classical Amber Trade in the Light of New Evidence", *Journal of Baltic Studies* 5:4 (1974), pp. 295–314

Henrietta Todorova, "The Neolithic, Eneolithic and Transitional Period in Bulgarian Prehistory" in Douglass Bailey, Ivan Panayotov, and Stefan Alexandrov (eds.), *Prehistoric Bulgaria* (Madison, WI, 1995), pp. 79–98

Francesca Trivellato, *The Familiarity of Strangers: The Sephardic diaspora, Livorno, and cross-cultural trade in the early modern period* (New Haven, 2009)
Francesca Trivellato, "Sephardic Merchants in the Early Modern Atlantic and Beyond: Towards a comparative historical approach to business cooperation" in Richard L. Kagan and Philip Morgan (eds.), *Atlantic Diasporas: Jews and Crypto-Jews in the Age of Mercantilism, 1500–1800* (Baltimore, 2005), pp. 101–3
Francesca Trivellato, Leor Halevi, and Catia Antunes (eds.), *Religion and Trade: Cross-Cultural Exchanges in World History* (Oxford, 2014)
Denis Twitchett, "The T'ang Market System", *Asia Major* 12:2 (1966), pp. 202–48
Étienne de la Vaissière, trans. James Ward, *Sogdian Traders: A history* (Leiden, 2005)
Emeri J. Van Donzel and Andrea Schmidt, *Gog and Magog in Early Syriac and Islamic Sources: Sallam's quest for Alexander's wall* (Leiden, 2009)
Willem Van Schendel and Itty Abraham, *Illicit Flows and Criminal Things: States, borders, and the other side of globalization* (Bloomington, IN, 2005)
Carter Vaughan, *The Turks in World History* (Oxford, 2005)
Filippo de Vivo, "Prospect or Refuge? Microhistory, History on the Large Scale", *Cultural and Social History* 7:3 (2010), pp. 387–97
Filippo de Vivo, "Microhistories of Long-Distance Information: Space, Movement and Agency in the Early Modern News", *Past & Present*, 12, Issue Supplement 14 (2019), pp. 179–214
Jan de Vries, "The Limits of Globalization in the Early Modern World", *The Economic History Review* 63:3 (2010), pp. 710–33
Arthur Waldron, *The Great Wall of China: From history to myth* (Cambridge, 1990)
Jessica Wang, "Reckoning with the Spatial Turn: Cartography, territoriality, and international history", *Diplomatic History* 41: 5 (2017), pp. 1010–18
Kenneth Wardle, "Wessex and Mycenae: A rapprochement?", *Athens University Review of Archaeology* 4 (2020), pp. 461–70
Andrew Watson, "Back to Gold – and Silver", *The Economic History Review* 20 (1967), pp. 30–1
Daniel Waugh, "Richthofen's 'Silk Roads': Towards the Archaeology of a Concept", *The Silk Road* 5:1 (2007)
Robert Wenke, *Patterns in Prehistory: Humankind's first three million years* (Oxford, 2006)
Susan Whitfield, "Was there a Silk Road?", *Asian Medicine* 3:2 (2008), p. 206, pp. 201–13
Ivor Wilks, "Wangara, Akan and Portuguese in the Fifteenth and Sixteenth Centuries, 1: The matter of Bitu", *The Journal of African History* 23:3 (1982), pp. 333–49
André Wink, *Al-Hind: The making of the Indo-Islamic World* (Leiden, 1990)
James Woodburn, "Silent Trade with Outsiders: Hunter Gatherers' Perspectives" in *HAU: Journal of Ethnographic Theory* 6:2 (2016), pp. 473–96
Sally Hovey Wriggins, *The Silk Road Journey with Xuanzang* (Colorado, 2004)
Stephanie Wynne-Jones and Adria LaViolette, *The Swahili World* (London, 2017)
Shiba Yoshinobu, "Sung Foreign Trade: Its scope and organization" in Morris Rossabi (ed.), *China Among Equals: The Middle Kingdom and its neighbors, 10th–14th centuries* (California, 1983), pp. 89–115
Bin Yang, "Horses, Silver and Cowries: Yunnan in global perspective", *Journal of World History* 15:3 (2004), pp. 281–322
Henry Yule, *Cathay and the Way Thither: Being a collection of medieval notices of China, vol. 3* (London, 1914)

Index

MIX
Papier | Fördert gute Waldnutzung
FSC® C083411

Kolibri 360 GmbH
Ferdinand-Jühlke-Straße 7
99095 Erfurt, Deutschland
produktsicherheit@kolibri360.de